The

ELECTRIC
PRESSURE
COOKER
COOKBOOK

for Two

The ELECTRIC PRESSURE COOKER COOKBOOK for Two

125 Easy, Perfectly-Portioned Recipes for the Electric Pressure Cooker and Multicooker

ERICA ACEVEDO

Creator of *The Crumby Kitchen*
Photography by Hélène Dujardin

ROCKRIDGE PRESS

For general information on our other products and services or to obtain technical support, please contact our Customer Care Department within the U.S. at (866) 744-2665, or outside the U.S. at (510) 253-0500.

Rockridge Press publishes its books in a variety of electronic and print formats. Some content that appears in print may not be available in electronic books, and vice versa.

Photography © Hélène Dujardin, 2018; food styling by Tami Hardeman

Cover, Chicken Cacciatore, p.124; Title page, Stuffed Acorn Squash, p.79, Cioppino, p.91, Mexican Street Corn (on the Cob), p.54.

ISBN: Print 978-1-64152-045-4 | eBook 978- 1-64152-046-1

For my nana Irene,
who taught me to find my passion,
and for my husband, Abel,
who helped me embrace it

CONTENTS

Introduction viii

One Fast Food Designed for Two 1

Two Breakfast and Brunch 19

Three Vegetables and Side Dishes 39

Four Meatless Main Dishes 59

Five Shellfish and Fish 83

Six Chicken and Turkey 109

Seven Pork and Beef 139

Eight Kitchen Staples 165

Nine Desserts and Sweet Treats 185

Appendix A: Electric Pressure Cooking Time Charts 211
Appendix B: The Dirty Dozen™ and the Clean Fifteen™ 218
Appendix C: Measurements and Conversions 219
Recipe Title Index 220
Index 222

Introduction

IT SITS IN THE CUPBOARD, nestled between a Dutch oven and a few saucepans. My Nana's 40-year-old pressure cooker resonates with nostalgia.

I can still faintly hear the rattling sound it made as it hissed its way to what would soon be perfectly smooth and buttery mashed potatoes. Every New Year's Day, my nose perked up to the fragrance of pork and sauerkraut in the air, while an ethereal cloud of steam billowed out of the shiny cooking vessel. Many of the most memorable meals of my childhood were crafted with the help of that heavy steel stove-top pot, which I inherited. I rarely use it today, though, because in the twenty-first century, electric pressure cooking has taken over the old-school stove-top method. In fact, this currently adored style of cooking is an updated version of a method developed in the seventeenth century!

Times have indeed changed. When the original stove-top pressure cooker was new and big on the scene in the 1950s, the housewife career was much more common, and the new convenience of preparing dinner in less time was very appealing. But there was a catch: You still had to keep an eye on the clock while your dinner sputtered away on the stove, waiting to be turned off. Now, in our modern set-it-and-forget-it world, a meal can quickly cook in the electric pressure cooker after we have just pressed a few buttons.

Recipe purists can argue that there's nothing like duck confit simmered for two days, the way Julia Child did it. To be honest, they're right. But enjoying that same delicious meal in a fraction of the time is more attainable and equally satisfying.

When I think back to the days of my childhood, I remember how much food could be made relatively quickly in Nana's old pressure cooker, from beef pot roast to tapioca pudding. We would often have leftovers for two or three days, and Nana was always creative in the ways she repurposed foods. But these days, millennial foodies (like my husband and I) want to have varied meals from day to day.

Using cookbooks and websites, I've created many recipes since becoming a self-sufficient adult, and my husband and I often end up with leftovers that land on the compost heap. It wasn't until I started my own food blog in 2014 that I began to really learn the art of cooking and how to make a family-style meal scaled down for two. The addition of an electric pressure cooker to our kitchen has expanded our meal possibilities.

In this book, you'll find that each recipe perfectly feeds two hungry people. In other words, some of the meals (like the Beef Ragù with Pappardelle, on page 161, and the soups) may leave you with a bit "extra." But if your partner has an appetite anything like mine does, that won't be an issue. The Kitchen Staples chapter includes bulk recipes that can be used for multiple meals (stocks, sauces, etc.) and are easily frozen for future use. A few of the desserts are slightly larger than two servings, but who would only want just one slice of cake anyway?

In the recipes, the times listed for preparation, cooking, and serving may vary in your kitchen and for your particular electric pressure cooker. Some cooker brands pressurize in less time than others, but the recipes in this book work with any multi-cooker. The total time listed is meant to give you a general idea of how long it will take you to get from prepping to eating, and the manual to your cooker will guide you through proper timing for various recipes.

Once you get started cooking for two with your electric pressure cooker, your regular cookware—and your oven, for that matter—will just have to get used to sharing time with the cooker. Talk about changing with the times!

One

FAST FOOD DESIGNED FOR TWO

Whether you're a busy couple, a single-parent family, or empty nesters with adventurous palates, knowing how to cook for two is a handy skill. Leftovers are great, but using your electric pressure cooker to whip up your favorite recipes on a smaller scale not only keeps your taste buds happy, it also reduces waste. In this book, you'll find all kinds of tips and tricks on how to make your electric pressure cooker, a.k.a. multicooker, work for you.

THE BENEFITS OF ELECTRIC PRESSURE COOKING FOR TWO

Pressure cooking has come a long way from its modern mid-1900s popularity. Today's electric pressure cookers work the same way as their stove-top pot-and-lid predecessors (raising the boiling point of water or other liquid in a pressure-sealed vessel, thus allowing food to cook hotter and faster than it would on the stove top), by means of temperature and pressure regulation via smart sensors.

Using an electric pressure cooker is very similar to using a slow cooker in that the cooking is done inside an inner pot placed in a housing unit fitted with a heating element, but that's where the similarities end. The lid is fitted with a removable gasket to ensure a tight fit, keeping all of that steam inside until you're ready to safely let it out using the pressure-release valve.

Pressure cooking depends on liquids to make it happen, meaning not every type of meal can be cooked in a pressure cooker alone. Roasted, fried, and some baked recipes should be kept to their respective appliances, but that doesn't mean your pressure cooker can't play a part in their creation. For example, steaming frozen chicken (when you've forgotten to thaw the meat in advance) before breading and baking it into crispy tenders for a weeknight dinner. Or whipping up last-minute baked mac 'n' cheese in half the time it normally takes. These are just a couple of the ways your electric pressure cooker can make your life in the kitchen much easier.

WHY USE AN ELECTRIC PRESSURE COOKER?

In case you need a little convincing as to why an electric pressure cooker is right for you when you have perfectly good appliances already, read the following points:

It's safe. Chances are that if you cook, you've splashed yourself with hot oil or gotten a burn from an oven rack. Electric pressure cookers are built with consumer safety in mind, with lid locks and automatic temperature and pressure controls to keep you safe.

It's fast and convenient. Electric pressure cookers cut traditional cooking times by up to 70 percent, turning weekend dinners into weekday options. Why wait three hours to eat a thick braised cut of meat when you can be enjoying it in 45 minutes? Also, many electric pressure cookers are multicookers, offering numerous different preset function buttons to make cooking just about any food even easier. And no monitoring is needed; the ease of a set-it-and-forget-it function is a draw for any busy home cook.

It saves energy. Many pressure cooker recipes (especially the ones in this book) can be made exclusively in the pot, leaving your larger appliances off, your cooling bill low, and your messy kitchen nerves unfrazzled. The environment thanks you, too.

It's nutritious. Pressure-cooked foods offer more vitamins and minerals than those cooked for longer times in traditional cookware. Less liquid is used in electric pressure cookers, meaning fewer nutrients are leached from the food. Smells are also trapped inside the cooker instead of dispersed throughout the house, so all those delicious flavors stay in the food.

WHY COOK FOR TWO?

You don't have to follow the same cooking routine you're used to. Here are some basic reasons why cooking smaller portions for two can mean happier bellies and eased minds:

Less waste. Face it: You don't always eat those leftovers. Everyone is guilty of finding storage containers of old leftovers during their periodic refrigerator purges. Reducing your grocery bill and your landfill contribution by changing those large meals into smaller ones is a smart approach.

More meal choices. Say you've decided cooking for two is right for you, but you just can't give up that warehouse store membership. Admittedly, bulk food prices are a draw, but you can still buy that pack of six chicken breasts and that five-pound bag of lentils. Freeze the chicken; it can be cooked from frozen in 15 minutes and turned into everything from chicken noodle soup to chicken marsala in about 30 minutes. There's no need to soak those lentils before pressure cooking them, and you can be eating them in less time than it normally takes to soak them.

Less caloric intake. When cooking a recipe for two, there's little wiggle room for extra. The recipes in this book are specially crafted to satiate anyone with a hearty appetite. Many of them are even calculated around certain nutrition facts. There will be nothing left after the food has been portioned out, meaning there is no temptation to go back for seconds. This is a boon for those watching their weight, or for folks who simply like to rummage for guilty late-night snacks.

Electric Pressure Cooking Terminology

There are so many buttons on those multicookers, but don't be afraid of the technology. It's actually much easier than you think to get cooking. Here are some of the cooker functions:

NATURAL RELEASE. The food in the cooker continues to cook while the pressure is released slowly by leaving the pressure release valve in the sealed position after the cook time ends. This is performed by selecting the cancel/keep warm functions or doing nothing at all. A full natural release can take anywhere from 5 to 30 minutes, and the lid will not open before the cooker is completely depressurized. This is particularly good for soups and grains (which tend to foam) and larger cuts of meat that need resting time before serving.

QUICK RELEASE. This function stops the cooking process quickly to avoid overcooking. A quick release results in a strong jet of steam coming from the pressure release valve, so be careful when turning the pressure release valve to the venting position when the cook time ends. This is ideal for potatoes and vegetables.

MANUAL/PRESSURE COOK. There is a setting on most electric pressure cookers that allows you to input all of your cooking settings from time to pressure level.

KEEP WARM. Most electric pressure cookers have this function, which allows you to keep the food inside the cooker heated at a low temperature. Many cookers default to this setting at the end of a cooking time.

SIMMER/BROWNING/SAUTÉ. Simmer is a low-heat cooking method, best used for thickening sauces and soups. When you see "sauté on low" in a recipe, choose either the sauté or simmer function on your electric pressure cooker. Browning is a high-heat cooking method, best used for searing meats and browning root vegetables. When you see "sauté on high" in a recipe, select either the sauté or browning function on your electric pressure cooker.

POT-IN-POT COOKING. This method uses a heatproof dish for cooking your meal, side, or dessert placed in your electric pressure cooker, as opposed to cooking it directly inside the inner pot. This approach allows for cooking meals with low liquid content, reheating previously cooked meals, preparing multiple recipe items at once (such as rice and chicken), or steaming desserts like cheesecake.

SLING. This comes in handy for pot-in-pot cooking—a sling makes it easier to remove large pans from the inside of the cooker pot. You can make your own sling by taking an 18-inch strip of foil and folding it lengthwise into thirds. Center your pan in the middle of the sling, then carefully lower it into the pot, preferably onto a trivet or egg rack, and then tuck the ends away before securing the cooker lid. You can use the sling ends to lift the pan out of the cooker when done.

CHOOSING AN ELECTRIC PRESSURE COOKER

In a world full of convenient small appliances capable of making any kitchen task easier, the consumer market is literally exploding with countless electric pressure cookers and multicookers.

Which Type of Electric Pressure Cooker Should I Get?

To decide which cooker is right for you, first consider your cooking habits. What kinds of dishes do you commonly make? If you already own a stove-top pressure cooker and use it frequently, maybe you're just looking to move to an electric cooker to free you from babysitting the heat. In this case, a standard electric pressure cooker would be the way to go; this type of cooker has limited built-in functions but specializes in pressure cooking all of the foods you're used to cooking in your stove-top version.

Second, go into your kitchen and look around. How much counter space do you have? If you already have a collection of small appliances cluttering your counters, or your kitchen is tiny, a multicooker is the way to go. It will perform all the functions of a pressure cooker, and it can also double as an excellent slow cooker and rice cooker. Many models can even make yogurt and cakes; some even have a sterilize function for jars and baby bottles!

Third, how much money do you want to spend? Electric pressure cookers are relatively inexpensive compared with most multicookers, so if you already own appliances that do the things a multicooker can do and you're on a budget, saving some money by choosing a basic model might be a good idea.

What Size Cooker Is the Right Size for Two?

Most electric pressure cookers and multicookers range in capacity from 3 to 9 quarts. Unless you're strictly cooking extremely small-batch meals on a regular basis, a 5- or 6-quart cooker is probably the best choice for a household of two. The recipes in this book were written for a 6-quart cooker. Keep in mind that, as for any pot that's advertised to hold a certain volume, you won't use all of the cooker's available space. For example, 6-quart volume means the capacity of the cooker when filled all the way to the top, which is something you won't ever do.

If you think you will be batch-cooking weekly, or you plan to cook whole chickens, game hens, or large cuts of meat, you may want to go bigger and choose a cooker with an 8-quart capacity. It's wider and taller, so it will also take up more space on your counter.

Selecting a Particular Brand of Multicooker

If you're faced with choosing a brand of multicooker, consider their main differences:

Instant Pot. The original multicooker, the Instant Pot, is available in 3-, 6-, and 8-quart sizes, and also offers different models with particular functions. The Lux is the 6-in-1 model; it is the closest to a standard electric pressure cooker, and it also has slow cooker and rice cooker functions. The Duo 7-in-1, the most popular model, comes equipped with a yogurt function, allowing you to make homemade yogurt easily (Instant Pot also offers a Duo Plus 9-in-1). The Ultra 10-in-1 model is a fully automated Instant Pot, providing push-button pressure release, a user-friendly LCD display, and the ability to adjust for altitude, among other impressive features. In addition, the Smart model comes with Bluetooth connectivity.

Fagor LUX. A well-trusted brand for decades, Fagor is known for its stove-top pressure cookers, making the electric versions a popular option. The LUX multicooker is next to the Instant Pot for most popular brand, and is even widely recognized as a better cooker overall. In multiple tests, it pressurized and depressurized faster than any other brand of cooker, and its user-friendly controls are a hit among home cooks. It also comes in many colors to fit your kitchen aesthetic.

Power Pressure Cooker XL. One of the largest multicookers (10-quart) on the market, this is an excellent choice for larger families. An affordable option, this cooker has an easy-to-use interface, giving you one of the highest levels of functionality in the electric pressure cooker market.

Breville Fast Slow Pro. The pricey but flashy Breville offers 11 cooking modes and is almost completely automated for the ultimate hands-off cook. This model boasts a color-changing LED display system, making it easy to double-check how the cooking is coming along. It is also one of the safest models of electric pressure cooker, with numerous safety features that other brands don't have.

Crock-Pot Multi-Use Express Crock. The most popular slow cooker company has arrived to try to take back its convenience crown with the newest multicooker on the market. It has preset buttons that allow you to increase or decrease the cook time. It also comes with a nonstick inner pot instead of a stainless steel one, so there is less sticking, but also less browning of ingredients to enhance flavor.

Ninja 4-in-1 Cooking System. This cooker has a stove-top function and is a slow cooker, a steamer, and an oven all in one! The Ninja could very well take over all the cooking in your kitchen if you let it.

All electric pressure cookers work at standard PSI (pounds per square inch) ranges. The pressure rise inside the cooker directly correlates with the rise in the water's boiling point. Any recipe you decide to cook again will be easy to duplicate with equally delicious results.

ELECTRIC PRESSURE COOKING FOR TWO

If you're new to pressure cooking, you'll want to first get very familiar with the manual for your cooker. The manual is comprehensive, telling you how to operate the machine and how to cook various types of food, and it even offers some fun tips.

The Pressure Cooking Sequence

Here's a quick overview of the primary steps used in electric pressure cooking (after fully reading the recipe, of course):

1. Mise en place. A French culinary term often used in professional kitchens, *mise en place* means "everything in its place." As for any recipe, ingredient preparation is the first step, which may include anything from chopping an onion to measuring out a liquid to soaking dried chiles for 15 minutes. Having all of your prepped ingredients ready to go and placed nearby streamlines the cooking process.

2. Pre-pressurized cooking. You may need to do some pre-pressurized cooking in the inner pot, which basically includes any sautéing, browning, or searing that needs to be done before you put the lid on. Melt oil or butter and work your magic on those onions and garlic. Season the ingredients. Deglaze the pan with some wine and scrape up all those tasty browned bits to punch up the flavor. Those delicious flavors cannot develop in the wet heat of a sealed pressure cooker, so attending carefully to this step is well worth it.

3. Remember the liquid. If you're steaming something on a trivet or in a steamer basket in the cooker, do not forget to add the water! No liquid = no steam = no cooking. In many recipes, the liquid comes from the food itself, so less water is required, but check your manual for the minimum amount to use (every brand has one).

4. Check the pressure needed. Once you're ready to close the cooker, ensure that the lid is fitted with the sealing ring, then lock the lid on. Don't forget to check that the pressure release valve is set to the sealing function. It will happen—you'll forget, and a half hour later you'll wonder why there is steam pouring from the valve but nothing is cooking. Also, always double-check the recipe for the pressure setting. Most of the recipes in this book cook at high pressure, but there are a few that require a low pressure setting.

5. Set the timer. Pay attention to the time that pops up on the digital screen when setting your cooker and adjust accordingly. As long as you set the correct time, the cooker will do the arduous work for you. The pressure can take anywhere from 1 to 15 minutes to build up in the cooker, depending on what's in the pot before the cooking time begins. Sometimes a bit of steam may leak out during the pressurizing stage, which is okay.

6. Let it go. The pressure, that is. When your cooker beeps to let you know its job is done, make sure you're paying attention, especially if a quick pressure release is needed. There's nothing more discouraging at dinnertime than overcooked, mushy pasta that was meant to be al dente. Be careful when performing a quick release to avoid getting any body parts near the valve when you turn it—the steam is extremely hot. The lid will unlock when the pressure is completely dispersed and the float valve has dropped. Always be careful when removing the lid, titling the steam vent away from you.

7. Finish it off. Some recipes require some post-pressurized attention, in the form of shredding meat, thickening a sauce or gravy, or adding more ingredients and completing the cooking with the lid off. Don't forget to follow these final steps for a perfect home-cooked meal.

Some Useful Equipment

Any electric pressure cooker will be amazing right off the shelf (and many come with bonus items), but investing in some extra pieces of equipment can turn a once-in-a-while pressure cooking hobby into an obsession. Here are some items that you'll likely use often when pressure cooking for two.

Cooking thermometer. No more guessing about whether the pork chops are really done. This handy kitchen gadget helps you know whether the item you are cooking is exactly the right temperature. There are several types of kitchen thermometers (for meat, liquids, oven temperature, all-purpose, etc.).

Ramekins. These are small ceramic or glass custard cups, perfect for individually sized meals, side dishes, or desserts; they come in several sizes. Also useful are 4-inch springform pans, for slightly larger but still single-serve desserts. Before filling them, be sure to grease with butter, oil, or cooking spray.

Sealing rings. The pressure cooker lid comes with a removable sealing ring that should be cleaned after every use. No matter how much you clean it, it will retain some of the smells from previous recipes. If you're planning on making a sweet recipe, like oatmeal or flan, consider picking up one or two more rings to keep, for example, the garlic flavor from yesterday's Shakshuka out of today's Cannoli Cheesecake. The rings wear out eventually anyway, so it's wise to keep a few on hand.

Small cake pan. Any 6- or 7-inch round, square, or rectangular pan or dish (glass, ceramic, or metal) can be used in your cooker for anything from cakes to lasagna to frittatas. Grease them with butter, oil, or cooking spray before filling.

Steamer basket. Much like a trivet with holes and feet, a steamer basket keeps food up out of the water. It is great for steaming vegetables like potatoes, cauliflower, and broccoli, and makes removal of foods easy.

Trivet. A trivet is a rack with feet that keeps ingredients or pot-in-pot dishes off the bottom of the pressure cooker. Most brands include one in the cooker.

Dos and Don'ts

As with any new appliance, there are a few rules to abide by:

DO read the entire recipe before you begin. Varying seasonings is one thing, but eyeballing liquids is another, especially in an appliance that relies on liquids to work.

DO use the release method specified in the recipe. Using a natural release when you actually needed a quick release will leave you with overcooked food.

DO double recipes if you find a dish you really love or are having company over for dinner. All of the recipes in this book are easy to double.

DO keep your pressure cooker clean. A little TLC will keep your new favorite appliance around for years. Wash the inner pot in warm, soapy water after every use. Clean the lid with a wet cloth and wipe it dry. Remove and clean the sealing ring and allow it to dry before replacing it. If the pressure release valve has collected foam from cooking pasta or rice, you can remove it for cleaning.

DON'T add too much liquid in the cooker, and DON'T leave the liquid out completely. Pressure cookers trap steam, allowing you to cook with less liquid than traditional stove-top cooking allows. It also keeps your food from scorching.

DON'T overfill the pressure cooker. Resist the temptation to fill your pot to the top—in fact, try to keep it less than two-thirds full. If there isn't enough space above the food in the cooker, proper pressure won't be reached, and foods like rice or beans that create a lot of foam may block the valves.

✳ **DON'T** increase cooking time when doubling recipes. The pressure cooks all of the food inside at the same rate, so even with twice as many potatoes, it will really only take the same number of minutes.

DON'T be careless when using your electric pressure cooker. The cookers themselves are built for safety, but be mindful when operating. Ensure that the bottom of the inner pot and the heating plate are clean and dry before using. Make sure the lid is in good working condition—meaning the valve is clean and free of food buildup, and the sealing ring is secure. Always use caution when releasing pressure, and don't forget to unplug your pressure cooker when you're done with it.

How to Double Recipes

So, you're having company for dinner tomorrow and want to double a recipe? Easy. Prepare twice as much of every ingredient; sauté things the same way; butcher cuts of meat to the same thickness but sear them in batches. As long as the thickness of your ingredients is the same, you can generally follow the original recipe cook time. A fuller pot does take longer to both build and release pressure, in which case you may need to slightly decrease your cook time (since food continues to cook during pressure release). Be sure to never fill the pot above the maximum fill line—maximum capacity is typically two-thirds full, or half full for foods that foam when cooking.

SMART MEAL PLANNING

For many people, meal planning consists of nothing more than making large quantities of dishes, then packing the leftovers for lunch or dinner the next day. For some, it involves taking an afternoon to meticulously prepare individual components and portion them into different flavor combos for the whole week.

Both methods are smart in their own way, but what if there were another way? What if you could plan your meals and have a different one every night with no extra effort?

Meal planning for two is just as challenging as meal planning for a larger family, if not more so. A larger family means more mouths to eat the food prepared, but paring down your favorite recipes for only two people is totally possible. You don't have to eat the same meal three nights in a row—or worse, two nights, with the rest ending up in the trash.

If you're a busy couple, one of the best ways to keep yourselves organized in the kitchen is to actually plan a weekly menu. Dog-ear a page in a cookbook or find something tasty on Pinterest and print the recipe. Decide how much time you have to cook on a given night during the week and pop those recipes on a calendar. Being able to look ahead during the week to see what meals you'll be enjoying will keep your mind at ease when you're trying to get everything done.

Next to that calendar, keep a running shopping list. The same day you plan your weekly meals, check your fridge and pantry and jot down the ingredients you'll need to pick up on your trip to the grocery store. By planning and shopping for an entire week instead of stopping in the grocery store every night to pick up one or two things for a recipe, you'll save time and energy.

At the end of every week, take a look at your pantry items and organize your refrigerator to see what ingredients are left. Plan on including anything perishable in one or two of the following week's meals, then repeat the planning and shopping. No one likes to throw away food, so go ahead and plump up your weekend frittata with leftover greens or make a side of mac 'n' cheese with a leftover block of cheese.

One of the greatest time-saving meal planning tips is to prep extra proteins for one or two additional meals during the week. You could easily portion a pork loin, but you also have the option of cooking the whole thing at once and serving it differently every night with freshly cooked side dishes. For example, you can cook a roast pork loin with mashed potatoes and Brussels sprouts for a delicious, hearty Sunday dinner, and then you can use some of the leftover pork on Tuesday to top a salad for lunch, and finish off the meat in a quick and easy stir-fry supper on Wednesday night. Think of how much time you will have saved by cooking the large pork roast once. And in an electric pressure cooker, it's an even easier process.

A Well-Stocked Pantry

There's nothing worse than getting excited about a recipe, gathering up the ingredients, and realizing you're out of one of the main components. Keeping a well-stocked pantry and refrigerator is the best way to avoid a last-minute trip to the grocery store and keeps your pressure-cooking way of life as quick and painless as it's supposed to be. Make a habit of jotting down the staples you've run out of or don't have so you can pick them up on your next shopping trip. You'll be using the following staples (or their vegan/Paleo alternatives) often when cooking the recipes in this book.

BROTHS AND STOCKS. Make them yourself (the recipes are in this book) and freeze, or buy them. Chicken stock can be used in almost any soup, or to cook rice or beans, but if you're vegetarian or vegan, a vegetable or mushroom stock is the way to go.

BUTTER. Even if you try to stay away from butter, it's still better than eating margarine, and it is a delicious way to add loads of flavor to recipes. Buy a pound and freeze it, pulling out a stick as you need it.

CANNED TOMATOES AND TOMATO SAUCE. Homemade tomato sauce is delicious, but the convenience of canned is undeniable. Having a couple cans of fire-roasted diced tomatoes is also convenient for last-minute pasta dishes and chilis.

EGGS. These are a traditional quick protein, a lazy person's breakfast-for-dinner option, the binding agent in baked goods—and they are super nutritious.

FLOUR, SUGAR, AND BAKING SODA. Even an ordinary cook will benefit from stocking these basic dry goods in the pantry.

GARLIC. Honestly, it's in just about everything. Keep it in fresh bulbs or minced in a jar of oil, because you're going to need it. Some of the recipes here call for garlic powder, so consider having a jar of that in the pantry as well.

HONEY. The purest natural sweetener on the planet, it's a welcome flavor in numerous dishes.

KOSHER SALT AND BLACK PEPPERCORNS. No doubt about it—if you cook, you need these. Table salt often contains additives, so opt for kosher salt, sea salt, or Himalayan salt. As for pepper, it not only easily flavors your dishes, but it also contains way more health benefits than you would expect. Invest in a good pepper grinder and freshly grind black pepper for each recipe.

LENTILS AND DRIED BEANS. Toss them (soaked and/or cooked) into soups, salads, and rice bowls, purée them into hummus, or add them to chili or ragù-style dishes. This shelf-stable, low-cost protein can be stretched incredibly far.

MILK. Whether dairy or nondairy, even having just a pint in the house will come in handy for numerous recipes. Some recipes call for coconut milk, meaning the canned unsweetened variety, which tends to separate in the can. The thick portion is called coconut cream, and the watery part is called the coconut water or liquid. You can whip chilled coconut cream. Shake the can before opening to recombine the contents.

OIL. Any plant-based oil of your choice. Olive oil is always a popular choice, and if you can find one or two flavored oils (herb-infused), you'll thank yourself later. For a neutral, high-heat cooking option, avocado oil is probably the best.

ONIONS AND SHALLOTS. They add flavor to everything.

PASTA. Spaghetti and macaroni are ubiquitous. Whether it's standard white pasta or gluten-free, it's not just for Italian dishes anymore.

RICE. The fastest, cheapest grain, and the most versatile, it's the most widely consumed staple food around the world.

SHREDDED CHEESE. The fact that you can freeze it is reason enough to buy the big bag, if it even lasts long enough to make it to the freezer.

SPICES, ESPECIALLY RED PEPPER FLAKES, PAPRIKA, AND DRIED HERBS. Pick your favorites and use them in lots of recipes.

VINEGAR. White wine and champagne vinegars are perfect for brightening up salads or raw veggies. Red wine and apple cider vinegars are meant for heartier dishes, while rice vinegar (mirin) is appropriate for milder meals, especially Asian-inspired dinners.

Shopping for Two

Shop at warehouse stores for long-shelf-life items. Oils, nut butters, rice, and most pantry staples are much cheaper when bought in bulk—and you'll save travel money by only having to buy them once in a great while.

BUY PROTEINS IN BULK AND DIVIDE THEM UP INTO ONE-MEAL SERVINGS. Like the long-shelf-life items, bulk proteins are often priced lower by the pound. Even if you're buying three to four times as much as you'd need in a week, double-bagging and freezing the extra portions makes practical (and financial) sense.

SHOP THE SALES ADS. Grocery stores send out those flyers for a reason! Use your coupons, take advantage of buy-one-get-one-free deals, and always check the clearance shelves for perfectly good but discontinued items that will enhance your cooking.

FIND A GOOD FARMERS' MARKET. There's nothing like farm-fresh produce, both in taste and cost, especially seasonal items (because grocery store produce prices include a markup incurred by their packaging and shipping costs). Make it a point to stop at the farmers' market once a week to pick up just the fruits and veggies you'll need for your meals.

SHOP WITH A FRIEND AND SPLIT THE COST OF SOME OF THOSE WAREHOUSE STORE MUST-HAVE BULK ITEMS. Maybe you can't eat 10 pounds of carrots in a week, but 5 pounds is doable. Not only will splitting save you from wasting half of the bag, but you'll also have half of those dollars to spend on something else.

DON'T BUY WHAT YOU DON'T NEED. Keep your shopping list limited to what you will absolutely eat. That family-size jug of apple cider may be on sale, but if only one of you drinks it, then you'll be stuck trying to finish it on your own.

Time-Saving Tips

I've learned many time-savers since cooking for two with our multicooker. Here are some that may be useful to you:

MAKE A SHOPPING LIST. They say you should never shop hungry; you should also never shop aimlessly. If you're a pro meal prepper, or even an aspiring one, keep a running shopping list on your fridge. Make a note when you're running low or are completely out of something you need and add it to the list when you set your meal plan for the week. Having a shopping list and sticking to it can save so much time in the grocery store!

DON'T BE AFRAID OF LEFTOVERS, AT LEAST WHEN IT COMES TO PROTEINS, RICE, AND BEANS. Pressure-cook three times as much chicken on Monday as you need for dinner. The following day, you can shred it and have two different lunch and dinner options halfway done. Store in the refrigerator in airtight containers to keep fresh.

KEEP YOUR KITCHEN IN ORDER. A labeled spice rack or cabinet, an organized pantry, a big drawer or cupboard just for pots and pans . . . sounds like a dream, right? Invest in a onetime overhaul of your kitchen, and it will require only very little maintenance while making your cooking life easier.

LEARN TO LOVE POT-IN-POT COOKING. What's not to love about a one-pot meal? With a trivet, a steamer basket, and a stainless steel bowl, you can cook your veggie, protein, and side dish at the same time (depending on what they are, of course) in the cooker. One-pot meals also mean fewer dirty dishes!

PREP YOUR STAPLES. Spend an hour a week mincing garlic, chopping onions, and turning those gorgeous heads of broccoli and cauliflower into small florets. Prepping the veggies and herbs you know you'll need in the next few days will help cut down on the amount of time you spend in the kitchen every day. Store in airtight containers in the refrigerator.

USE THE RIGHT TOOLS. A good set of knives is an invaluable kitchen tool. The sharper the knife, the faster you can slice through all those veggies and meats that are going into your dinner. A mandoline is also an option; it's a handy tool to have for thin slices. Having those extra pressure cooker equipment items handy (steamer basket, rame-kins, etc.) will keep you from hunting around your kitchen for the perfectly sized cooking vessel, or from chasing stray Brussels sprouts around the pan.

The Best (and Worst) Foods to Pressure Cook

The convenience of an electric pressure cooker is motivating, and after a few successful meals, you're bound to start feeling experimental. But not everything is meant to be made in a pressure cooker. Here are some examples of the best and worst foods to cook in the pressure cooker:

BEST

BOILED EGGS. Soft- or hard-boiled, the perfect egg is finally within reach! They cook perfectly every time and peel like a dream.

BROTHS. One hour and done. No matter what kind of broth you need, just pop your ingredients in the multicooker and go about your day.

POTATOES. Whether they're baked, mashed, Russet, or sweet, nothing will cook your potatoes as well as an electric pressure cooker.

RISOTTO. This is a difficult dish to master even for some chefs. Put a little love into sautéing and deglazing before a 6-minute cooking time, and you'll be eating the most tender, creamiest risotto of your life.

ROASTS AND TOUGH CUTS OF MEAT. Grandma's all-day oven pot roast is achievable in 1 hour, thanks to your electric pressure cooker taking care of the old-fashioned low-and-slow cooking method.

WORST

BREADS AND PASTRIES. Cheesecakes and flans are perfect desserts for the pressure cooker, but some sweets just need the dry heat that only an oven can provide.

CERTAIN SHELLFISH SUCH AS SCALLOPS AND SHRIMP. You'll notice that there are several shrimp recipes in this book, but the shrimp is always added after the pressure-cooking time. Shrimp and scallops are delicate proteins that need special treatment.

TENDER CUTS OF BEEF LIKE RIB EYE OR NEW YORK STRIP. Steaks never met a grill or cast-iron pan they didn't like, so don't ruin them in a pressure cooker.

WHOLE CHICKEN. It is very possible to cook a chicken in most cookers, but . . . just don't do it. Cut up the chicken ahead of time if you want to, and cook the light and dark meat separately. Cook half of it at a time; the amount of water needed to cook a whole chicken goes way above the recommended fill line and takes forever to pressurize, and you'll likely be left with overcooked white meat by the time the dark meat is done.

ABOUT THE RECIPES

The recipes in this book are easy to understand and use. For each one, I've provided the prep time (including minutes for chopping, sautéing, and finishing), cook time (how long you should set your pressure cooker timer for), and total time (an approximate overall time from start of prep to sitting down to eat). I also have included the number of servings (every recipe is for two, even the desserts), the cooker pressure and release settings, and some ingredient substitution tips. I've provided "to serve" suggestions at the end of the ingredient lists.

The special characteristics of the recipes are also clearly labeled to make your recipe choice as easy as possible. For example:

5-INGREDIENT. The recipe uses five or fewer main ingredients. A few basic pantry staples (salt, pepper, oil, etc.) do not count toward these primary five ingredients.

30 MINUTES OR LESS. The recipe requires 30 minutes or less to make from start to finish. This includes prep time, the time it takes to reach cooker pressure, and the time it takes to completely release the pressure.

COMFORT FOOD. The recipe makes one of those classic, nostalgic dishes that you just feel good eating.

ONE-POT MEAL. The recipe makes a complete meal requiring only your electric pressure cooker to prepare, so cleanup is a snap.

WORTH THE WAIT. The recipe may take 1 hour or longer from start to finish, but the delicious results make up for the extra time required.

Each recipe also includes specific nutrition information and labels indicating whether the recipe fulfills special dietary needs (or can be modified to fulfill that need):

LIGHT AND HEALTHY. The recipe is relatively low in calories, sodium, and fat, or it offers substitution/modification suggestions to make the dish low in calories, sodium, and fat.

PALEO/PALEO-FRIENDLY. The recipe follows the Paleo diet or offers substitution/ modification suggestions to make the dish follow the guidelines of the Paleo diet.

VEGAN/VEGAN-FRIENDLY. The ingredients in the recipe adhere to the vegan diet, or the recipe offers substitution/modification suggestions to make the dish without animal products.

VEGETARIAN/VEGETARIAN-FRIENDLY. The ingredients in the recipe adhere to the vegetarian diet, or the recipe offers substitution/modification suggestions to make the dish without meat.

Two

BREAKFAST AND BRUNCH

Your pressure cooker loves breakfast almost as much as you do. Whether you're craving oatmeal, an egg-based meal, or something sweet, your cooker can quickly fulfill most of your hankerings. The recipes in this chapter run the gamut of flavor profiles and are sure to satisfy. You will need a trivet, 1-cup-size ramekins, and a small cake pan or heatproof bowls for most of these dishes—not only for making small portions but also for making cleanup a breeze.

Tomato-Basil Eggs en Cocotte, page 22

Savory Oatmeal with Eggs and Chorizo 21

Tomato-Basil Eggs en Cocotte 22

Arugula and Feta Frittata 24

Shakshuka 25

Eggs and Smoked Sausage Bake 26

Turkey and Sweet Potato Egg Breakfast Cups 27

French Toast Casserole 28

Southwestern Hash 29

Biscuits with Sausage Gravy 30

Maple-Pecan Steel-Cut Oatmeal 31

Blueberries and Cream Clafouti 32

Raspberry-Almond Breakfast Cake 33

Chocolate Chip Banana Bread 35

Baked Apples with Coconut Muesli 36

Chocolate-Covered-Strawberry Breakfast Quinoa 37

PRESSURE LEVEL: High
RELEASE: Natural

2 links Spanish chorizo, sliced

½ cup uncooked steel-cut oats

1½ cups water

½ tablespoon unsalted butter

Pinch kosher salt

2 fried eggs

TO SERVE
- Shredded cheese
- Chopped scallions
- Freshly ground
  black pepper

SAVORY OATMEAL WITH EGGS AND CHORIZO

5-INGREDIENT | 30 MINUTES OR LESS

People usually enjoy their oatmeal on the sweeter side, loaded with cinnamon, brown sugar, and fruit. Using savory ingredients occasionally, though, makes a heartier, more nourishing breakfast possible in less time than it takes to hop in your morning shower. The steel-cut oats in this recipe are infused with the flavor of Spanish chorizo before they're cooked and can be made chewy or creamy depending on your preference.

1. Preheat the pressure cooker pot on sauté mode. When the display reads hot, add the chorizo and brown for 2 to 3 minutes. Transfer to a bowl and set aside, leaving any grease in the cooker pot.

2. Add the oats to the cooker and toast for about 2 minutes, stirring to avoid burning. Add the water, butter, and salt, and stir to combine.

3. Secure the lid and cook on high pressure for 11 minutes for chewier oats or 13 minutes for creamier oats. Allow a natural release at the end of the cook time. Carefully remove the lid.

4. Divide the cooked oats between two cereal bowls and top with an egg and the chorizo. To serve, sprinkle with cheese and chopped scallions, and season with salt and pepper.

Nutrition Tip Make this breakfast vegetarian by leaving out the chorizo and instead toasting the oats in a plant-based oil. Lower the calorie count even more by omitting the cheese and spooning on a little Greek yogurt instead.

PER SERVING Calories: 780; Total fat: 50g; Saturated fat: 23g; Cholesterol: 463mg; Carbohydrates: 32g; Fiber: 4g; Protein: 43g

SERVES 2
PREP TIME: 30 minutes
COOK TIME: 8 minutes
TOTAL TIME: 45 minutes

PRESSURE LEVEL: High
RELEASE: Quick

1 cup grape tomatoes, halved

2 teaspoons kosher salt

Unsalted butter, softened, for greasing

1 teaspoon oil

1 garlic clove, minced

1 tablespoon freshly squeezed lemon juice

½ teaspoon sugar

3 cups chopped mushrooms

1 tablespoon chopped fresh basil

4 tablespoons heavy cream

4 eggs

2 tablespoons shredded Parmesan cheese (optional)

Freshly ground black pepper (optional)

Hot sauce (optional)

TOMATO-BASIL EGGS EN COCOTTE

VEGETARIAN

Switch up your familiar eggs-for-breakfast game with this elegant yet easy presentation. Known as *oeufs en cocotte* in French, this dish is named for the small vessels—ramekins or cocottes—in which the eggs are cooked. This appealing meal is reminiscent of tomato bisque in flavor and is delicious served with runny yolks and crusty bread or English muffins.

1. Place the tomatoes in a fine-mesh strainer set over a medium bowl and sprinkle with salt. Massage the salt into the tomatoes and allow them to drain for 20 to 30 minutes.

2. Add 1 cup of water to the pressure cooker pot and place the trivet or egg rack in the bottom. Coat four ramekins with butter and set aside.

3. On the stove top, heat the oil in a medium saucepan over medium heat. Add the garlic and brown lightly, stirring often, until fragrant, about 1 minute. Add the drained tomatoes. Reduce the heat to low, cover, and simmer for 5 to 6 minutes until softened.

4. Add the lemon juice and sugar and stir to combine. Stir in the mushrooms and cook for 2 to 3 minutes, continuing to stir frequently. Remove from the heat and stir in the basil.

5. Distribute the tomato-mushroom mixture evenly among the prepared ramekins. Add 1 tablespoon of cream to each ramekin, then crack an egg into each one. Sprinkle some Parmesan cheese over each egg (if using). Place three ramekins on the trivet in a three-leaf clover arrangement, then center the fourth one on top of the others.

6. Secure the lid and cook on high pressure for 2 to 4 minutes, depending on how soft you want the yolks. Quick release the pressure, then remove the lid.

7. Carefully remove the ramekins from the pot. Season with salt, pepper, and hot sauce (as desired).

Variation Tip   For a different, more umami flavor profile, replace the tomato-mushroom mixture with bacon or cooked crumbled breakfast sausage. Layer on some fresh baby spinach before adding the cream and the egg, then top with some crumbled goat cheese before cooking.

PER SERVING Calories: 486; Total fat: 41g; Saturated fat: 22g; Cholesterol: 464mg; Carbohydrates: 8.4g; Fiber: 1g; Protein: 24g

PRESSURE LEVEL: High

RELEASE: Natural

Unsalted butter, at room temperature, for greasing

3 eggs, beaten

¼ red onion, chopped

¼ cup loosely packed arugula

¼ cup feta cheese crumbles

¼ teaspoon garlic powder

Kosher salt

Freshly ground black pepper

TO SERVE

- Sliced avocado
- Marinated tomatoes

ARUGULA AND FETA FRITTATA

30 MINUTES OR LESS | LIGHT AND HEALTHY
PALEO-FRIENDLY | VEGETARIAN

A frittata is easy enough when started on the stove top and then popped into the oven to continue cooking, but being able to set it and forget it in your electric pressure cooker is so convenient on a busy morning. This classic egg-based Italian breakfast is a perfect, low-calorie way to use any veggies and cheeses you have in your refrigerator. Serve with some sun-dried or marinated tomatoes and sliced avocado for even more nutritional value and flavor.

1. Add 1 cup of water to your cooker pot and place the trivet or egg rack in the bottom. Coat a 7-inch baking vessel (round cake pan, ramekin, or bowl) with butter and set aside.

2. In a medium bowl, stir together the eggs, onion, arugula, feta, and garlic powder, and season with salt and pepper. Add to the prepared pan. Cover with foil.

3. Carefully put the frittata mixture on top of the trivet.

4. Secure the lid and cook on high pressure for 5 minutes, then allow the pressure to naturally release, about 10 minutes. Open the vent at the top and remove the lid. Remove the frittata. Serve hot with sliced avocado and marinated tomatoes.

Variation Tip Craving some breakfast meat? Add another egg and mix in some crumbled sausage, chopped bacon, or leftover turkey. For a Paleo frittata, skip the cheese and add some more hearty veggies.

PER SERVING Calories: 152; Total fat: 11g; Saturated fat: 5g; Cholesterol: 262mg; Carbohydrates: 3g; Fiber: 0.4g; Protein: 11g

SERVES 2
PREP TIME: 5 minutes
COOK TIME: 10 minutes
TOTAL TIME: 25 minutes

PRESSURE LEVEL: High
RELEASE: Quick

1 tablespoon oil

½ large onion, chopped

½ bell pepper, chopped

1 jalapeño pepper, seeded and diced

2 large garlic cloves, minced

1 (14.5-ounce) can crushed tomatoes, mostly drained

2 teaspoons paprika

1 teaspoon ground cumin

¼ teaspoon red pepper flakes

Freshly ground black pepper

1 cup loosely packed fresh baby spinach

4 eggs

TO SERVE
- Thickly sliced fresh rustic bread
- Hot sauce (optional)

SHAKSHUKA

30 MINUTES OR LESS | LIGHT AND HEALTHY | VEGETARIAN

Also known as Eggs in Purgatory, this simple Middle Eastern breakfast is made of eggs poached in a spicy tomato-pepper sauce, with a little added spinach for extra nutrition. The heat is variable based on the chef's preference, and it's delicious served with a slice or two of crusty bread to soak up all the tasty juices.

1. Preheat the cooker pot on sauté mode. When the display reads hot, add the oil. Add the onion, bell pepper, and jalapeño, and sauté until softened, 4 to 5 minutes. Add the garlic and cook, stirring often, for 1 minute.

2. Stir in the tomatoes, paprika, cumin, red pepper flakes, and black pepper to combine well.

3. Secure the lid and cook on high pressure for 10 minutes, then quick release the pressure in the cooker and remove the lid. Select sauté.

4. Layer the spinach on top and let wilt for 1 to 2 minutes. Crack the eggs, one at a time, into a small bowl, then gently lower each one onto the bubbling sauce.

5. Cook, loosely covered, until the egg whites are set but the yolks are still runny, 3 to 4 minutes.

6. Serve with bread and hot sauce (if using).

Serving Tip To cool off your soon-to-be-hot mouth, serve this dish with sliced avocado and a sprinkling of shredded cheese.

PER SERVING Calories: 323; Total fat: 17g; Saturated fat: 4g; Cholesterol: 327mg; Carbohydrates: 29g; Fiber: 10g; Protein: 18g

SERVES 2
PREP TIME: 10 minutes
COOK TIME: 15 minutes
TOTAL TIME: 25 minutes

PRESSURE LEVEL: High
RELEASE: Quick

Unsalted butter, at room temperature, or oil, for greasing

4 ounces ready-to-eat smoked sausage, chopped

1½ cups shredded hash browns

4 eggs

¼ cup milk

¼ cup shredded Cheddar cheese

1 teaspoon kosher salt

½ teaspoon freshly ground black pepper

EGGS AND SMOKED SAUSAGE BAKE

30 MINUTES OR LESS

A hearty breakfast, this little casserole combines smoky sausage with hash browns, eggs, and cheese into one simple, delicious meal. Top with extra cheese and broil at the end for a yummy, crispy top.

1. Add 1 cup of water to the pressure cooker pot and place the trivet in the bottom. Coat a heatproof 7-inch bowl with butter and set aside. Place a small pan on the trivet.

2. Preheat the pressure cooker on sauté mode. When the display reads hot, add the sausage to the pan on the trivet and sauté for 2 to 3 minutes, or until browned. Add the hash browns and cook for 2 to 3 minutes, or until the liquid evaporates. Transfer the sausage mixture to the prepared bowl.

3. In a medium bowl, whisk together the eggs, milk, cheese, salt, and pepper. Pour over the sausage and hash browns. Place the bowl on top of the trivet.

4. Secure the lid and cook on high pressure for 15 minutes, then quick release the pressure in the cooker and remove the lid. Remove the bowl from the cooker, let cool for 5 minutes, and serve.

Ingredient Tip Adding veggies to this casserole will not only help clean out your crisper drawer, but it will also boost your vitamin intake for the day. Chopped onion, bell pepper, spinach, or mushrooms are all tasty, low-calorie additions.

PER SERVING Calories: 715; Total fat: 45g; Saturated fat: 14g; Cholesterol: 387mg; Carbohydrates: 44g; Fiber: 4g; Protein: 33g

SERVES 2

PREP TIME: 5 minutes

COOK TIME: 5 minutes

TOTAL TIME: 25 minutes

PRESSURE LEVEL: High
RELEASE: Natural

4 slices deli turkey

½ cup shredded sweet
potatoes

2 teaspoons butter, melted

⅓ cup shredded
Cheddar cheese

2 eggs

2 teaspoons milk

Kosher salt

Freshly ground black pepper

1 scallion, sliced

TURKEY AND SWEET POTATO EGG BREAKFAST CUPS

30 MINUTES OR LESS | LIGHT AND HEALTHY

They say that breakfast is the most important meal of the day, but it's also the most ignored, especially when you're habitually running late. Having handy, on-the-go bites like these delicious protein- and antioxidant-loaded egg breakfast cups will keep you strong until your next meal.

1. Add 1 cup of water to the pressure cooker pot and place the trivet or egg rack in the bottom.

2. Line 4 cups of a muffin tin with the turkey slices.

3. In a medium bowl, combine the sweet potatoes with the butter. Spoon into the turkey-lined breakfast cups. Sprinkle with the cheese.

4. In a medium bowl, whisk together the eggs and milk, and season with salt and pepper. Pour the egg mixture over the potatoes and cheese in the breakfast cups. Top with the scallion.

5. Place the breakfast cups on the trivet.

6. Secure the lid and cook on high pressure for 5 minutes, then allow the pressure to naturally release, about 10 minutes. Open the vent at the top and remove the lid.

7. Let the breakfast cups cool slightly and enjoy them warm, or refrigerate in a covered container and reheat in the microwave when ready to eat.

Ingredient Tip These easy breakfast cups are a great way to use what's in the produce bin in your refrigerator. Add some sliced mushrooms, chopped tomato, or bell pepper to some of the cups, introducing a variety of flavors to the batch.

PER SERVING Calories: 249; Total fat: 16g; Saturated fat: 8g; Cholesterol: 220mg; Carbohydrates: 9g; Fiber: 1g; Protein: 17g

SERVES 2

PREP TIME: 30 minutes

COOK TIME: 25 minutes

TOTAL TIME: 45 minutes

PRESSURE LEVEL: High

RELEASE: Quick

1 tablespoon butter, melted,
plus more for greasing

¼ cup packed brown sugar

¾ cup whole milk

2 eggs, beaten

½ teaspoon ground cinnamon

½ teaspoon vanilla extract

½ teaspoon salt

6 slices thick-cut brioche
bread, cubed and
lightly toasted

¼ cup raisins

FRENCH TOAST CASSEROLE

VEGETARIAN

Pressure cooker French toast casserole is as close as you can get to having dessert for breakfast! Steaming the casserole versus baking it turns it into a cinnamon-sweet bread pudding that tastes so delicious with your morning cup of coffee or a tall glass of milk.

1. Add 1 cup of water to the pressure cooker pot and place the trivet or egg rack in the bottom. Coat a 7-inch round cake pan with butter and set aside.

2. In a large bowl, whisk together 1 tablespoon of melted butter and the brown sugar. Whisk in the milk, eggs, cinnamon, vanilla, and salt. Stir in the bread and raisins. Let rest for 5 minutes, or until the bread absorbs all of the milk, tossing occasionally.

3. Spread the cubed bread mixture into the prepared pan. Cover with a paper towel, then a piece of aluminum foil.

4. Prepare a foil sling (see page 4), center the pan on it, and lower the pan into the cooker. Arrange the sling ends across the pan.

5. Secure the lid and cook on high pressure for 15 minutes, then quick release the pressure in the pot and remove the lid. Remove the pan from the pot using the tails of the sling.

6. Let the casserole cool slightly, then slice and serve warm.

Cooking Tip For a crispy top, sprinkle the French toast with coarse sugar and set it under the broiler for a few minutes to brown up. To make an extra-decadent treat, drizzle each piece with some sweetened condensed milk and/or serve with a dollop of whipped heavy cream.

PER SERVING Calories: 950; Total fat: 33g; Saturated fat: 15g; Cholesterol: 188mg; Carbohydrates: 136g; Fiber: 8g; Protein: 24g

SERVES 2
PREP TIME: 20 minutes
COOK TIME: 5 minutes
TOTAL TIME: 30 minutes

PRESSURE LEVEL: High
RELEASE: Quick

3 links Spanish chorizo, sliced

½ onion, sliced

2 teaspoons oil

3 small Russet potatoes, cubed

1 teaspoon fresh rosemary leaves, minced

Kosher salt

Freshly ground black pepper

½ cup roasted corn kernels

¼ cup chopped roasted red bell pepper

⅓ cup shredded mozzarella cheese

2 fried eggs

Adobo Barbacoa Sauce (page 175), for drizzling

SOUTHWESTERN HASH

30 MINUTES OR LESS

Inspired by a delicious dish at a charming little Florida bistro, this hash has everything you could want in a Southwestern breakfast. Crispy rosemary potatoes and spicy chorizo are complemented by roasted corn, a runny egg, and a bit of chipotle chile-inflected Adobo Barbacoa Sauce (page 175) for an earthy flair.

1. Preheat the pressure cooker pot on sauté mode. When the display reads hot, add the chorizo, sautéing until browned, 2 to 3 minutes. Transfer to a medium bowl and set aside, leaving any grease behind in the cooker.

2. Add the onion and sauté until lightly browned, 5 to 6 minutes. Transfer to the bowl with the chorizo.

3. Add the oil to the pot, allowing it to heat for 1 to 2 minutes. Add the potatoes and the rosemary. Season with salt and pepper. Cook the potatoes for 4 to 5 minutes, gently stirring to brown on all sides.

4. Add ½ cup of water to the potatoes. Secure the lid and cook on high pressure for 5 minutes, then quick release the pressure in the pot and remove the lid.

5. Transfer the potatoes to the bowl with the chorizo-onion mixture. Add the corn and roasted red pepper. Season with salt and pepper and stir to combine.

6. Immediately divide the mixture between two bowls. Top with the shredded mozzarella and fried eggs. Drizzle with some adobo sauce as desired and serve.

Variation Tip If you're not a fan of chorizo, chopped chicken or tofu bathed in adobo sauce are equally delicious and satisfying—and lower in cholesterol.

PER SERVING Calories: 477; Total fat: 22g; Saturated fat: 6g; Cholesterol: 194mg; Carbohydrates: 50g; Fiber: 8g; Protein: 22g

SERVES 2
PREP TIME: 10 minutes
COOK TIME: 2 minutes
TOTAL TIME: 20 minutes

PRESSURE LEVEL: Low
RELEASE: Quick

4 store-bought large
buttermilk biscuits

½ pound pork sausage

2 tablespoons flour

1 cup whole milk

¼ teaspoon kosher salt

¼ teaspoon freshly
ground black pepper

BISCUITS WITH SAUSAGE GRAVY

5-INGREDIENT | 30 MINUTES OR LESS | COMFORT FOOD

This traditional Southern recipe of creamy sausage gravy over fluffy buttermilk biscuits will leave you full and satisfied in no time. Make it a complete breakfast or brunch by serving it with eggs, some wilted spinach, and a side of fruit. The biscuits are available in the dairy case of the supermarket.

1. Bake the biscuits in the oven according to the package instructions.

2. While the biscuits bake, prepare the gravy. Preheat the pressure cooker pot on sauté mode. When the display reads hot, add the sausage, breaking it up with a wooden spoon and browning for 5 to 6 minutes, or until it's almost fully cooked.

3. Sprinkle the flour on the sausage and stir until it's blended with the meat. Pour in the milk and stir until combined. Add the salt and pepper.

4. Secure the lid and cook on low pressure for 2 minutes, then quick release the pressure in the pot, remove the lid, and stir. Season with more salt and pepper, if needed.

5. Slice the biscuits in half and serve the gravy over them.

Variation Tip For even more flavor (and a few more calories), sauté some bacon with the pork sausage and add 1 tablespoon butter.

PER SERVING Calories: 775; Total fat: 39g; Saturated fat: 12g; Cholesterol: 105mg; Carbohydrates: 70g; Fiber: 2g; Protein: 35g

SERVES 2
PREP TIME: 2 minutes
COOK TIME: 11 minutes
TOTAL TIME: 30 minutes

PRESSURE LEVEL: High
RELEASE: Natural

½ cup steel-cut oats

1½ cups water

¼ cup maple syrup, plus more for serving

2 tablespoons packed brown sugar

¼ teaspoon ground cinnamon

Pinch kosher salt

1 tablespoon unsalted butter

TO SERVE
- Toasted chopped pecans
- Fresh fruit or Greek yogurt

MAPLE-PECAN STEEL-CUT OATMEAL

5-INGREDIENT | 30 MINUTES OR LESS | ONE-POT MEAL
PALEO-FRIENDLY | VEGAN-FRIENDLY | VEGETARIAN

Ditch your normal morning cereal and try a bowl of heart-healthy steel-cut oatmeal instead. The chewier, less processed cousin of familiar rolled oats, steel-cut oats are equal in nutrition but have a characteristic crunchy texture and body. Cooking them with maple syrup and brown sugar will remind you of your childhood but fill you up like an adult.

1. Preheat the pressure cooker pot on sauté mode. Add the oats and toast for about 2 minutes, stirring to avoid burning. Press cancel, then add the water, ¼ cup of maple syrup, the brown sugar, cinnamon, and a pinch of salt.

2. Secure the lid and cook on high pressure for 11 minutes for chewier oats or 13 minutes for creamier oats. Allow the pressure to naturally release, about 10 minutes, then open the vent at the top and remove the lid.

3. Stir the oats and taste, adding additional maple syrup or salt if desired. For softer oats, replace the lid unlocked and allow to sit 5 to 10 minutes. When ready to serve, stir in the butter. Divide the cooked oats between two bowls and top with pecans, if desired. Serve with fresh fruit or Greek yogurt.

Variation Tip To make this recipe vegan or Paleo, simply leave out the butter and brown sugar; instead, use additional maple syrup to sweeten to your liking. Skip the yogurt topping.

PER SERVING Calories: 475; Total fat: 29g; Saturated fat: 6g; Cholesterol: 15mg; Carbohydrates: 54g; Fiber: 5g; Protein: 6g

SERVES 2

PREP TIME: 5 minutes

COOK TIME: 11 minutes

TOTAL TIME: 25 minutes

PRESSURE LEVEL: High
RELEASE: Quick

Butter, at room temperature, for greasing

3 tablespoons granulated sugar, plus more for sprinkling

½ cup fresh blueberries

1 egg

1 tablespoon all-purpose flour

1 teaspoon rum

¼ cup heavy cream

¼ cup whole milk

¼ teaspoon grated lemon zest

¼ teaspoon vanilla extract

Pinch salt

Powdered sugar, for garnish

BLUEBERRIES AND CREAM CLAFOUTI

30 MINUTES OR LESS | VEGETARIAN

Browned on top but creamy within, this simple but elegant soufflé-style custard cake is a lovely finale to a special breakfast. Dust with powdered sugar before serving, or make it extra decadent with a dollop of heavy whipped cream.

1. Add 1 cup of water to the pressure cooker pot and place the trivet or egg rack in the bottom.

2. Butter two 1-cup ramekins, then sprinkle a bit of granulated sugar in each of them and tip to coat. Divide the blueberries between the ramekins and set aside.

3. In a medium bowl, vigorously whisk the egg and 3 tablespoons of granulated sugar until combined. Mix in the flour, rum, cream, milk, lemon zest, vanilla, and salt for about 1 minute until smooth. Pour the batter over the berries, filling the ramekins about three-quarters full.

4. Put the ramekins on the trivet and place a square of aluminum foil loosely on top.

5. Secure the lid and cook on high pressure for 11 minutes. Quick release the pressure in the pot, remove the lid, and immediately remove the ramekins.

6. Transfer the ramekins to a baking sheet and preheat the oven broiler. Broil on high for 3 to 4 minutes to brown the top, then transfer to a cooling rack and let cool for 10 to 15 minutes. Garnish with powdered sugar and serve.

Variation Tip Originating in France, this dish is traditionally made with dark cherries. The base, however, can be a wonderfully blank canvas: substitute the blueberries with sliced plums, pears, peaches, or seasonal cranberries for a different flavor.

PER SERVING Calories: 284; Total fat: 15g; Saturated fat: 8g; Cholesterol: 121mg; Carbohydrates: 34g; Fiber: 1g; Protein: 5g

SERVES 2, TWICE
PREP TIME: 10 minutes
COOK TIME: 30 minutes
TOTAL TIME: 1 hour

PRESSURE LEVEL: High
RELEASE: Quick

¼ cup unsalted butter,
at room temperature,
plus more for greasing

1 cup all-purpose flour, plus
more for dusting and coating

1 teaspoon baking powder

¼ teaspoon salt

⅓ cup granulated sugar

1 egg, at room temperature

½ teaspoon vanilla extract

½ teaspoon almond extract

¼ cup buttermilk

1 cup fresh raspberries

Powdered sugar, for garnish
(optional)

RASPBERRY-ALMOND BREAKFAST CAKE

VEGETARIAN | WORTH THE WAIT

Many breakfast cakes involve sugar-laden streusel toppings, but this cake is very fruit-forward and rather light on the sweetness. It's a perfect slice to serve for those lazy summer brunches, where morning and afternoon seem to meld together.

1. Add 1 cup of water to the pressure cooker pot and place the trivet or egg rack in the bottom.

2. Coat a 7-inch cake pan with butter and then with flour. Set aside.

3. In a small bowl, mix 1 cup of flour, the baking powder, and the salt. Reserve 2 tablespoons of the flour mixture in another small bowl for Step 5.

4. In a large bowl, using an electric hand mixer, mix the granulated sugar and ¼ cup of butter until thoroughly combined, scraping down the sides of the bowl as necessary. Add the egg, vanilla, and almond extract and mix to combine. →

5. Add the flour mixture and the buttermilk in alternating batches to the batter, mixing well after each addition.

6. In a medium bowl, lightly toss the raspberries with some flour to coat. Gently fold the berries into the cake batter. Pour the batter into the prepared pan and put the pan on the trivet in the pressure cooker.

7. Secure the lid and cook on high pressure for 30 minutes. Quick release the pressure in the pot, then remove the lid and immediately transfer the cake to a cooling rack.

8. Let cool for 10 to 15 minutes, then dust with powdered sugar (if desired). Serve warm.

Serving Tip For a tastier topping, serve this cake with a dollop of Greek yogurt or coconut whipped cream. Make the coconut whipped cream by whipping the cream that floats to the top of a can of coconut milk that has been chilled for at least 8 hours until it's smooth and fluffy.

PER SERVING Calories: 319; Total fat: 13g; Saturated fat: 8g; Cholesterol: 72mg; Carbohydrates: 46g; Fiber: 3g; Protein: 6g

SERVES 2

PREP TIME: 10 minutes

COOK TIME: 40 minutes

TOTAL TIME: 1 hour 30 minutes

PRESSURE LEVEL: High

RELEASE: Natural

3 tablespoons unsalted butter, at room temperature, plus more for greasing

¼ cup applesauce

2 tablespoons packed brown sugar

1 egg, at room temperature

2 very ripe bananas, mashed

¼ cup milk

½ teaspoon vanilla extract

1 cup flour

1 teaspoon baking soda

¼ teaspoon kosher salt

⅓ cup chocolate chips

CHOCOLATE CHIP BANANA BREAD

VEGETARIAN | WORTH THE WAIT

Normally cooked in the oven, this version of banana bread is considerably denser than a traditional loaf of quick bread, but it's just as delicious. Steaming versus baking really brings out the fresh banana flavor, and cutting down the fat with applesauce makes each bite feel a little less guilt-ridden.

1. Add 1 cup of water to your pressure cooker pot and place the trivet or egg rack in the bottom.

2. Coat a 7-inch loaf pan with butter and set aside.

3. In a medium bowl, mix together 3 tablespoons of butter, the applesauce, and the brown sugar. Add the egg and stir in the mashed bananas, milk, and vanilla.

4. Stir in the flour, baking soda, and salt. Fold in the chocolate chips. Pour the batter into the prepared loaf pan and cover with foil, then place on the trivet inside the pot.

5. Secure the lid and cook on high pressure for 40 minutes, then allow the pressure to naturally release, about 10 minutes. Open the vent at the top and remove the lid.

6. Carefully remove the pan and place on a cooling rack. Remove the foil, being sure to avoid dripping any condensation onto the bread. Test the bread with a toothpick to make sure the center is fully cooked; no more than a few moist crumbs should be on the toothpick. If it needs more time, place the bread back in the cooker, cover with the foil again, and set on high pressure for another 5 minutes, ending with a quick release. Let cool at room temperature for at least 45 minutes.

7. Once the banana bread has thoroughly cooled, cut into thick slices.

Variation Tip Not a chocolate fan? Substitute your favorite nuts, raisins, or some shredded coconut for a little tasty texture.

PER SERVING Calories: 727; Total fat: 29g; Saturated fat: 18g; Cholesterol: 137mg; Carbohydrates: 104g; Fiber: 6g; Protein: 14g

SERVES 2

PREP TIME: 10 minutes

COOK TIME: 3 minutes

TOTAL TIME: 25 minutes

PRESSURE LEVEL: Low

RELEASE: Natural

2 large unpeeled organic apples, cored

½ cup coconut muesli

2 tablespoons butter, cubed

2 teaspoons packed brown sugar

½ teaspoon ground cinnamon

⅓ cup water

TO SERVE

• Plain Greek yogurt

BAKED APPLES WITH COCONUT MUESLI

5-INGREDIENT | 30 MINUTES OR LESS | VEGETARIAN

Baked apples are often considered a dessert, but when they're stuffed with muesli and served with Greek yogurt instead, they can easily be considered a hearty part of a balanced breakfast. Coconut muesli is available in most grocery stores, either in bulk or boxed in the cereal aisle.

1. Remove the tops of the apples. If necessary, slice the bottoms off just enough to help the apples sit flat in the cooker pot.

2. In a bowl, mix together the muesli, butter, brown sugar, and cinnamon, mashing gently with a fork until combined.

3. Stuff each apple with the muesli mixture, then place them in the bottom of the cooker pot. Add the water to the pot. Secure the lid and cook on low pressure for 2 to 4 minutes, depending on how large the apples are. Allow the pressure to naturally release, about 10 minutes, then carefully remove the lid.

4. Serve with Greek yogurt.

Cooking Tip If you prefer firmer apples, perform a quick release and remove the lid after 10 minutes.

PER SERVING Calories: 256; Total fat: 12g; Saturated fat: 7g; Cholesterol: 31mg; Carbohydrates: 40g; Fiber: 7g; Protein: 2g

SERVES 2

PREP TIME: 5 minutes

COOK TIME: 12 minutes

TOTAL TIME: 30 minutes

PRESSURE LEVEL: Low

RELEASE: Natural

½ cup uncooked quinoa

¾ cup unsweetened coconut milk, plus more for serving

½ cup water

2 tablespoons maple syrup

1 tablespoon unsweetened cocoa powder

½ teaspoon vanilla extract (optional)

Pinch kosher salt

TO SERVE

- Sliced fresh strawberries
- Chocolate shavings

CHOCOLATE-COVERED-STRAWBERRY BREAKFAST QUINOA

5-INGREDIENT | 30 MINUTES OR LESS | LIGHT AND HEALTHY
ONE-POT MEAL | VEGETARIAN

When you want a satisfying change from oatmeal, a warm bowl of breakfast quinoa can hit the spot. Look forward to waking up to a bowl of naturally sweetened crunchy goodness that not only offers the taste of chocolate and strawberries but is also full of protein. Add a splash of vanilla to enhance the flavors of all the ingredients even more.

1. Thoroughly rinse the quinoa in a fine-mesh strainer for 2 minutes, using your hands to sort through and pick out any discolored pieces or pebbles.

2. Put the quinoa in the bowl of your cooker and stir in the coconut milk, water, maple syrup, cocoa powder, vanilla (if using), and salt. Seal the lid with the vent shut and press the button for the rice setting to cook on low pressure for 12 minutes.

3. Allow the pressure to naturally release, about 10 minutes, then open the vent at the top and remove the lid.

4. Fluff the quinoa with a fork and spoon it into two cereal bowls. Add more coconut milk, and top with strawberries and chocolate shavings.

Variation Tip For a unique and indulgent chocolate flavor, swap out the cocoa powder for your favorite chocolate-hazelnut spread and add crushed hazelnuts on top.

PER SERVING Calories: 436; Total fat: 25g; Saturated fat: 20g; Cholesterol: 0mg; Carbohydrates: 50g; Fiber: 7g; Protein: 9g

Three

VEGETABLES AND SIDE DISHES

Electric pressure cookers were practically invented for the cooking of vegetables and sides. They are perfect for making the fastest, creamiest macaroni and cheese you'll ever eat, achieving a perfect risotto in half the time, and creating a small batch of kettle corn perfect for date night. Not only is cooking time reduced, but preparing vegetables in this way—in an enclosed pot that prevents the steam from escaping—retains more of their vitamins and minerals. The recipes in this chapter are scaled for two but can easily be doubled if you want to make them into main dishes.

Mexican Street Corn (on the Cob), page 54

Cacio e Pepe Spaghetti Squash 41

Takeout-Style Fried Rice 43

Mushroom Risotto 44

Creamy Four-Cheese Macaroni and Cheese 45

Creamy Buttered Mashed Potatoes 46

Broccoli-Cheddar Scalloped Potatoes 47

Lightened-Up Southern-Style Potato Salad 48

Loaded "Baked" Sweet Potatoes 49

Cilantro-Lime Cauliflower Rice 50

Southern Beans and Greens 51

Balsamic Brown Sugar Brussels Sprouts 52

Hot Honey Maple Carrots 53

Mexican Street Corn (on the Cob) 54

Green Chile Corn Bread 55

Flea Market Kettle Corn 57

PRESSURE LEVEL: High
RELEASE: Quick

1 whole spaghetti squash

Kosher salt

3 tablespoons unsalted butter

1 teaspoon freshly squeezed lemon juice

½ cup Pecorino Romano cheese

¼ cup Parmesan cheese, plus more for serving

1½ teaspoons freshly ground black pepper

CACIO E PEPE SPAGHETTI SQUASH

5-INGREDIENT | 30 MINUTES OR LESS | ONE-POT MEAL | VEGETARIAN

When you're cutting back on carbs or trying to adjust to a gluten-free diet, this simple "cheese and pepper" spaghetti squash dish is just about the tastiest way to kick that pasta craving. When cooked, the squash can be scraped into spaghetti-like strands. Unlike its winter cousins, it is very mild in flavor and melds beautifully with a classic buttery Italian cheese sauce.

1. Using a hefty, sharp knife, carefully cut the spaghetti squash in half lengthwise (this will result in longer strands of squash flesh). With a spoon, scrape out the seeds in the middle.

2. Place a trivet or steamer basket in the pressure cooker pot; add 1 cup of water and half of the squash. (Wrap the other half in plastic wrap and refrigerate for another meal.)

3. Secure the lid and cook on high pressure for 7 minutes, using a quick release at the end of the cook time. Select cancel and open the lid carefully.

4. Transfer the spaghetti squash to a work surface and let cool until it can be handled. Using a fork or large spoon, gently pull the flesh away from the skin and break into long spaghetti-like strands. →

5. Remove the trivet from the cooker pot. Select sauté and adjust to low. Season the water with salt. Add the butter and lemon juice and stir until melted.

6. Gradually sprinkle in the Pecorino Romano cheese and stir until completely melted. Repeat with the ¼ cup of Parmesan cheese. Add the spaghetti squash strands and stir until the cheese is melted and smooth (the cheese will initially clump before melting into a sauce). Stir in the pepper and season with salt. Serve topped with more Parmesan cheese.

Serving Tip Spaghetti squash can be used to replace any sort of starch, and will be equally delicious in place of the pasta in these recipes: Easy Spaghetti and Meatballs (page 153), Mussels Fra Diavolo with Linguine (page 96), or tossed with Beef Ragù with Pappardelle (page 161).

PER SERVING Calories: 509; Total fat: 40g; Saturated fat: 29g; Cholesterol: 126mg; Carbohydrates: 12g; Fiber: 3g; Protein: 24g

PRESSURE LEVEL: High

RELEASE: Natural

½ cup jasmine rice, rinsed well

¾ cup water

½ tablespoon oil

¼ cup diced yellow onion

½ tablespoon unsalted butter

¼ cup chopped carrots

¼ cup green peas

1 egg, lightly beaten

1 tablespoon low-sodium soy sauce

1 scallion, chopped

Sesame seeds, for garnish

TAKEOUT-STYLE FRIED RICE

ONE-POT MEAL | VEGAN-FRIENDLY | VEGETARIAN

This fried rice is as close to Chinese takeout as you can get without using a wok. This veggie version is easily adaptable and is a fantastic way to use leftovers. You could toss in chopped chicken, pork, or shrimp to add protein to this recipe.

1. Add the rice and water to the cooker pot. Stir.

2. Secure the lid and cook on high pressure for 12 minutes, then allowing the pressure to release naturally, 10 minutes. Carefully remove the lid. Press cancel.

3. Fluff the rice with a fork and transfer to a medium bowl; cover and set aside.

4. Select sauté. Add the oil to the cooker pot and heat until the display reads hot, then add the onion. Cook for 2 minutes, stirring frequently, until softened. Add the butter, carrots, and peas and cook for 2 minutes.

5. Select sauté and adjust to low. Move the veggies to the side of the pot and pour the beaten egg into the empty side. Stir constantly as the egg scrambles to avoid sticking. Once the egg is almost cooked, stir it into the vegetables.

6. Stir in the cooked rice, soy sauce, and scallion. Cook everything together for 8 to 10 minutes, stirring occasionally. Portion into bowls and sprinkle with sesame seeds.

Ingredient Tip Leftover white rice is perfect for this recipe. Using it cuts the cook time in half. Make this recipe completely vegan by substituting more oil for the butter and omitting the egg.

PER SERVING Calories: 299; Total fat: 9g; Saturated fat: 3g; Cholesterol: 86mg; Carbohydrates: 45g; Fiber: 3g; Protein: 8g

SERVES 2

PREP TIME: 20 minutes

COOK TIME: 5 minutes

TOTAL TIME: 30 minutes

PRESSURE LEVEL: Low

RELEASE: Quick

1 tablespoon oil

8 ounces cremini mushrooms, sliced

¼ teaspoon kosher salt

2 shallots, chopped

2 garlic cloves, minced

1 cup Arborio rice

½ cup dry white wine, such as Chardonnay or Chablis

3 cups Vegetable Stock (page 170)

½ teaspoon fresh thyme

2 tablespoons unsalted butter

2 cups fresh baby spinach (optional)

¼ cup freshly grated Parmesan cheese, plus more for garnish

MUSHROOM RISOTTO

30 MINUTES OR LESS | COMFORT FOOD | ONE-POT MEAL | VEGETARIAN

Gone are the days of standing at the stove, stressing over making the perfect risotto. Let your pressure cooker do the hard work, and you can just enjoy the creamy, rich, luscious results in half the time.

1. Select the sauté setting on the pressure cooker. Heat the oil in the cooker pot until the display reads hot. Add the mushrooms and salt and cook for 8 minutes, or until the mushrooms are tender, stirring frequently.

2. Add the shallots and garlic and cook for 3 minutes more, stirring often.

3. Add the rice and cook for 3 to 4 minutes, stirring often, until the rice kernel edges start to become translucent.

4. Add the wine and cook, stirring, until the alcohol aroma has cooked off and the wine has almost fully evaporated, about 2 minutes.

5. Add the stock and thyme. Make sure all of the ingredients are submerged.

6. Secure the lid and cook on low pressure for 5 minutes, using a quick release at the end of the cook time. Carefully remove the lid.

7. Add the butter and spinach (if using) to the rice mixture and stir to wilt spinach. Stir in the ¼ cup of Parmesan cheese and season with salt if desired. Serve with an additional sprinkle of cheese.

Serving Tip This recipe is perfect for two main dishes, but if you're using it as a side dish, be ready to have leftovers for lunch the following day. Or better yet, turn the remaining risotto into arancini for a fancy appetizer: Mix 1 cup risotto with 1 egg, ¼ cup bread crumbs, and ¼ cup Parmesan cheese. Form the mixture into 2 tablespoon-size balls, roll in more bread crumbs, and fry in 3 inches of 350°F oil (measured with a cooking thermometer) until browned, about 4 minutes.

PER SERVING Calories: 702; Total fat: 24g; Saturated fat: 12g; Cholesterol: 49mg; Carbohydrates: 85g; Fiber: 3g; Protein: 22g

SERVES 2
PREP TIME: 5 minutes
COOK TIME: 5 minutes
TOTAL TIME: 20 minutes

PRESSURE LEVEL: High
RELEASE: Quick

6 ounces elbow macaroni

¾ cup Vegetable Stock
(page 170) or water, plus
more if necessary

½ teaspoon kosher salt

1 tablespoon unsalted butter

2 ounces cream cheese

⅓ cup whole milk

½ tablespoon hot sauce
(optional)

½ tablespoon Dijon mustard

⅓ cup shredded
Cheddar cheese

⅓ cup shredded
Gruyère cheese

⅓ cup shredded
fontina cheese

Freshly ground black pepper

CREAMY FOUR-CHEESE MACARONI AND CHEESE

30 MINUTES OR LESS | COMFORT FOOD | ONE-POT MEAL | VEGETARIAN

Sweet dreams are made of cheese, especially ones that are this adaptable. Any kind of pasta works in this classic, creamy, dreamy mac 'n' cheese. Feel free to use chickpea noodles for a gluten-free side dish that you'll both love. The cheese can also be switched out, so if your cheese drawer is overflowing with scraps of Swiss or Gouda, shred them up and make all your cheese dreams come true.

1. Add the macaroni, stock (enough to cover the macaroni), and salt to the cooker pot and stir to combine. Secure the lid and cook on high pressure for 5 minutes, using a quick release at the end of the cook time. Carefully remove the lid.

2. Select sauté and adjust to low; stir the butter into the pasta until it melts. Add the cream cheese, milk, hot sauce (if using), and mustard. Mix well, then switch the pot to the keep warm setting.

3. Add the shredded cheeses about ⅓ cup at a time, stirring well after each addition to fully melt and incorporate the cheese. Season with salt and pepper.

Ingredient Tip Use Chicken Stock (page 167) instead of vegetable for more depth of flavor. And for something super special, top off the finished product with some crumbled crispy bacon, fresh chopped chives, or crunchy bread crumbs and bake at 400°F for 10 to 15 minutes.

PER SERVING Calories: 727; Total fat: 36g; Saturated fat: 22g; Cholesterol: 111mg; Carbohydrates: 67g; Fiber: 3g; Protein: 31g

SERVES 2

PREP TIME: 10 minutes

COOK TIME: 8 minutes

TOTAL TIME: 30 minutes

PRESSURE LEVEL: High

RELEASE: Quick

1 pound Russet potatoes, peeled and quartered

2 garlic cloves, minced

1 teaspoon kosher salt

¼ cup butter

¼ cup milk

¼ cup cream cheese (optional)

Freshly ground black pepper

Fresh chives, chopped (optional)

CREAMY BUTTERED MASHED POTATOES

30 MINUTES OR LESS | COMFORT FOOD | ONE-POT MEAL | VEGETARIAN

There is no faster way to achieve perfectly creamy mashed potatoes than in your electric pressure cooker! These potatoes are the creamiest and smoothest you can imagine, thanks to the addition of cream cheese to the recipe.

1. Put the potatoes in the cooker pot, add the garlic, and season with salt. Cover the potatoes with water.

2. Secure the lid and cook on high pressure for 8 minutes, using a quick release at the end of the cook time. Carefully remove the pot from the cooker, drain the water through a large sieve or colander over a large bowl, reserve the cooking liquid, and set aside.

3. Return the potatoes to the pot and mash them using a potato masher or the back of a wooden spoon. Mix in the butter, milk, and cream cheese (if using). Add some of the reserved potato water, if needed, to get the desired creaminess. Season with salt and pepper.

4. Serve topped with chives (if desired).

Cooking Tip Making a double recipe of these potatoes is a good idea. Turn the leftovers into potato pancakes the next morning by mixing them with an egg, 2 tablespoons flour, and some salt and pepper, and then browning them in butter in a skillet. Serve the potato pancakes with eggs and bacon for the most satisfying breakfast of your week.

PER SERVING Calories: 380; Total fat: 24g; Saturated fat: 15g; Cholesterol: 64mg; Carbohydrates: 38g; Fiber: 6g; Protein: 5g

SERVES 2

PREP TIME: 20 minutes

COOK TIME: 5 minutes

TOTAL TIME: 30 minutes

PRESSURE LEVEL: High

RELEASE: Quick

1½ tablespoons unsalted butter, divided

¼ yellow onion, chopped

¾ cup Chicken Stock (page 167)

½ teaspoon garlic powder

¼ teaspoon kosher salt

Pinch freshly ground black pepper

3 medium Yukon Gold potatoes, sliced ⅛ inch thick

1 cup broccoli florets, chopped

3 tablespoons sour cream

½ cup shredded Cheddar cheese, divided

⅓ cup shredded Monterey Jack cheese, divided

BROCCOLI-CHEDDAR SCALLOPED POTATOES

30 MINUTES OR LESS

Savory, cheesy scalloped potatoes are such a delightful addition to any weeknight dinner—especially when they're made in only 30 minutes. Most of the work is done in the pressure cooker, with the crispy top coming from a few minutes under the broiler. The addition of broccoli makes this dish similar to a casserole and adds a good dose of vitamins.

1. Select sauté on the pressure cooker. Melt 1 tablespoon of butter in the pot until the display reads hot. Add the onion and cook for 4 to 5 minutes, or until softened, then stir in the stock, garlic powder, salt, and pepper.

2. Place a steamer basket in the cooker pot. Add the potatoes and broccoli. Secure the lid and cook on high pressure for 5 minutes, using a quick release at the end of the cook time. Select cancel and open the lid. Carefully remove the steamer basket from the pot.

3. Preheat the oven broiler. Coat a small ovenproof casserole dish with the remaining ½ tablespoon of butter. Transfer the potatoes and broccoli to the prepared dish.

4. To the cooking liquid in the cooker pot, add the sour cream, half of the Cheddar cheese, and half of the Monterey Jack cheese and stir until melted and smooth. Pour over the potatoes and broccoli, making sure not to come above the top edge of the dish.

5. Top with the remaining cheeses, place in a baking pan, and broil until golden brown, 6 to 7 minutes.

Variation Tip For an even more filling casserole-style side dish, add ½ cup chopped ham to the recipe before baking.

PER SERVING Calories: 325; Total fat: 22g; Saturated fat: 14g; Cholesterol: 62mg; Carbohydrates: 18g; Fiber: 4g; Protein: 15g

SERVES 2

PREP TIME: 10 minutes

COOK TIME: 4 minutes

TOTAL TIME: 20 minutes

PRESSURE LEVEL: High

RELEASE: Quick

4 medium Russet potatoes, peeled and cubed

2 eggs

1 celery stalk, chopped

¼ red onion, chopped

¼ cup plain Greek yogurt

2 tablespoons yellow mustard

Kosher salt

Freshly ground black pepper

Paprika, for garnish

LIGHTENED-UP SOUTHERN-STYLE POTATO SALAD

30 MINUTES OR LESS | COMFORT FOOD | LIGHT AND HEALTHY VEGETARIAN

This salad is a perfect summer side dish. Though potato salad is normally served at picnics and barbecues, it can be enjoyed any time of year. In my version, I've lightened it up, replacing the mayonnaise with Greek yogurt to reduce the calories but retain the familiar creaminess.

1. Put 1 cup of water and the potatoes into the cooker pot. Put the whole eggs (in their shells) on top of the potatoes.

2. Secure the lid and cook on high pressure for 4 minutes. Use a quick release at the end of the cook time. Remove the lid and take out the eggs. Carefully remove the cooker pot, then drain the potatoes through a large sieve or colander and set aside.

3. Rinse the eggs under cold water until they are no longer steaming. Place them into a bowl of cold water to chill. When cooled, peel and roughly chop them.

4. In a medium bowl, combine the potatoes, eggs, celery, onion, yogurt, and mustard, then season with salt and pepper.

5. Transfer the potato salad to a serving bowl, sprinkle with paprika, and cover and refrigerate until ready to serve.

Variation Tip For a delicious herby twist, use skin-on baby red potatoes instead of Russet, skip the red onion in favor of chopped scallions, and sprinkle with fresh dill.

PER SERVING Calories: 397; Total fat: 6g; Saturated fat: 2g; Cholesterol: 167mg; Carbohydrates: 71g; Fiber: 11g; Protein: 17g

SERVES 2

PREP TIME: 10 minutes

COOK TIME: 15 minutes

TOTAL TIME: 45 minutes

PRESSURE LEVEL: High

RELEASE: Natural

2 medium sweet potatoes

4 tablespoons butter, at room temperature

2 teaspoons ground cinnamon

¼ cup packed brown sugar

¼ cup chopped pecans

1 cup mini marshmallows

LOADED "BAKED" SWEET POTATOES

COMFORT FOOD | VEGETARIAN-FRIENDLY

These sweet little tubers are great for when you've got a taste for sweet potato casserole in summer. They're the perfect accompaniment to a full barbecue spread, and opting for sweet over baked white potatoes is so much more nutritious, even with the added sugars and fats.

1. Put a steamer basket in the pressure cooker pot and add 1 cup of water.

2. Place the sweet potatoes on the steamer basket inside the pot.

3. Secure the lid and cook on high pressure for 15 minutes (time will vary if you are cooking larger potatoes). Allow the pressure to naturally release for 10 minutes, then vent the remaining steam.

4. Put the butter in a small bowl. Sprinkle on the cinnamon and mix together until fully combined.

5. Preheat the broiler in the oven.

6. Remove the pressure cooker lid. Transfer the potatoes to a clean work surface and let cool a bit. Cut both potatoes open, mash the flesh a bit, and divide the butter mixture between them. Sprinkle with the brown sugar, pecans, and marshmallows.

7. Put the potatoes in a baking dish and broil for 3 to 4 minutes, or until the marshmallows are lightly browned. Serve hot.

Variation Tip For a savory vegetarian baked sweet potato, omit the cinnamon, sugar, and marshmallows, and top with black beans, chopped kale, and avocado pesto.

PER SERVING Calories: 598; Total fat: 43g; Saturated fat: 17g; Cholesterol: 61mg; Carbohydrates: 53g; Fiber: 8g; Protein: 6g

SERVES 2

PREP TIME: 5 minutes

COOK TIME: 1 minutes

TOTAL TIME: 15 minutes

PRESSURE LEVEL: High

RELEASE: Quick

1 medium to large head cauliflower, broken into florets

2 tablespoons olive oil

¼ teaspoon kosher salt

1 cup chopped fresh cilantro

Juice of 1 lime

CILANTRO-LIME CAULIFLOWER RICE

5-INGREDIENT | 30 MINUTES OR LESS | PALEO | VEGAN | VEGETARIAN

Standard rice can often leave you feeling sluggish after a hearty lunch. To cut back on the starch and extra carbs, riced cauliflower is a delicious and nutritious substitute. It can be flavored any way you would normally flavor your favorite rice—like this Mexican-inspired cilantro-lime combination. It's the perfect side for a spicy or super-flavorful main dish.

1. Place a steamer basket in the cooker pot and add 1 cup of water. Put the cauliflower florets into the steamer basket.

2. Secure the lid and cook on high pressure for 1 minute, using a quick release at the end of the cook time. Select cancel and open the lid carefully.

3. Transfer the cauliflower to a plate. Carefully drain the water from the pot, wipe the pot dry, and put it back in the cooker.

4. Select sauté and adjust to low. Heat the olive oil in the pot until the display reads hot. Add the cooked cauliflower and break it up with a potato masher.

5. Season with the salt, add the cilantro, and stir gently while the cauliflower rice heats. Add the lime juice and stir. Serve.

Serving Tip Try this tasty rice substitute in a batch of Chipotle Chicken Fajita Lettuce Cups (page 121) or layered in a Kalua Pork Rice Bowl (page 151).

PER SERVING Calories: 202; Total fat: 14g; Saturated fat: 2g; Cholesterol: 0mg; Carbohydrates: 19g; Fiber: 8g; Protein: 6g

SERVES 2

PREP TIME: 10 minutes

COOK TIME: 10 minutes

TOTAL TIME: 1 hour 20 minutes

PRESSURE LEVEL: High

RELEASE: Natural

1 tablespoon oil

½ yellow onion, diced

2 garlic cloves, minced

1 cup Chicken Stock
(page 167)

½ pound dried
black-eyed peas

2 cups chopped Swiss
chard or kale

1½ teaspoons red
pepper flakes

2 fresh thyme sprigs or
½ teaspoon dried thyme

½ tablespoon kosher salt

¼ teaspoon freshly ground
black pepper

1 tablespoon apple
cider vinegar

1 to 2 teaspoons hot sauce
(optional)

SOUTHERN BEANS AND GREENS

COMFORT FOOD | ONE-POT MEAL | VEGAN-FRIENDLY
VEGETARIAN-FRIENDLY | WORTH THE WAIT

A healthier spin on a New Year's Day tradition in the South, this recipe tastes delicious with any of your favorite greens. Feel free to sub out the Swiss chard for collards, kale, spinach, or any combination of greens you like. Serve this dish with corn bread for a traditional presentation.

1. Select sauté on the pressure cooker. Add the oil to the cooker pot, heat until the display reads hot, and add the onion. Cook, stirring often, for 2 minutes, or until softened. Add the garlic and cook, stirring, until fragrant, about 1 minute.

2. Add the stock, peas, Swiss chard, red pepper flakes, thyme, salt, and pepper. Deglaze the pot by scraping all the flavorful brown bits up off the bottom of the pot with a wooden spoon, then mix well.

3. Secure the lid and cook on high pressure for 10 minutes, then allow the pressure to naturally release for 10 minutes. Carefully remove the lid and press cancel.

4. Stir in the vinegar and hot sauce (if using). Adjust seasoning if desired. Serve.

Ingredient Tip Make this side dish vegan by using water or vegetable stock in place of the chicken stock. You can also make the recipe even more savory by adding a ham hock before the pressure cooking, then using a fork to shred the ham meat off the bone and into the greens.

PER SERVING Calories: 385; Total fat: 8g; Saturated fat: 1g; Cholesterol: 0mg; Carbohydrates: 77g; Fiber: 32g; Protein: 31g

PRESSURE LEVEL: High

RELEASE: Quick

8 ounces fresh Brussels sprouts, halved

4 uncooked bacon slices, chopped

1 tablespoon packed brown sugar

2 tablespoons balsamic vinegar

Pinch kosher salt

Pinch freshly ground black pepper

BALSAMIC BROWN SUGAR BRUSSELS SPROUTS

5-INGREDIENT | 30 MINUTES OR LESS | VEGETARIAN-FRIENDLY

Quickly steamed, then fried with bacon and brown sugar and drizzled with balsamic vinegar, these Brussels sprouts are nothing like the ones you were fed as a kid! And quickly preparing the sprouts in the pressure cooker also prevents their smell from permeating the entire house.

1. Place a steamer basket in the pressure cooker pot. Add 1 cup of water and arrange the Brussels sprouts evenly in the steamer basket.

2. Secure the lid and cook on high pressure for 1 minute, using a quick release at the end of the cook time. Open the lid carefully and press cancel.

3. Carefully remove the steamer basket and transfer the Brussels sprouts to a medium bowl. Drain and discard the water from the pot, then wipe it dry and return it to the cooker.

4. Select sauté and adjust to normal. When the display reads hot, add the bacon to the pot and cook for 5 minutes, stirring often, until the bacon browns and begins to crisp. Add the Brussels sprouts to the pot and stir, coating them in the bacon grease and sprinkling with the brown sugar. Cook for 2 to 3 minutes more, stirring constantly to keep the sugar from scorching.

5. Transfer the sprouts and bacon to a serving dish. Drizzle with the vinegar, season with salt and pepper, and toss to coat. Serve immediately.

Variation Tip Make this dish vegetarian by leaving out the bacon. Brown the sprouts in a plant-based oil with some minced garlic, then dress them with balsamic vinegar and serve topped with crumbled feta cheese.

PER SERVING Calories: 275; Total fat: 16g; Saturated fat: 5g; Cholesterol: 42mg; Carbohydrates: 16g; Fiber: 4g; Protein: 18g

PRESSURE LEVEL: High
RELEASE: Quick

½ tablespoon oil

½ pound carrots, sliced

2 teaspoons honey, plus more for topping (optional)

1 teaspoon maple syrup

1 teaspoon ground cayenne pepper

Pinch kosher salt

½ cup water

HOT HONEY MAPLE CARROTS

5-INGREDIENT | 30 MINUTES OR LESS | ONE-POT MEAL | PALEO
VEGAN-FRIENDLY | VEGETARIAN

Sweet and spicy veggies should have a place on every dinner table. Honey-glazed carrots are prepared the standard way, but when maple syrup and cayenne pepper are introduced, they become so much more than a Sunday-dinner side dish. This dish is fairly spicy, but you can adjust the heat level by using more or less cayenne.

1. Select the sauté setting on the pressure cooker. Put the oil in the pot and heat until the display reads hot. Add the carrots.

2. Add 2 teaspoons of honey, the maple syrup, cayenne pepper, salt, and water and stir to mix well.

3. Secure the lid and cook on high pressure for 4 minutes, then use a quick release at the end of the cook time. Carefully remove the lid.

4. Mix the carrots in the liquid and top with additional honey (if desired). Serve hot.

Substitution Tip You can make this recipe vegan by substituting agave nectar for the honey.

PER SERVING Calories: 104; Total fat: 4g; Saturated fat: 0.5g; Cholesterol: 0mg; Carbohydrates: 18g; Fiber: 3g; Protein: 1g

SERVES 2

PREP TIME: 10 minutes

COOK TIME: 10 minutes

TOTAL TIME: 25 minutes

PRESSURE LEVEL: High

RELEASE: Quick

2 ears corn, shucked and broken in half

2 teaspoons oil

½ cup sour cream

2 tablespoons mayonnaise

1 teaspoon garlic, minced

Juice of ½ lime

¼ teaspoon ground ancho chile powder

2 tablespoons chopped fresh cilantro, plus more for serving

¼ cup Cotija cheese crumbles, plus more for serving

Freshly ground black pepper (optional)

Lime wedges, for serving

MEXICAN STREET CORN (ON THE COB)

30 MINUTES OR LESS | VEGETARIAN

Once you try this classic Mexican street food, you may never go back to conventional grilled corn. These sweet ears of corn are grilled to perfection and slathered in a chili-and-lime-spiked creamy sauce with lots of cheese and cilantro. Precooking the corn in your pressure cooker means you get to indulge in this tasty veggie in half the time it would normally take.

1. Warm up a barbecue grill until hot, or heat a stove-top grill pan over high heat.

2. Place the trivet or steamer basket in the pressure cooker pot. Add 1 cup of water and the corn.

3. Secure the lid and cook on high pressure for 2 minutes, then quick release the pressure in the pot. Open the lid carefully.

4. Transfer the corn to a plate. Drizzle it with the oil and place on the hot grill or grill pan for 2 to 3 minutes per side, turning until a few sides have grill marks. Return to the plate.

5. In a medium bowl, whisk together the sour cream, mayonnaise, garlic, lime juice, chile powder, 2 tablespoons of cilantro, and ¼ cup of Cotija cheese until well combined. Spread the mixture onto the corn.

6. Sprinkle the corn with more cilantro and cheese, then sprinkle with black pepper (if using). Serve with lime wedges.

Serving Tip This street corn, also known as *elote*, will be the perfect side dish for Carnitas Tacos with Avocado Crema (page 149) or the Barbacoa Bella Burrito Bowls (page 78). Double the recipe and use the leftover corn kernels in the Southwestern Hash (page 29).

PER SERVING Calories: 461; Total fat: 31g; Saturated fat: 14g; Cholesterol: 59mg; Carbohydrates: 38g; Fiber: 5g; Protein: 14g

PRESSURE LEVEL: High

RELEASE: Natural

2 tablespoons melted butter, plus more at room temperature, for greasing

¾ cup yellow cornmeal, plus more for dusting

⅓ cup all-purpose flour

½ tablespoon baking powder

1 teaspoon kosher salt

½ cup buttermilk

⅓ cup sour cream

2 tablespoons honey

1 egg

1 cup creamed corn

1 (4.5-ounce) can diced fire-roasted jalapeño peppers

TO SERVE
- Softened butter
- Honey

GREEN CHILE CORN BREAD

VEGETARIAN | WORTH THE WAIT

Corn bread is an American national treasure, prepared differently in the Northern (sweeter) and Southern (bacon) states. This version is sweetened with honey instead of sugar and is made super moist by the addition of creamed corn. The chiles give the bread a mild kick of heat that will have your taste buds dancing.

1. Add 1 cup of water to the pressure cooker pot and put the trivet or egg rack in the bottom. Coat a 7-inch round cake pan with butter and dust it with cornmeal; set aside.

2. In a large mixing bowl, stir together the ¾ cup of cornmeal, the flour, baking powder, and salt.

3. In a medium bowl, whisk together the buttermilk, sour cream, honey, the 2 tablespoons of melted butter, and the egg.

4. Pour the buttermilk mixture over the cornmeal mixture and stir gently with a rubber spatula until just combined. Fold in the creamed corn and the jalapeños and stir to combine. ⟶

5. Pour the batter into the prepared cake pan. Place a paper towel over the cake pan, then cover it with aluminum foil and secure the aluminum foil around the cake pan (to prevent any moisture from getting into the pan). Prepare a foil sling (see page 4), center the pan on it, lower it into the pressure cooker, and arrange the sling ends across the pan.

6. Secure the lid and cook on high pressure for 25 minutes, then allow the pressure to naturally release for 10 minutes. Carefully remove the lid and, using the sling ends, lift the pan and transfer to a cooling rack.

7. Allow the corn bread to cool slightly, then slice and serve warm with softened butter and honey.

Serving Tip Pairing this corn bread with the Southern Beans and Greens (page 51) for a New Year's Day meal is a classic, but it will also be the perfect accompaniment for a big bowl of Quick Texas Chili con Carne (page 156) or Chicken-Bacon Stew (page 113).

PER SERVING Calories: 320; Total fat: 12g; Saturated fat: 7g; Cholesterol: 66mg; Carbohydrates: 49g; Fiber: 3g; Protein: 7g

SERVES 2
PREP TIME: 5 minutes
COOK TIME: 10 minutes
TOTAL TIME: 15 minutes

PRESSURE LEVEL: None
RELEASE: None

2 tablespoons unsalted butter

2 tablespoons coconut oil

½ cup popcorn kernels

¼ cup powdered sugar

2 tablespoons granulated sugar

Kosher salt, to taste

FLEA MARKET KETTLE CORN

5-INGREDIENT | 30 MINUTES OR LESS | ONE-POT MEAL | VEGETARIAN

Kettle corn is considered a veggie, right? At least it was in a former life. Make those at-home date nights extra special: rent a movie On Demand, fire up this salty-sweet snack, and make the entire house smell like an evening at the theater.

1. Preheat the pressure cooker on sauté mode. When the display reads hot, add the butter and coconut oil to the pot and melt them completely, until they start to sizzle. Add 3 popcorn kernels (as a test), wait for one or two to pop, then add the rest of the kernels.

2. Place a glass lid on top of the pot, or loosely set your pressure cooker lid on top. In 2 to 3 minutes, the popcorn will begin popping. Using pot holders, remove the cooker pot and shake it occasionally as the popcorn pops rapidly, then return it to the cooker. Do this a few times and listen for the popping to slow after 3 to 5 minutes, then select cancel to turn off the cooker. Sprinkle the popcorn with the powdered sugar and granulated sugar, cover, and shake the pot until the popping stops completely.

3. Using pot holders, carefully remove the pot from the cooker. Lift the lid and season the popcorn with salt. Replace the lid and, using the pot holders to hold the pot, shake to distribute the salt and pop any remaining kernels.

4. Pour the popped corn into a large bowl and serve.

Variation Tip To switch up the flavors, leave out the sugar and toss the popcorn with some dried herbs and garlic salt, or with a few spritzes of malt vinegar and extra salt for a more savory flavor.

PER SERVING Calories: 355; Total fat: 26g; Saturated fat: 20g; Cholesterol: 31mg; Carbohydrates: 32g; Fiber: 1g; Protein: 1g

Four
MEATLESS MAIN DISHES

Whether you are a meatless-Monday eater, have sworn off animal products completely, or have special dietary needs (either medically necessary or elective), you'll love this chapter devoted to delicious entrées sans meat! A perfectly healthy diet is totally possible without meat, a fact proven by the next 15 recipes. From soups to sandwiches to stuffed squash, even carnivores will find these meals satisfying and flavorful, all without the inclusion of tofu or meat substitutes.

Stuffed Acorn Squash, page 79

Tomato–Basil Bisque 61

Cheesy Broccoli and Cauliflower Soup 62

Tuscan Bean and Kale Soup 63

Sweet Potato Lentil Soup 64

Vegetarian Quinoa Chili Verde 65

Ratatouille 66

Chinese Vegetable Stir-Fry with Brown Rice 68

Refried Bean and Cheese Burritos 70

Deviled Egg Salad Sandwiches 72

Butternut Squash and Broccoli Rabe Lasagna 73

Penne alla Vodka 75

Vegetable Shepherd's Pie 76

Barbacoa Bella Burrito Bowls 78

Stuffed Acorn Squash 79

Vegan Sloppy Joes 81

SERVES 2
PREP TIME: 15 minutes
COOK TIME: 5 minutes
TOTAL TIME: 30 minutes

PRESSURE LEVEL: High
RELEASE: Natural

2 tablespoons butter

1 cup diced onion

1 celery stalk, diced

1 carrot, chopped

2 garlic cloves, minced

1½ cups Vegetable Stock (page 170)

1 (28-ounce) can whole tomatoes with their juices

¼ cup fresh basil

1 tablespoon tomato paste

Pinch sugar

½ teaspoon kosher salt

¼ teaspoon freshly ground black pepper

⅓ cup shredded Parmesan cheese

½ cup heavy cream

TO SERVE
- Shredded Parmesan cheese
- Crème fraîche
- Crusty bread

TOMATO-BASIL BISQUE

30 MINUTES OR LESS | LIGHT AND HEALTHY | ONE-POT MEAL VEGETARIAN

This thick and hearty bisque is nothing like the canned tomato soup you remember from your childhood. The puréed vegetables meld with the sweet, acidic tomatoes in a delicious and surprisingly light soup, while the basil will make you wish summer produce was in season all the time. Serve with a grilled cheese sandwich or garlic toast for a completely nostalgic meal.

1. Preheat the pressure cooker on sauté. When the display reads hot, put the butter in the pot. Add the onion, celery, and carrot and cook, stirring frequently, until softened, 3 to 4 minutes. Add the garlic and cook, stirring, until fragrant, 1 minute.

2. Add the stock, tomatoes and their juices, basil, tomato paste, sugar, salt, and pepper. Stir to combine well.

3. Secure the lid and cook on high pressure for 5 minutes, then allow the pressure to naturally release for 10 minutes. Open the vent at the top and remove the lid. Press cancel.

4. Using an immersion blender, carefully purée the soup until smooth. (Alternatively, you can use a countertop blender.)

5. Press sauté on the pressure cooker. Add the Parmesan cheese and heavy cream and stir until fully combined and the cheese is melted. Season with salt and pepper. Serve with more cheese, crème fraîche, and crusty bread.

Ingredient Tip If you prefer your tomato soup chunky, reserve some of the cooked tomatoes before puréeing, then add them back into the soup before serving.

PER SERVING Calories: 460; Total fat: 33g; Saturated fat: 21g; Cholesterol: 102mg; Carbohydrates: 15g; Fiber: 4g; Protein: 21g

SERVES 2

PREP TIME: 15 minutes
COOK TIME: 8 minutes
TOTAL TIME: 30 minutes

PRESSURE LEVEL: High
RELEASE: Quick

½ tablespoon oil

½ large onion, chopped

1 cup chopped carrots

2 garlic cloves, minced

2 tablespoons flour

2 cups Vegetable Stock
(page 170)

2 cups chopped broccoli
(including stems), plus 1 cup
florets reserved

1 cup chopped cauliflower
(including stems)

2 cups shredded low-fat
Cheddar cheese

½ teaspoon paprika

¼ teaspoon nutmeg

½ cup whole milk

Kosher salt

Freshly ground black pepper

CHEESY BROCCOLI AND CAULIFLOWER SOUP

30 MINUTES OR LESS | LIGHT AND HEALTHY | ONE-POT MEAL
VEGETARIAN

You just might fall in love with vegetables you disliked as a kid with this soup! Low-carb and gluten-free-friendly (if you leave out the flour), it meets just about every specialty diet need, so everyone can enjoy it. The cauliflower simply offers more nutrients, and you may not even notice it's there.

1. Preheat the pressure cooker on sauté. When the display reads hot, add the oil. Add the onion and carrots and cook until softened, 3 to 4 minutes. Add the garlic and flour and stir for 1 minute. Add the stock and continue stirring until no flour lumps remain.

2. Add the 2 cups of chopped broccoli and the chopped cauliflower to the pot. Secure the lid and cook on high pressure for 8 minutes, then quick release the pressure in the pot and remove the lid. Press cancel.

3. Using an immersion blender, carefully purée the soup until smooth. (Alternatively, you can use a countertop blender.)

4. Press sauté on the pressure cooker. Add the Cheddar cheese, paprika, and nutmeg and stir until fully combined and the cheese is melted. Stir in the milk and season with salt and pepper.

5. Press cancel. Add the reserved 1 cup of broccoli florets and stir well, then loosely cover the pot and let sit for 4 to 5 minutes before serving.

Serving Tip To make this meal even more filling, serve it in a sourdough bread bowl, à la your favorite bistro. Even with the added carbs and calories from the bread, the low-calorie soup will leave you feeling mostly guilt-free and completely satisfied.

PER SERVING Calories: 394; Total fat: 14g; Saturated fat: 7g; Cholesterol: 30mg; Carbohydrates: 33g; Fiber: 6g; Protein: 35g

PRESSURE LEVEL: High

RELEASE: Natural

½ tablespoon oil

½ onion, chopped

1 medium carrot, thickly sliced

1 garlic clove, finely chopped

1 thyme sprig

1 (15.5-ounce) can cannellini beans, drained and rinsed

2½ cups Vegetable Stock (page 170) or water

1 cup diced tomatoes with their juices

¼ teaspoon red pepper flakes

1 small Parmesan chunk with rind, plus shaved Parmesan cheese for garnish

Kosher salt

Freshly ground black pepper

2 cups chopped kale

TUSCAN BEAN AND KALE SOUP

30 MINUTES OR LESS | **LIGHT AND HEALTHY** | **ONE-POT MEAL**
VEGAN-FRIENDLY | **VEGETARIAN**

This soup, a riff on ribollita, gets Tuscany through Italian winters, and it will get you through chilly weather as well. It's a peasant soup, a collection of odds and ends: beans, chunks of root vegetables, a bit of Parmesan rind, and some superfood kale, which is a winter crop that loves growing in the snow.

1. Preheat the pressure cooker on sauté mode. When the display reads hot, add the oil. Add the onion and carrot and cook until softened, 4 to 5 minutes. Add the garlic and cook until fragrant, 1 minute.

2. Add the thyme, beans, stock, tomatoes and their juices, red pepper flakes, and Parmesan rind. Season with salt and pepper.

3. Secure the lid and cook on high pressure for 8 minutes, then allow the pressure to naturally release for 10 minutes. Open the vent at the top and remove the lid.

4. Remove the thyme stem and the Parmesan rind and stir in the kale. Taste and season with salt and pepper as desired. Serve garnished with shaved Parmesan cheese.

Ingredient Tip This soup can also be made with 6 ounces of soaked dried cannellini beans instead of canned. Prepare the recipe the same way but cook on high pressure for 20 minutes and allow a full natural release. To make this recipe vegan, omit the cheese.

PER SERVING Calories: 395; Total fat: 8g; Saturated fat: 3g; Cholesterol: 10mg; Carbohydrates: 61g; Fiber: 15g; Protein: 23g

SERVES 2

PREP TIME: 5 minutes
COOK TIME: 18 minutes
TOTAL TIME: 30 minutes

PRESSURE LEVEL: High
RELEASE: Quick

2 teaspoons oil

½ cup diced yellow onion

½ cup diced celery

½ cup chopped carrot

1 large sweet potato, peeled and cubed

4 garlic cloves, minced

1 teaspoon ground cumin

1 teaspoon ground turmeric

½ teaspoon herbes de Provence

Kosher salt

Freshly ground black pepper

¾ cup dry lentils

¼ cup dry split peas (or more lentils)

4 cups Vegetable Stock (page 170)

½ cup baby spinach

1 teaspoon red wine vinegar

SWEET POTATO LENTIL SOUP

30 MINUTES OR LESS | LIGHT AND HEALTHY | ONE-POT MEAL
VEGAN | VEGETARIAN

Hearty but healthy, this comforting soup is a fabulous way to reset your body after the holidays, vacation, or some other long period of indulgent eating. It's also the easiest thing to make when you need to go grocery shopping but aren't in the mood; it's made up almost exclusively of pantry staples. The addition of nutritious sweet potato and spinach combined with a kiss of red wine vinegar will make this your new favorite cold-weather meal.

1. Preheat the pressure cooker pot on sauté mode. When the display reads hot, add the oil and heat until shimmering. Stir in the onion, celery, carrot, and sweet potato and sauté until the vegetables begin to soften, about 5 minutes.

2. Stir in the garlic, cumin, turmeric, and herbes de Provence and cook for an additional 1 minute. Season with salt and pepper. Add the lentils, split peas, and stock. Stir together.

3. Secure the lid and cook on high pressure for 12 minutes, then quick release the pressure in the pot and remove the lid.

4. Stir in the spinach and vinegar and season with salt and pepper.

Pressure Cooker Tip The soup function can be used for this recipe if your cooker has one. Select soup and set your time for 12 minutes.

PER SERVING Calories: 702; Total fat: 23g; Saturated fat: 4g; Cholesterol: 0mg; Carbohydrates: 88g; Fiber: 34g; Protein: 38g

SERVES 2
PREP TIME: 15 minutes
COOK TIME: 15 minutes
TOTAL TIME: 45 minutes

PRESSURE LEVEL: High
RELEASE: Natural

2 tablespoons oil

½ cup chopped onion

3 large tomatillos

1 medium (6-ounce) sweet potato, peeled and cubed

3 garlic cloves, chopped

1 fresh jalapeño pepper, stemmed, seeded, and chopped

1 fresh poblano chile, stemmed, seeded, and chopped

1 tablespoon chopped fresh oregano

3 teaspoons ground cumin

Kosher salt

Freshly ground black pepper

1 cup Vegetable Stock (page 170)

1 (7-ounce) can diced mild green chiles, drained

1 bunch fresh cilantro, chopped

¼ cup quinoa, rinsed well

¼ cup dried lentils, sorted and rinsed well

1 (15-ounce) can black beans, drained and rinsed

VEGETARIAN QUINOA CHILI VERDE

LIGHT AND HEALTHY | VEGAN | VEGETARIAN

Southwestern chili verde is made with pork shoulder, but this vegan version is just as delightful. It gets heartiness from chunks of sweet potato, quinoa, lentils, and black beans, and will please the palate of even the staunchest carnivore.

1. Preheat the pressure cooker pot on sauté mode. When the display reads hot, add the oil. Add the onion, tomatillos, sweet potato, garlic, jalapeño, and poblano. Loosely cover with the cooker lid and let sweat for 5 to 6 minutes, stirring frequently. Mix in the oregano and cumin and season with salt and pepper. Add the stock and stir, then bring to a simmer.

2. Place the green chiles and cilantro in a blender or food processor. Blend just until smooth, then add to the pressure cooker pot.

3. Add the quinoa, lentils, and beans to the pot and stir well. Secure the lid and cook on high pressure for 15 minutes, then allow the pressure to naturally release for 10 minutes. Open the vent at the top, remove the lid, and stir the chili. Press cancel and let the chili thicken with the lid off, if desired.

4. Season with more salt and pepper, if desired. Serve with your favorite toppings.

Serving Tip This recipe is completely vegan, even with toppings such as fresh chopped cilantro, chopped green onions, sliced avocado, pico de gallo, lime wedges, or tortilla chips. Non-vegans can garnish with anything else they like, including Cheddar or crumbled feta cheese, sour cream, or Greek Yogurt (page 176).

Serve with a slice of Green Chile Corn Bread (page 55) for a perfectly balanced meal.

PER SERVING Calories: 558; Total fat: 19g; Saturated fat: 2g; Cholesterol: 0mg; Carbohydrates: 79g; Fiber: 23g; Protein: 23g

SERVES 2
PREP TIME: 25 minutes
COOK TIME: 6 minutes
TOTAL TIME: 45 minutes

PRESSURE LEVEL: High
RELEASE: Natural

1 small eggplant, chopped

Kosher salt

2 tablespoons oil, divided

1 small onion, chopped

1 garlic clove, minced

1 tablespoon mashed roasted garlic (see Ingredient Tip below)

1 zucchini, chopped

1 yellow summer squash, chopped

1 green bell pepper, seeded and chopped

¼ cup dry white wine

½ cup Vegetable Stock (page 170) or water

2 basil leaves

½ teaspoon herbes de Provence

Freshly ground black pepper

1 (14-ounce) can crushed tomatoes with their juices

TO SERVE
- Chopped fresh basil
- Grated Parmesan or vegan cheese

RATATOUILLE

LIGHT AND HEALTHY | PALEO-FRIENDLY | VEGAN-FRIENDLY
VEGETARIAN

Serve this French country dish over pasta, polenta, or your favorite cooked grain for a classic French dinner. Alternatively, you can turn the ratatouille into a Spanish-style breakfast-for-dinner by topping it with Manchego cheese and a fried egg, and serving it with hearty bread.

1. In a colander set over a medium bowl, sprinkle salt on the eggplant, toss to coat, and let drain.

2. Preheat the pressure cooker pot on sauté mode. When the display reads hot, add 1 tablespoon of oil to the pot. Add the onion and sauté until softened, 4 to 5 minutes. Add the minced garlic and roasted garlic and cook until fragrant, 1 minute.

3. Add the zucchini, squash, and bell pepper and cook until softened, 4 to 5 minutes. Add the wine and deglaze the pot, scraping up any browned bits from the bottom and allowing the mixture to reduce by half, about 2 minutes. Carefully transfer the mixture to a large bowl and set aside.

4. Heat the remaining 1 tablespoon of oil in the pot. Add the eggplant and brown, stirring frequently, 2 to 3 minutes. Press cancel.

5. Return the vegetables to the pot, stir in the stock, basil, and herbes de Provence, and season with salt and pepper. Stir well, then add the tomatoes and their juices.

6. Secure the lid and cook on high pressure for 6 minutes, then allow the pressure to naturally release for 5 minutes. Open the vent at the top and remove the lid. Press cancel, then select sauté.

7. Stir the contents of the pot and let simmer until thickened, about 5 minutes.

8. Serve sprinkled with chopped basil and grated Parmesan or vegan cheese.

Ingredient Tip Roasted garlic can be purchased at some specialty stores, but you can also make it yourself—in your pressure cooker! Slice off the top quarter of 1 garlic bulb and place it in a steamer basket over ½ cup of water in the cooker pot. Secure the lid and cook on high pressure for 6 minutes, then allow a 10-minute natural release. Preheat the broiler in the oven. Peel the garlic cloves into a small bowl, drizzle generously with olive oil, and broil for 5 minutes until caramelized. Smash the roasted garlic cloves with a fork and use in recipes or spread on toasted baguette slices. To store, place in an airtight container and cover completely in olive oil. Refrigerate for up to 1 week.

Variation Tip For a Paleo or vegan version, omit the Parmesan cheese and wine.

PER SERVING Calories: 360; Total fat: 15g; Saturated fat: 2g; Cholesterol: 0mg; Carbohydrates: 46g; Fiber: 18g; Protein: 12g

SERVES 2

PREP TIME: 10 minutes

COOK TIME: 15 minutes

TOTAL TIME: 30 minutes

PRESSURE LEVEL: High

RELEASE: Natural

3 tablespoons sesame oil, divided, plus more for greasing

¾ cup long-grain brown rice

¾ cup water, plus 3 tablespoons

Kosher salt

1 tablespoon cornstarch

2 garlic cloves, crushed

1½ teaspoons peeled minced fresh ginger, divided

1 cup broccoli florets

½ cup julienned carrots

¾ cup snow peas, trimmed

3 fresh shiitake mushrooms, sliced

¼ cup drained sliced water chestnuts

2 to 3 tablespoons low-sodium soy sauce

¼ cup chopped onion

CHINESE VEGETABLE STIR-FRY WITH BROWN RICE

30 MINUTES OR LESS | LIGHT AND HEALTHY | VEGAN | VEGETARIAN

This simple stir-fry recipe calls for cooking the veggies in your favorite wok, and then using your pressure cooker to make a set-it-and-forget-it brown rice. Feel free to use any vegetables you have in the refrigerator—in fact, the more the better!

1. Coat the inside of the pressure cooker pot with sesame oil. Put the pot in the cooker.

2. Add the rice and ¾ cup of water and season with salt. Secure the lid and cook on high pressure for 15 minutes, then allow the pressure to naturally release for 5 minutes. Open the vent at the top and remove the lid.

3. While the rice is cooking, prepare the vegetables. In a large bowl, stir together the cornstarch, garlic, ½ teaspoon of ginger, and 2 tablespoons of sesame oil until combined and the cornstarch is dissolved. Add the broccoli, carrots, snow peas, mushrooms, and water chestnuts and toss to lightly coat.

4. Heat the remaining 1 tablespoon of sesame oil in a wok over medium heat. Increase the heat to medium-high and add the vegetables. Cook for 2 minutes, tossing constantly to prevent burning.

5. Stir in the soy sauce and remaining 3 tablespoons of water. Add the onion and remaining 1 teaspoon of ginger and season with salt. Cook, stirring constantly, until the vegetables are tender but still crisp, 1 to 2 minutes.

6. Divide the brown rice between two plates and top with the stir-fried vegetables.

Variation Tip Prefer white rice? That's fine. Rinse it thoroughly, then add a 1-to-1 ratio of rice to water to your cooker; cook on high pressure for 3 minutes, then allow a 10-minute natural release, or just use your cooker's rice setting.

PER SERVING Calories: 618; Total fat: 23g; Saturated fat: 3g; Cholesterol: 0mg; Carbohydrates: 94g; Fiber: 9g; Protein: 10g

SERVES 2
PREP TIME: 20 minutes
COOK TIME: 35 minutes
TOTAL TIME: 1 hour 10 minutes
(including baking time)

PRESSURE LEVEL: High
RELEASE: Natural

1 tablespoon olive oil

2 tablespoons chopped
red onion

½ jalapeño pepper, stemmed,
seeded, and finely chopped

1 garlic clove, finely minced

½ cup canned pinto beans,
rinsed and drained

2 cups water

½ teaspoon ground cumin

Kosher salt

Freshly ground black pepper

½ cup shredded
Cheddar cheese

4 (8-inch) flour tortillas

TO SERVE
• Cooked white rice
• Fresh salsa

REFRIED BEAN AND CHEESE BURRITOS

LIGHT AND HEALTHY | VEGETARIAN

Homemade burritos are much easier to make than you might think, and they are healthier. Plus, they're freezer-friendly and very inexpensive. While they can be enjoyed by themselves, a side of rice and salsa will make for a satisfying meal.

1. Preheat the oven to 350°F. Line a baking sheet with aluminum foil.

2. Preheat the pressure cooker on sauté mode. When the display reads hot, add the olive oil. Add the onion, jalapeño, and garlic and cook for 1 to 2 minutes, stirring often.

3. Add the beans, water, and cumin and season with salt and pepper.

4. Secure the lid and cook on high pressure for 35 minutes, then allow the pressure to naturally release for 10 minutes. Open the vent at the top and remove the lid.

5. Drain the beans, reserving 2 cups of the cooking liquid in a bowl. Using an immersion blender or potato masher, process or mash the beans to your desired consistency, adding some of the reserved cooking water if needed for a smoother purée.

6. In a medium bowl, mix together the beans and Cheddar cheese.

7. Lay out the tortillas on a work surface. Scoop about ¼ cup of the bean mixture onto one tortilla just below center. Fold the bottom edge of the tortilla up and over the filling. Fold the sides in, overlapping them to enclose the filling. Roll up the tortilla from the bottom, then place seam-side down on the prepared baking sheet. Repeat with the remaining tortillas and filling.

8. Bake the burritos in the oven for 12 to 15 minutes, or until heated through. Serve with white rice and fresh salsa.

Ingredient Tip These burritos are also a perfect grab-and-go snack. Double or triple the recipe, wrap the burritos individually in foil, and store them in plastic zip-top bags in your freezer for up to 3 months until ready to eat. They toast nicely in the oven but are enjoyable microwaved as well.

PER SERVING Calories: 631; Total fat: 23g; Saturated fat: 9g; Cholesterol: 30mg; Carbohydrates: 80g; Fiber: 10g; Protein: 26g

SERVES 2

PREP TIME: 10 minutes
COOK TIME: 5 minutes
TOTAL TIME: 30 minutes

PRESSURE LEVEL: High
RELEASE: Natural

6 eggs

¼ cup chopped celery

2 tablespoons chopped scallions

¼ cup mayonnaise

2 tablespoons Dijon mustard

½ teaspoon hot sauce

½ teaspoon kosher salt

¼ teaspoon freshly ground black pepper

¼ teaspoon paprika

4 slices sandwich bread

DEVILED EGG SALAD SANDWICHES

30 MINUTES OR LESS | PALEO-FRIENDLY | VEGETARIAN

The addition of paprika and hot sauce elevates an ordinary egg salad to deviled egg status in this quick weekday lunch recipe. Using your electric pressure cooker is the easiest way to consistently produce perfectly boiled eggs! The egg salad can also be served over salad greens.

1. Add 1 cup of water to the pressure cooker pot and place the egg rack in the bottom. Put the eggs on the rack.

2. Secure the lid and cook on high pressure for 5 minutes for hard-boiled eggs. When the timer beeps, select cancel and allow the pressure to release naturally for 2 to 3 minutes. Open the vent at the top, then carefully remove the lid.

3. Transfer the eggs to a large bowl and place under cold running water to stop the cooking process. Peel and chop the eggs as soon as they are cool enough to handle. Transfer to a medium bowl and add the celery and scallions.

4. In a small bowl, mix together the mayonnaise, mustard, and hot sauce. Gently stir the mayo dressing into the egg mixture. Season with the salt, pepper, and paprika.

5. Serve some of the egg salad on the sandwich bread (use about 1 cup for each sandwich). Store the remaining egg salad in an airtight container in the refrigerator for up to 3 days.

Pressure Cooker Tip Craving plain soft-boiled eggs instead? Reduce the time on your pressure cooker to 2 minutes and enjoy an egg with some sliced toast strips, a breakfast dish known as boiled eggs and soldiers.

Variation Tip Make a Paleo version of this recipe by omitting the bread.

PER SERVING Calories: 319; Total fat: 24g; Saturated fat: 6g; Cholesterol: 499mg; Carbohydrates: 10g; Fiber: 1g; Protein: 18g

SERVES 2

PREP TIME: 30 minutes

COOK TIME: 20 minutes

TOTAL TIME: 1 hour 30 minutes
(including broiling time)

PRESSURE LEVEL: High

RELEASE: Natural

⅓ package no-boil
lasagna noodles

1 (12-ounce) bag cubed steam-
in-bag butternut squash

Kosher salt

Freshly ground black pepper

3 tablespoons unsalted butter,
plus more for greasing

½ small onion, diced

3 tablespoons flour

1½ cups whole milk

1 tablespoon mashed roasted
garlic (see Ingredient Tip on
page 67)

1 pound broccoli rabe, woody
ends trimmed

½ cup grated Parmesan
cheese, divided

1 cup ricotta cheese

½ tablespoon chopped fresh
sage, plus more for garnish

¼ teaspoon grated lemon zest

1 cup shredded
mozzarella cheese

BUTTERNUT SQUASH AND BROCCOLI RABE LASAGNA

VEGETARIAN | WORTH THE WAIT

You've never had lasagna like this before! This rich meal is totally worth the effort, as puréed butternut squash and a broccoli rabe (rapini) Mornay sauce join a traditional ricotta mixture, layered between chewy sheets of pasta. It's a perfect fall dinner for vegetarians and meat lovers alike.

1. Fill a large bowl with hot water and soak the lasagna noodles for 20 minutes, checking occasionally to make sure they aren't sticking together. (This step is optional, but it ensures that the noodles cook thoroughly and gives them a fresher texture.) Transfer to a paper towel-lined plate to drain.

2. Cook the squash according to the package directions, then purée until smooth, either in a blender or in a bowl using an immersion blender. Season with salt and pepper and set aside.

3. Preheat the pressure cooker on sauté mode. When the display reads hot, melt the 3 tablespoons of butter, then add the onion and sauté until browned and softened, 5 to 7 minutes. Add the flour and cook, stirring, for 1 to 2 minutes.

4. Press cancel, then select sauté. Gradually whisk in the milk, ½ cup at a time, stirring constantly. Add the garlic and bring the sauce to a boil, stirring frequently. Add the broccoli rabe and cook until the sauce thickens. Select cancel, stir in ¼ cup of Parmesan cheese, and season with salt and pepper. Transfer the sauce to a bowl, then carefully remove and wash the inner pot, wipe it dry, and return it to the cooker.

5. In a small bowl, mix together the ricotta cheese, the remaining ¼ cup of Parmesan cheese, the ½ tablespoon of sage, and the lemon zest until smooth. Season with salt and pepper to taste. Set aside. →

6. Coat a 7-inch round cake or springform pan with butter. Spread half of the broccoli rabe sauce on the bottom of the pan. Cover with a layer of lasagna noodles, gently pressing down to compress slightly. Spread half of the butternut squash purée on top, then cover with another layer of noodles. Spread the ricotta cheese mixture on top, then cover with an additional layer of noodles. Top with the remaining butternut purée and a final layer of lasagna noodles. Top with the remaining broccoli rabe sauce and sprinkle with the mozzarella.

7. Cover the baking dish with aluminum foil that's been sprayed with a little cooking spray.

8. Add 1 cup of water to the pressure cooker pot and place the trivet in the bottom. Prepare a foil sling (see page 4), center the pan on it, lower it into the pressure cooker, and arrange the sling ends across the pan.

9. Secure the lid and cook on high pressure for 20 minutes, then allow the pressure to naturally release, about 10 minutes. Open the vent at the top and remove the lid.

10. Using the sling ends, carefully remove the lasagna pan from the inner pot. Remove the foil, then place the dish under the broiler for a few minutes to brown the cheese. Let rest for 10 minutes, then garnish with chopped sage and serve.

Ingredient Tip If you can't find precut butternut squash, you can easily steam a whole squash in your electric pressure cooker. Simply cut it in half and scoop out the seeds, then place it in a steamer basket over 1 cup of water. Cook on high for 12 minutes, then allow a 5-minute natural release before venting. Scoop out 1½ cups of squash and follow the rest of the recipe as written.

PER SERVING Calories: 1,223; Total fat: 51g; Saturated fat: 30g; Cholesterol: 180mg; Carbohydrates: 134g; Fiber: 9g; Protein: 63g

SERVES 2
PREP TIME: 10 minutes
COOK TIME: 4 minutes
TOTAL TIME: 25 minutes

PRESSURE LEVEL: High
RELEASE: Quick

½ tablespoon olive oil

½ cup diced onion

3 garlic cloves, minced

1 teaspoon red pepper flakes (optional)

¼ cup vodka

1 (14.5-ounce) can crushed tomatoes with their juices

2 teaspoons tomato paste

8 ounces penne pasta

Kosher salt

1 cup water

⅓ cup heavy cream

2 tablespoons grated Parmesan cheese

2 basil sprigs, chopped, for garnish

PENNE ALLA VODKA

30 MINUTES OR LESS | ONE-POT MEAL | VEGETARIAN

Cream sauce and red sauce are an unusual combination; they generally do not mesh well, as the acidity of the tomatoes often causes the oil and cream to separate. The vodka in this recipe serves as an emulsifier, allowing everything to come together into one cohesive sauce. Vodka is also thought to release certain flavors from the tomatoes that would otherwise go unnoticed.

1. Preheat the pressure cooker on sauté mode. When the display reads hot, add the olive oil. Add the onion and sauté until softened, 2 to 3 minutes. Add the garlic and red pepper flakes (if using) and cook for 1 minute.

2. Stir in the vodka and cook for 2 minutes, stirring often, until reduced by half.

3. Add the tomatoes and their juices, the tomato paste, and pasta, then season with salt, and add the water.

4. Secure the lid and cook on high pressure for 4 minutes, then quick release the pressure in the pot. Remove the lid and press cancel.

5. Stir in the cream and Parmesan cheese and mix well. Serve hot, garnished with chopped basil.

Variation Tip Add some color to this plain-looking dish by sautéing sliced mushrooms with the onion, adding frozen peas before cooking, and wilting spinach in with the cream and cheese addition. To turn this into a meaty meal, add shredded cooked chicken or browned ground beef with the cream and cheese, and allow it to warm through before serving.

PER SERVING Calories: 617; Total fat: 15g; Saturated fat: 7g; Cholesterol: 115mg; Carbohydrates: 85g; Fiber: 8g; Protein: 21g

SERVES 2

PREP TIME: 35 minutes

COOK TIME: 20 minutes

TOTAL TIME: 1 hour 15 minutes
(including baking time)

PRESSURE LEVEL: High

RELEASE: Natural

1 pound potatoes, peeled
and quartered

2 tablespoons butter, divided,
plus more for greasing

2 teaspoons oil

1 small onion, diced

2 garlic cloves, minced

¾ cup dried brown or green
lentils, rinsed, sorted,
and drained

2 cups Vegetable Stock
(page 170)

½ tablespoon tomato paste

1 teaspoon fresh thyme or
½ teaspoon dried thyme

Kosher salt

Freshly ground black pepper

1 cup shredded
Cheddar cheese

¼ cup whole milk

1 tablespoon cornstarch

2 tablespoons cold water

6 ounces frozen mixed
vegetables

VEGETABLE SHEPHERD'S PIE

VEGAN-FRIENDLY | VEGETARIAN | WORTH THE WAIT

Shepherd's pie doesn't have to be made with meat
when lentils can satisfy hungry bellies just the same.
The juicy filling in this version is very vegetable forward,
full of flavor and nutrition.

1. Add 1 cup of water to the pressure cooker pot. Place the
steamer basket in the bottom of the pot and put the potatoes in it.

2. Secure the lid and cook on high pressure for 5 minutes, then
quick release the pressure in the pot and remove the lid.

3. Remove the potatoes and the steamer basket from the pot and
set aside. Carefully drain the water from the pot, wipe dry, and
return to the pressure cooker.

4. Preheat the oven to 400°F. Coat a medium casserole dish with
butter and set aside.

5. On the cooker, select sauté. When the display reads hot, add
the oil. Add the onion and sauté until softened, 3 minutes. Add
the garlic and sauté for 1 minute. Press cancel.

6. To the cooker pot, add the lentils, stock, tomato paste, and
thyme and season with salt and pepper. Secure the lid and cook
on high pressure for 15 minutes.

7. Meanwhile, transfer the potatoes to a medium bowl and mash
with a potato masher. Stir in the cheese, milk, and the 2 tablespoons of butter and season with salt and pepper. Set aside.

8. When the cooking time is up on the lentil mixture, allow about a 10-minute natural release, then open the vent at the top and remove the lid. Select sauté.

9. In a small bowl, combine the cornstarch and cold water and whisk to mix well. Add to the pot and bring to a simmer, stirring frequently, until thickened. Add the frozen mixed vegetables to the lentil mixture.

10. Transfer the filling to the prepared casserole dish. Spread the mashed potatoes evenly over the filling, up to the edge of the dish. Season with salt and pepper.

11. Put the casserole dish on a baking sheet and bake until the potatoes are lightly golden brown, 20 to 25 minutes.

Variation Tip Make this recipe vegan by substituting in dairy-free milk, butter, and cheese.

PER SERVING Calories: 907; Total fat: 37g; Saturated fat: 21g; Cholesterol: 93mg; Carbohydrates: 104g; Fiber: 32g; Protein: 41g

SERVES 2

PREP TIME: 5 minutes

COOK TIME: 5 minutes

TOTAL TIME: 30 minutes

PRESSURE LEVEL: High

RELEASE: Natural

2 cups Adobo Barbacoa
Sauce (page 175)

8 ounces portobello
mushrooms, chopped

Juice of ½ lime

1 bay leaf

Kosher salt

¾ cup cooked white rice

½ cup cooked black beans

½ cup shredded
Cheddar cheese

TO SERVE
- Shredded romaine lettuce
- Pico de gallo
- Guacamole
- Sour cream

BARBACOA BELLA BURRITO BOWLS

30 MINUTES OR LESS | LIGHT AND HEALTHY | ONE-POT MEAL
PALEO-FRIENDLY | VEGAN-FRIENDLY | VEGETARIAN

Forget tofu; the tastiest meat replacement is definitely portobello mushrooms. Inspired by the popular burrito bowls at Chipotle Mexican Grill, this copycat barbacoa is strictly vegan, using chopped mushrooms in place of the signature beef. You have a good chance of surprising your carnivorous loved ones with this dish.

1. Pour the barbacoa sauce into the cooker pot and add the mushrooms, lime juice, and bay leaf. Stir together.

2. Secure the lid and cook on high pressure for 5 minutes, then allow the pressure to naturally release for 10 minutes. Open the vent at the top, then remove the lid.

3. Put the pot on sauté mode. Remove the bay leaf, then allow the contents to simmer for about 5 minutes, or until thickened. Season to taste with salt.

4. Serve in bowls over the cooked rice and black beans, topped with the Cheddar cheese and, as desired, shredded lettuce, pico de gallo, guacamole, and sour cream.

Variation Tip For an even heartier burrito bowl, add 1½ cups raw, unpeeled, cubed sweet potato to the pot with the barbacoa sauce and mushrooms. You'll be boosting your vitamin and antioxidant intake, as well as regulating your digestive system, with just one serving of this colorful superfood. For a vegan version, leave out the dairy. For a Paleo version, omit the dairy and rice and use Adobo Barbacoa Sauce that hasn't been made with wine or sugar (see page 175).

PER SERVING Calories: 562; Total fat: 16g; Saturated fat: 7g; Cholesterol: 32mg; Carbohydrates: 81g; Fiber: 9g; Protein: 22g

PRESSURE LEVEL: High
RELEASE: Natural

1 small (1-pound) acorn squash, halved lengthwise and seeded

1 tablespoon olive oil

1 medium shallot, finely chopped

1 celery stalk, diced

3 ounces portobello mushrooms, finely chopped

1 garlic clove, minced

1 teaspoon chopped fresh sage

½ teaspoon chopped fresh thyme

¼ teaspoon chopped fresh rosemary

½ cup Vegetable Stock (page 170) or water, divided

½ cup wild rice, rinsed

2 tablespoons soy sauce

1 cup canned chickpeas, rinsed and drained

¼ cup chopped dried cranberries

¼ cup chopped pecans

2 tablespoons balsamic vinegar

Kosher salt

Freshly ground black pepper

TO SERVE
• Shaved Parmesan or vegan cheese (optional)

STUFFED ACORN SQUASH

LIGHT AND HEALTHY | VEGAN-FRIENDLY | VEGETARIAN
WORTH THE WAIT

Whether served on Thanksgiving Day or in June, this seasonal squash dish, stuffed with wild rice, mushrooms, and chickpeas, is the flavorful vegetarian meal you've been craving. A sprinkle of shaved Parmesan or vegan cheese makes it extra special.

1. Add ½ cup of water to the pressure cooker pot and place the steamer basket in the bottom. Place the squash halves cut-side up in the steamer basket. Secure the lid and cook on high pressure for 4 minutes, then allow the pressure to naturally release, about 5 minutes. Open the vent at the top and remove the lid.

2. Transfer the squash to a plate and set aside. Carefully remove the steamer basket, then lift the inner pot from the cooker and carefully drain the water. Dry the pot thoroughly and return to the cooker.

3. Preheat the pressure cooker on sauté mode. When the display reads hot, add the oil. Add the shallot, celery, and mushrooms and sauté until softened, 3 minutes. Add the garlic, sage, thyme, rosemary, and a splash of stock and cook until fragrant, 2 to 3 minutes. Press cancel.

4. Add the remaining stock, the rice, and soy sauce. Stir to combine.

5. Secure the lid and cook on high pressure for 25 minutes, then allow the pressure to naturally release, about 10 minutes. Open the vent at the top and remove the lid. ⟶

6. Stir in the chickpeas, cranberries, pecans, and balsamic vinegar. Season with salt and pepper and stir to combine. Allow to warm through for 3 to 4 minutes.

7. Spoon the filling into the squash halves and serve topped with shaved Parmesan or vegan cheese (if desired).

Variation Tip If you're craving a fall meal and you're a meat eater, substitute some browned Italian pork sausage for the chickpeas. To make the dish vegan, omit the Parmesan cheese.

PER SERVING Calories: 540; Total fat: 12g; Saturated fat: 1g; Cholesterol: 0mg; Carbohydrates: 96g; Fiber: 13g; Protein: 18g

SERVES 2

PREP TIME: 10 minutes

COOK TIME: 18 minutes

TOTAL TIME: 45 minutes

PRESSURE LEVEL: High

RELEASE: Natural

2 tablespoons oil

½ onion, minced

2 garlic cloves, minced

½ green bell pepper, seeded and diced

1 carrot, grated

2 teaspoons kosher salt

½ tablespoon chili powder, plus more for seasoning (optional)

½ teaspoon dried oregano

Pinch paprika

2 tablespoons tomato paste

1 (14-ounce) can crushed roasted tomatoes with their juices

1 tablespoon apple cider vinegar

1 tablespoon vegan Worcestershire sauce, such as Annie's brand

1½ cups Vegetable Stock (page 170) or water

1 cup dried lentils, sorted and rinsed

1 tablespoon maple syrup (optional)

4 large portobello mushroom caps, roasted

VEGAN SLOPPY JOES

LIGHT AND HEALTHY | ONE-POT MEAL | VEGAN | VEGETARIAN

This sandwich might be the cheapest one you'll ever eat. The "meaty" vegan filling—made hearty with a few diced vegetables, lentils, and plenty of pantry items—can be served on a fluffy bun, but to keep this meal truly vegan (plus carb-free!), roasted portobello mushroom caps are used here. You can also serve the filling over cooked rice or cauliflower rice instead.

1. Preheat the pressure cooker on sauté mode. When the display reads hot, add the oil. Add the onion, garlic, bell pepper, and carrot and sauté until softened, 3 minutes. Stir in the salt, ½ tablespoon of chili powder, the oregano, and paprika. Add the tomato paste and cook, stirring, for 1 minute.

2. Add the tomatoes and their juices, the vinegar, Worcestershire sauce, stock, and lentils and stir well, scraping up any browned bits from the bottom of the pot.

3. Secure the lid and cook on high pressure for 13 minutes, then allow the pressure to naturally release, about 10 minutes. Open the vent at the top and remove the lid.

4. Stir the sloppy joe filling, seasoning with more chili powder (if desired) and adding the maple syrup (if using). Divide the filling between two of the portobello caps, then top with the remaining portobello caps and serve.

Variation Tip To add even more heartiness to this vegan meal, stir ½ cup of vegetable meat substitute or chopped mushrooms into the completed sloppy joe filling and simmer on sauté before serving.

PER SERVING Calories: 609; Total fat: 16g; Saturated fat: 2g; Cholesterol: 0mg; Carbohydrates: 85g; Fiber: 34g; Protein: 30g

Five

SHELLFISH AND FISH

Your electric pressure cooker inherently has a love/hate relationship with seafood. The humid, steamy cooking environment is perfect for mollusks, poached fish, and seafood soups. Shrimp, however, a prevalent ingredient in this chapter, is a bit tougher to get right. To avoid overcooked shrimp and fish, it is important to follow the recipes carefully, whether that means adding the shrimp after the pressure cooking is finished or flipping the pressure release valve as soon as the cooking time is finished.

Cioppino, page 91

Shrimp and Grits 85

Quick Shrimp Scampi 87

Shrimp Paella 88

Cajun Shrimp Boil 89

Seafood Gumbo 90

Cioppino 91

Clam Chowder 93

Seafood Coconut Curry 95

Mussels Fra Diavolo with Linguine 96

Perfect Lobster Tails with Lemon-Butter Sauce 98

Steamed Cod and Vegetables 100

California Fish Tacos 102

Salsa-Poached Red Snapper 104

Teriyaki Salmon Salad 105

Tuna Casserole 107

SERVES 2

PREP TIME: 10 minutes

COOK TIME: 28 minutes

TOTAL TIME: 40 minutes

PRESSURE LEVEL: High

RELEASE: Natural

3 uncooked bacon slices, chopped

2 shallots, chopped

¼ green bell pepper, chopped

¼ cup chopped celery

1 garlic clove, minced

Splash dry white wine or stock

½ cup fresh or canned diced tomatoes

⅓ cup Chicken Stock (page 167)

1 tablespoon freshly squeezed lemon juice

Kosher salt

Freshly ground black pepper

½ cup dry grits

1 cup milk

1 cup water

½ pound uncooked shrimp, tails removed, peeled and deveined

1 tablespoon butter

¾ cup shredded Cheddar cheese

2 tablespoons heavy cream

TO SERVE

• Chopped scallions
• Hot sauce

SHRIMP AND GRITS

Made from ground corn, grits do not have a distinctive taste on their own, but they soak up the flavors of whatever they are mixed with during and after cooking, such as lots of butter, Cheddar cheese, and bacon—the trifecta of American breakfast indulgence. When topped with perfectly poached shrimp and crispy bacon, it's no wonder they're on the menu all day.

1. Preheat the pressure cooker on sauté mode. When the display reads hot, add the bacon to the pot and cook until crispy, 5 to 6 minutes. Transfer to a paper towel-lined plate to drain. Do not wipe out the pot. Add the shallots, bell pepper, and celery to the bacon grease in the pot and sauté, stirring occasionally, for 2 to 3 minutes.

2. Press the cancel button and stir in the garlic. Sauté for 1 minute.

3. Stir in the wine and deglaze the pot, scraping up the browned bits from the bottom. Allow the liquid to reduce for 1 to 2 minutes, stirring frequently, then add the diced tomatoes, stock, and lemon juice. Stir and season with salt and pepper. Pour the tomato sauce into a large bowl, cover, and set aside. Rinse out the cooker pot, wipe dry, and place back in the cooker.

4. In a heatproof medium glass or metal bowl, stir together the grits, milk, and water and season with salt and pepper. Put a trivet or egg rack in the cooker pot and set the grits bowl on top.

5. Secure the lid and cook on high pressure for 10 minutes, then allow the pressure to naturally release for about 10 minutes. Open the vent at the top. Remove the lid, then carefully remove the bowl of grits from the cooker pot and set aside. →

6. Put the shrimp in the cooker pot, add the tomato sauce, and stir. Replace the lid and allow the shrimp to cook in the residual heat for 7 to 8 minutes, stirring once or twice, to evenly cook on both sides.

7. Meanwhile, fluff the grits with a fork and stir in the butter and shredded cheese. Cover the bowl with plastic wrap to keep warm.

8. When the shrimp is almost finished cooking, stir in the cream and allow it to warm through.

9. Divide the grits between two bowls and top with the shrimp and tomato sauce. Sprinkle the chopped bacon on top and serve with scallions and hot sauce.

Ingredient Tip Corn grits can be either yellow or white, depending on the color of the corn used; the more finely ground white grits, however, are favored for this recipe. Yellow grits, also known as polenta, are more coarsely textured when cooked.

PER SERVING Calories: 765; Total fat: 51g; Saturated fat: 25g; Cholesterol: 383mg; Carbohydrates: 24g; Fiber: 2g; Protein: 50g

PRESSURE LEVEL: High
RELEASE: Quick

6 ounces linguine

1 tablespoon oil

1 tablespoon butter

1 shallot, chopped

1 tablespoon minced garlic

Pinch red pepper flakes, plus more for seasoning (optional)

¼ cup white wine

¼ cup Chicken Stock (page 167)

1 tablespoon freshly squeezed lemon juice

¾ pound thawed frozen raw jumbo shrimp, tails removed, peeled and deveined

Kosher salt

Freshly ground black pepper

TO SERVE
• Chopped parsley
• Crusty bread

QUICK SHRIMP SCAMPI

30 MINUTES OR LESS | LIGHT AND HEALTHY | PALEO-FRIENDLY

Quick 15-minute dinners on weekdays are the best! This buttery, garlicky scampi dish turns a ho-hum meal into a gourmet dinner that you'll be craving at least once a week.

1. Cook the pasta according to package directions while you cook everything else in the pressure cooker. Drain the pasta but do not rinse, transfer to a serving bowl, cover, and set aside.

2. Preheat the pressure cooker pot on sauté mode. When the display reads hot, add the oil and butter and stir to melt. Add the shallot, garlic, and red pepper flakes and sauté for 2 minutes.

3. Pour in the wine and deglaze the pot, scraping up the browned bits from the bottom using a wooden spoon and stirring them into the liquid. Let cook for 1 minute to reduce by half. Press cancel.

4. Add the stock, lemon juice, and shrimp. Secure the lid. Set the cooker timer for 0 minutes, which will cause the cooker to come to pressure, then immediately depressurize. Quick release the pressure in the pot, then remove the lid. Press cancel.

5. Season with salt, pepper, and additional red pepper flakes (if desired) and stir in the parsley. Pour into the serving bowl with the pasta and toss. Serve with slices of crusty bread.

Cooking Tip Whether you use fresh or frozen shrimp, peel on or off, if it ever looks underdone after pressure cooking, simply select sauté and let it simmer for 1 to 2 more minutes, until pink.

Variation Tip For a Paleo version, omit the wine, substitute the butter with more oil, and substitute zucchini noodles for the linguine.

PER SERVING Calories: 596; Total fat: 14g; Saturated fat: 5g; Cholesterol: 705mg; Carbohydrates: 46g; Fiber: 2g; Protein: 68g

SERVES 2

PREP TIME: 10 minutes

COOK TIME: 5 minutes

TOTAL TIME: 20 minutes

PRESSURE LEVEL: High

RELEASE: Quick

2 tablespoons oil

½ onion, chopped

2 garlic cloves, minced

Kosher salt

Freshly ground black pepper

1 teaspoon paprika

¼ teaspoon red pepper flakes

Pinch saffron threads

¼ cup white wine

½ cup basmati rice

1 (14-ounce) can diced
tomatoes and chiles, with
their juices

½ cup Chicken Stock
(page 167)

½ pound peel-on large raw
shrimp, deveined

TO SERVE
- Chopped fresh cilantro
- Lime wedges

SHRIMP PAELLA

30 MINUTES OR LESS | LIGHT AND HEALTHY | ONE-POT MEAL
PALEO-FRIENDLY

This low-fat, low-calorie paella is a simplified but
mouthwatering version of the traditional Spanish preparation and shows off your electric pressure cooker's
one-pot capabilities. Shrimp is one of the easiest
proteins to overcook, so be sure to stir it into the rice
after the pressure-cooking cycle is completed.

1. Preheat the pressure cooker pot on sauté mode. When the
display reads hot, add the oil. Add the onion and sauté until
softened, 3 minutes. Add the garlic and cook, stirring frequently,
for 1 minute. Season with salt and pepper, then add the paprika,
red pepper flakes, and saffron, stirring until well combined.

2. Pour in the wine and deglaze the pot, scraping up the browned
bits from the bottom. Stir in the rice, then add the tomatoes and
chiles and their juices, and the stock. Stir and make sure all the
rice is covered.

3. Secure the lid and cook on high pressure for 5 minutes, then
quick release the pressure in the pot and remove the lid. Press
cancel, then select sauté.

4. Stir the shrimp into the rice, cover the pot with the lid loosely,
and cook for 3 to 5 minutes, or until pink. Serve with chopped
fresh cilantro and lime wedges.

Variation Tip To make a heartier, more traditional paella, add
½ pound browned and sliced Spanish chorizo, 1 chopped chicken
breast, an additional ¼ cup of stock, and toss in ½ pound cleaned
clams or mussels (see page 216) before pressure cooking. To make
the dish Paleo, omit the wine and don't add chorizo.

PER SERVING Calories: 439; Total fat: 12g; Saturated fat: 7g; Cholesterol: 193mg;
Carbohydrates: 50g; Fiber: 5g; Protein: 28g

SERVES 2
PREP TIME: 5 minutes
COOK TIME: 4 minutes
TOTAL TIME: 15 minutes

PRESSURE LEVEL: High
RELEASE: Quick

1 cup water

½ pound red potatoes, halved

1 medium sweet
onion, chopped

2 ears of corn, shucked and
broken in half

½ pound fully cooked kielbasa
sausage, cut into 2-inch slices

2 tablespoons Old Bay
seasoning, plus more for
seasoning

2 tablespoons crab boil
seasoning (optional)

½ teaspoon kosher salt

1 pound peel-on large raw
shrimp, deveined

TO SERVE
- Melted butter
- Lemon wedges
- Crusty bread

CAJUN SHRIMP BOIL

30 MINUTES OR LESS | ONE-POT MEAL | PALEO-FRIENDLY

A shrimp boil is perfect for a big summer gathering, but you can enjoy the warm-weather feelings on a smaller scale—and in half the time—by using your electric pressure cooker. For full effect, spread the finished product over layered newspapers on your kitchen table, and serve with melted butter.

1. In the pressure cooker pot, combine the water, potatoes, onion, corn, kielbasa, 2 tablespoons of Old Bay, the crab boil seasoning (if using), and salt.

2. Secure the lid and cook on high pressure for 4 minutes, then quick release the pressure in the pot and remove the lid. Press cancel.

3. Stir in the shrimp, replace the lid loosely, and let cook in the residual heat for 3 to 4 minutes. Season with more salt and Old Bay. Drain in a large colander.

4. Serve in large, shallow bowls with a side of melted butter, some lemon wedges, and crusty bread for dipping.

Ingredient Tip There are many boil seasonings on the market, so feel free to discover your favorite brand or use whatever you have on hand. Increase the Old Bay for a more richly seasoned boil. The crab boil seasoning is optional but makes for spicier, Louisiana-style results.

Variation Tip For a Paleo version, replace the corn with whole mushrooms or artichokes, and use a sugar-free sausage.

PER SERVING Calories: 986; Total fat: 40g; Saturated fat: 14g; Cholesterol: 492mg; Carbohydrates: 46g; Fiber: 5g; Protein: 114g

SERVES 2

PREP TIME: 30 minutes

COOK TIME: 4 minutes

TOTAL TIME: 1 hour

PRESSURE LEVEL: High

RELEASE: Quick

3 tablespoons oil, divided

½ pound andouille sausage, cut into ½-inch slices

1 small onion, diced

1 celery stalk, diced

1 cup diced green bell pepper

3 garlic cloves, minced

2 tablespoons butter

3 tablespoons all-purpose flour

3 cups Chicken Stock (page 167)

1 cup sliced okra

2 tablespoons tomato paste

1 tablespoon Creole seasoning, plus more for seasoning (optional)

¼ teaspoon cayenne pepper, plus more for seasoning (optional)

Kosher salt

Freshly ground black pepper

1 medium tomato, diced

½ pound raw medium shrimp, tail-on, peeled and deveined

¼ pound lump crabmeat, picked over

Gumbo filé powder (optional)

TO SERVE

- Cooked white rice
- Chopped scallions

SEAFOOD GUMBO

PALEO-FRIENDLY | WORTH THE WAIT

Traditional gumbo is prepared over several hours, but this recipe is considerably faster and, while it isn't exactly everything a Creole gumbo should be, it is definitely a flavorful variation. For a Paleo version, choose a sugar-free sausage and don't serve it with rice.

1. Preheat the pressure cooker pot on sauté mode. When the display reads hot, add 2 tablespoons of oil. Add the sausage, onion, celery, and bell pepper and sauté until browned, 6 to 8 minutes. Add the garlic and cook, stirring, for 1 minute. Transfer the mixture to a plate and set aside.

2. Add the remaining 1 tablespoon of oil and the butter to the pot to melt. Sprinkle in the flour and whisk to combine. Cook for 12 to 15 minutes, whisking constantly to avoid burning, until the roux is a medium to dark brown (the darker the roux, the more intense the flavor).

3. Stir in the sausage mixture, stock, okra, tomato paste, Creole seasoning, and cayenne pepper. Season with salt and black pepper to taste. Add the tomato.

4. Secure the lid and cook on high pressure for 4 minutes, then quick release the pressure in the pot and remove the lid. Select sauté. Taste and adjust the seasonings, adding more cayenne pepper or Creole seasoning if needed.

5. Stir in the shrimp, sprinkle the crabmeat loosely on the top, and let cook 4 to 5 minutes, or until the shrimp are pink. Add gumbo filé powder (if using).

6. Serve with white rice and a sprinkle of scallions.

Variation Tip To make a more authentic gumbo, replace the butter and oil with bacon grease and add ½ teaspoon gumbo filé powder (found at most grocery stores) before pressure cooking.

PER SERVING Calories: 1,026; Total fat: 68g; Saturated fat: 22g; Cholesterol: 375mg; Carbohydrates: 34g; Fiber: 6g; Protein: 70g

SERVES 2

PREP TIME: 15 minutes

COOK TIME: 10 minutes

TOTAL TIME: 45 minutes

PRESSURE LEVEL: High

RELEASE: Natural

2 tablespoons butter

1 tablespoon oil

1 shallot, thinly sliced

½ small fennel bulb, thinly sliced

2 garlic cloves, minced

½ teaspoon red pepper flakes, plus more for seasoning (optional)

½ teaspoon dried oregano

Pinch kosher salt

1 (14-ounce) can diced tomatoes with their juices

¾ cup canned clam juice

1 cup white wine

Freshly ground black pepper

½ pound mussels, rinsed, scrubbed, and debearded

½ pound manila clams, scrubbed

½ pound flaky white fish, such as cod or flounder

½ pound medium shrimp, tail-on, peeled and deveined

TO SERVE
- Chopped fresh parsley
- Lemon wedges
- Toasted crusty bread slices

CIOPPINO

ONE-POT MEAL | PALEO-FRIENDLY

The name of this dish may sound fancy and foreign, but cioppino was actually developed in the late 1800s by fishermen in San Francisco. When they returned from a day at sea empty-handed, they would walk around with a pot asking other fishermen to donate whatever they could spare, and that became their dinner.

1. Preheat the pressure cooker on sauté mode. When the display reads hot, melt the butter into the oil. Add the shallot and fennel and sauté until softened, about 2 minutes. Add the garlic, ½ teaspoon of red pepper flakes, the oregano, and a pinch of salt and cook for 1 minute.

2. Stir in the tomatoes and their juices, the clam juice, and wine. Season with salt and pepper. Secure the lid and cook on high pressure for 10 minutes, then allow the pressure to naturally release for about 10 minutes. Open the vent at the top and remove the lid. Press cancel. →

3. Select sauté. Add the mussels and clams to the pot and cook, uncovered, for 5 to 6 minutes, or until the clams and mussels begin to open. Add the fish and shrimp and simmer for 3 to 4 minutes, or until cooked through. Discard any mussels or clams that do not open. Taste and season with salt and more red pepper flakes (if desired).

4. Divide the cioppino between two large bowls and serve with a sprinkling of chopped parsley, lemon wedges, and toasted crusty bread.

Recipe Tip This hearty, tomato-and-wine-based seafood dish is very much a "kitchen sink–style" stew and can be made from whatever the catch of the day is—or whatever seafood happens to be in your refrigerator or freezer. For complete satisfaction, serve it with lots of crusty sourdough bread to soak up the broth.

Variation Tip For a Paleo version of this recipe, omit the wine and don't serve with bread.

PER SERVING Calories: 733; Total fat: 25g; Saturated fat: 9g; Cholesterol: 368mg; Carbohydrates: 36g; Fiber: 6g; Protein: 72g

SERVES 2

PREP TIME: 25 minutes

COOK TIME: 5 minutes

TOTAL TIME: 45 minutes

PRESSURE LEVEL: High
RELEASE: Quick

4 uncooked bacon
slices, chopped

2 tablespoons butter

1 small onion, diced

1 garlic clove, minced

¼ cup white wine

1 cup clam juice

1 cup Chicken Stock
(page 167) or water

1 large Russet potato, cubed
(2 cups)

2 thyme sprigs or ¼ teaspoon
dried thyme

½ teaspoon red pepper flakes
(optional)

Kosher salt

Freshly ground black or
white pepper

1 tablespoon cornstarch

3 (6.5-ounce) cans clams,
whole, chopped, or minced,
or 1½ pounds fresh clams in
the shell

1 cup heavy cream

½ cup whole milk

CLAM CHOWDER

This soup is the kind that begs for extra carbohydrates in the form of a bread bowl and oyster crackers. Of course, those additions are optional if you're interested in a lower-carb version.

1. Preheat the pressure cooker on sauté mode. When the display reads hot, add the bacon and cook until barely crispy, about 5 minutes. Transfer to a paper towel—lined plate to drain. Do not wipe out the pot.

2. Melt the butter in the bacon grease in the pot. Add the onion and garlic and sauté until softened, 3 to 4 minutes.

3. Add the wine and deglaze the pot, scraping up the browned bits from the bottom. Let the liquid reduce by half and press cancel.

4. Add the clam juice, stock, potato, thyme, and red pepper flakes (if using) and season with salt and pepper. Stir well.

5. Secure the lid and cook on high pressure for 5 minutes, then quick release the pressure in the pot and remove the lid. Press cancel. →

6. Remove the thyme sprigs. Using a potato masher, carefully mash some or all of the potato cubes. Select sauté. In a small bowl, whisk 2 tablespoons of the chowder with the cornstarch until dissolved.

7. Stir the cornstarch mixture back into the pot, along with the clams, cream, and milk. Let simmer for about 5 minutes before serving.

Ingredient Tip If you're preparing this chowder with fresh clams, you can save some money and make your own clam juice in your pressure cooker. Place the cleaned clams in a steamer basket set over 1 cup of water in the cooker pot. Cook on high for 5 minutes, performing a quick release at the end of the cook time. Open the lid and let the clams cool enough to handle, then open them over the pot and allow the juices to mingle with the clam water. Use the liquid as your clam juice (strain it through a fine-mesh sieve lined with cheesecloth to remove sand), adding water as needed to yield 1 cup.

PER SERVING Calories: 722; Total fat: 37g; Saturated fat: 18g; Cholesterol: 119mg; Carbohydrates: 63g; Fiber: 6g; Protein: 29g

SERVES 2
PREP TIME: 10 minutes
COOK TIME: 2 to 3 minutes
TOTAL TIME: 20 minutes

PRESSURE LEVEL: High
RELEASE: Quick

2 teaspoons oil

5 to 6 curry leaves or kaffir lime leaves, plus more for garnish

½ onion, sliced

1 green chile (preferably serrano or jalapeño), stemmed, seeded, and sliced

2 garlic cloves, minced

½ tablespoon grated peeled fresh ginger

2 tablespoons curry powder

1 cup unsweetened coconut milk

¾ cup cherry tomatoes

¼ cup chopped fresh cilantro

½ pound fresh or thawed frozen tilapia fillets, cut into bite-size pieces

Kosher salt

1 tablespoon freshly squeezed lime juice

¼ pound raw medium shrimp, peeled and deveined

TO SERVE
- Cooked jasmine rice
- Lime wedges
- Unsweetened shredded coconut

SEAFOOD COCONUT CURRY

30 MINUTES OR LESS | PALEO

This curry recipe is extremely versatile—you can use any seafood you have on hand—and is always a delicious and fast dinner choice. Having prepared curry powder on hand makes the recipe even faster and easier, cutting down on the time it takes to measure individual spices to achieve the right flavor profile.

1. Preheat the pressure cooker pot on sauté mode. When the display reads hot, add the oil. Add the curry leaves and sauté for 1 minute, then add the onion, chile, garlic, and ginger and sauté until softened, 30 seconds.

2. Stir in the curry powder and sauté for 30 seconds. Add the coconut milk and mix well, deglazing the pot and scraping up any browned bits from the bottom. Let simmer for 30 to 60 seconds.

3. Add the tomatoes, cilantro, and tilapia pieces. Stir gently to coat the fish.

4. Secure the lid and cook on high pressure for 2 to 3 minutes, depending on how thick the fish pieces are, then quick release the pressure in the pot and remove the lid. Press cancel.

5. Season with salt and add the lime juice. Stir in the shrimp and loosely cover the pot with the lid, allowing the shrimp to cook in the residual heat for 3 to 4 minutes, or until pink. Serve in bowls with cooked jasmine rice, lime wedges, and shredded coconut, garnished with more curry leaves.

Ingredient Tip Curry and kaffir lime leaves can be found at Indian and Asian markets, or on Amazon.com. Curry powder can be found in the spice aisle of the grocery store.

PER SERVING Calories: 522; Total fat: 36g; Saturated fat: 27g; Cholesterol: 167mg; Carbohydrates: 23g; Fiber: 8g; Protein: 38g

PRESSURE LEVEL: High

RELEASE: Quick

6 ounces linguine

1 tablespoon oil, plus more for the pasta

½ large onion, chopped

3 garlic cloves, minced

2 tablespoons red pepper flakes

½ cup dry white wine

1 (14-ounce) can fire-roasted crushed tomatoes with their juices

4 ounces canned clam juice

Kosher salt

Freshly ground black pepper

1 pound fresh mussels, rinsed, scrubbed, and debearded

⅓ cup fresh chopped basil

TO SERVE
- Lime wedges
- Crusty bread

MUSSELS FRA DIAVOLO WITH LINGUINE

30 MINUTES OR LESS | PALEO-FRIENDLY

Fra diavolo means "brother devil" in Italian, which is exactly what to expect from this tasty pasta dish. Plump, juicy mussels bathed in a spicy, garlicky tomato sauce are served over a bed of linguine (or zucchini noodles, a.k.a. "zoodles," if you don't want so many carbs). Don't forget to serve with crusty bread to sop up all that glorious spicy goodness!

1. Cook the pasta according to package directions. Drain and toss with some oil.

2. Sort through the mussels and discard any that aren't fully closed or have broken shells.

3. Preheat the pressure cooker pot on sauté mode. When the display reads hot, add 1 tablespoon of oil. Add the onion and sauté until softened, 2 minutes. Add the garlic and red pepper flakes and sauté until fragrant, about 1 minute.

4. Pour in the wine and deglaze the pot, scraping up the browned bits from the bottom. Cook for 1 to 2 minutes, or until the wine is reduced by half.

5. Add the tomatoes and their juices and the clam juice and stir well. Season with salt and pepper. Let the mixture simmer briefly, then stir in the mussels.

6. Secure the lid and cook on high pressure for 3 minutes, then quick release the pressure in the pot and remove the lid. Press cancel.

7. Stir in the chopped basil. Season with more salt and pepper as desired.

8. Portion the pasta into bowls and immediately ladle the mussels and sauce on top. Serve with lime wedges and crusty bread.

Variation Tip If you're looking for an alternative to mollusks, this recipe can be made with shrimp or lobster instead of mussels. Fra diavolo sauce can be found in many grocery and specialty stores if you want a quick sauce solution. Alternatively, you can add red pepper flakes to Easy Marinara Sauce (page 171) and use that. To make this recipe Paleo, omit the linguine and wine and don't serve with bread.

PER SERVING Calories: 631; Total fat: 15g; Saturated fat: 3g; Cholesterol: 108mg; Carbohydrates: 76g; Fiber: 6g; Protein: 45g

SERVES 2

PREP TIME: 5 minutes
COOK TIME: 3 minutes
TOTAL TIME: 15 minutes

PRESSURE LEVEL: High
RELEASE: Quick

1 cup Chicken Stock
(page 167) or water

1 teaspoon Old Bay seasoning

2 (about 1-pound) fresh Maine
lobster tails

Juice of 1 lemon, divided

½ cup butter, melted

½ tablespoon minced garlic

½ lemon, cut into wedges

PERFECT LOBSTER TAILS WITH LEMON-BUTTER SAUCE

30 MINUTES OR LESS

There are so many ways to prepare lobster tails, but electric pressure cookers do it the quickest, and with the best results. This simple recipe yields perfectly tender lobster tails, and the butter sauce is so good, you might want to make double! For a special surf 'n' turf meal, serve this up with a nicely grilled steak and steamed baby potatoes.

1. Add the stock and Old Bay to your pressure cooker pot and place the trivet in the bottom. Place each lobster tail shell-side down, meat-side up on the trivet. Drizzle half of the lemon juice over the lobster.

2. Secure the cooker lid and cook on high pressure for 3 minutes. Quick release the pressure in the pot, then remove the lid.

3. While the pressure releases, fill a large bowl with ice water. Using tongs, immediately transfer the lobster tails to the ice bath to avoid overcooking. Let chill for 1 to 2 minutes.

4. In a small bowl, whisk together the butter, the remaining lemon juice, and the garlic.

5. Transfer the lobster tails to a dish towel-covered cutting board. Butterfly the lobster tail using kitchen shears or a large knife: with the meat side of the tail up, cut the underside of the tail down the center.

6. Serve with the lemon wedges and the lemon-butter sauce for dipping.

Serving Tip Want a meal that's a little more than just lobster tails? Skip the butter sauce, toast up a couple of hoagie buns, and make some delicious Maine lobster rolls! Remove the lobster tails from their shells and chop. Transfer to a medium bowl. Add ⅓ cup mayonnaise, 2 tablespoons melted butter, ¼ cup chopped celery, 1 chopped scallion, some lemon juice, and some Old Bay. Chill the mixture for 2 hours, pile it into the hoagie buns, and serve. Yum!

PER SERVING Calories: 572; Total fat: 48g; Saturated fat: 29g; Cholesterol: 222mg; Carbohydrates: 7g; Fiber: 1g; Protein: 32g

SERVES 2
PREP TIME: 5 minutes
COOK TIME: 2 to 4 minutes
TOTAL TIME: 15 minutes

PRESSURE LEVEL: High
RELEASE: Quick

2 (6-ounce) cod fillets

Kosher salt

Freshly ground black pepper

2 tablespoons melted butter

2 tablespoons freshly
squeezed lemon juice, divided

1 garlic clove, minced

1 cup cherry tomatoes

1 zucchini or yellow summer
squash, cut into thick slices

1 cup whole Brussels sprouts

2 thyme sprigs or ½ teaspoon
dried thyme

TO SERVE

• Cooked rice or couscous
• Lemon wedges

STEAMED COD AND VEGETABLES

30 MINUTES OR LESS | LIGHT AND HEALTHY

This simple and fast cooking method can be employed for any kind of white fish, both fresh and frozen fillets. The vegetables benefit from the garlic butter-brushed fish, since it drips into the steamer basket during cooking, flavoring everything at once. If you're considering substituting in other vegetables, be mindful of which ones you use—many require much less or more cooking time than the squash and Brussels sprouts used here. Consult your pressure cooker manual for cooking times before steaming.

1. Add ½ cup of water to the pressure cooker pot and put the steamer basket in the bottom.

2. Season the fish with salt and pepper. In a small bowl, combine the butter, 1 tablespoon of the lemon juice, and the garlic. Set aside.

3. Place the tomatoes in the steamer basket, then add the zucchini and Brussels sprouts. Season with salt and pepper, then drizzle with the remaining 1 tablespoon of lemon juice.

4. Set the fish fillets on top of the vegetables. Brush with the garlic-lemon butter, then flip the fish and repeat on the other side. Drizzle any remaining butter over the vegetables. Top with the thyme sprigs.

5. Secure the cooker lid and cook on high pressure for 2 to 4 minutes, depending on the thickness of the fish, then quick release the pressure in the pot and remove the lid.

6. Serve the vegetables topped with the fish, and pair them with cooked rice or couscous and lemon wedges.

Cooking Tip This recipe is a great candidate for pot-in-pot cooking! Pour 1 cup of water into the cooker pot with ½ cup of couscous. Set the trivet inside and place the steamer basket on it. Add the vegetables and set the fish on top. Proceed with cooking for 2 to 3 minutes. If using frozen fish or vegetables, use ½ cup basmati rice and ½ cup of water instead, and add 1 to 2 minutes of cooking time.

PER SERVING Calories: 271; Total fat: 13g; Saturated fat: 8g; Cholesterol: 86mg; Carbohydrates: 17g; Fiber: 6g; Protein: 25g

SERVES 2
PREP TIME: 15 minutes
COOK TIME: 8 minutes
TOTAL TIME: 30 minutes

PRESSURE LEVEL: High
RELEASE: Quick

FOR THE MANGO SALSA

1 cup mango, diced

¼ cup red onion, diced

½ avocado, chopped

1 jalapeño pepper, stemmed, seeded and diced

1 tablespoon lime juice

FOR THE FISH

1 teaspoon kosher salt, divided

½ teaspoon ground cumin

½ teaspoon paprika

½ teaspoon garlic powder

¼ teaspoon cayenne pepper

12 ounces flaky white fish (cod, snapper, or mahi-mahi), cut into fingers

Juice of ½ lime, divided

TO SERVE

- Warmed flour or corn tortillas (see Tip)
- Shredded red cabbage
- Chopped fresh cilantro
- Lime wedges

CALIFORNIA FISH TACOS

30 MINUTES OR LESS | LIGHT AND HEALTHY | PALEO-FRIENDLY

The taste of summer in a tortilla! There's no need to fire up the grill or a frying pan to enjoy this Baja Peninsula staple. The smoky-seasoned white fish is steamed *en papillote* (in paper), keeping it moist and full of flavor, and is topped with a fresh mango and avocado salsa and crunchy shredded cabbage.

TO MAKE THE MANGO SALSA

Combine the mango, onion, avocado, jalapeño, and lime juice in a small bowl, cover, and refrigerate.

TO MAKE THE FISH

1. Mix ½ teaspoon of salt, the cumin, paprika, garlic powder, and cayenne pepper together in a small bowl.

2. Cut two oblong pieces of parchment paper, set them over the top of the pressure cooker, and fold both so there is about 1 inch of room on either side of the cooker. Transfer to a work surface.

3. Place half of the fish on one side of a piece of the parchment paper. Drizzle some of the lime juice on the fish, then rub on the seasoning mix. Fold the parchment packet closed and wrap in a large piece of aluminum foil. Repeat the process with the remaining fish to create another packet.

4. Add 1 cup of water to the pressure cooker pot and place the steamer basket in the bottom. Put the two packets in the steamer basket. Secure the lid and cook on high pressure for 8 minutes, then quick release the pressure in the pot and remove the lid.

5. Using tongs, transfer the packets to a work surface, open them carefully (the steam will be hot!), and remove the fish from the packets and put in a medium bowl. Flake the fish with a fork and toss with the remaining lime juice.

6. Serve wrapped in warmed flour or corn tortillas with the mango salsa, shredded cabbage, cilantro, and lime wedges.

Variation Tip Tacos are not inherently Paleo, but many specialty and health food stores carry grain-free tortillas that can fulfill every specialty dieter's Taco Tuesday dreams.

PER SERVING Calories: 774; Total fat: 16g; Saturated fat: 4g; Cholesterol: 372mg; Carbohydrates: 57g; Fiber: 12g; Protein: 102g

SERVES 2

PREP TIME: 5 minutes

COOK TIME: 3 to 4 minutes

TOTAL TIME: 15 minutes

PRESSURE LEVEL: High

RELEASE: Quick

2 (6-ounce) snapper fillets

1 teaspoon kosher salt

½ teaspoon freshly ground black pepper

1½ cups fresh salsa

¼ cup pale lager beer or water

½ lime

TO SERVE

- Cooked rice or quinoa
- Steamed vegetables
- Salsa
- Chopped fresh cilantro
- Lime wedges

SALSA-POACHED RED SNAPPER

5-INGREDIENT | 30 MINUTES OR LESS | LIGHT AND HEALTHY
ONE-POT MEAL | PALEO-FRIENDLY

Poaching is a great way to preserve the inherent moisture in fish and add flavor without adding fat to the healthy protein. Follow this cooking method for your favorite type of fish, whether it's lean like tilapia or fatty like salmon, for a tasty dinner every time.

1. Put the trivet in the bottom of the cooker pot.

2. Season the fish with the salt and pepper. Add the salsa and beer to the pot and place the fish on top. Squeeze the juice from the lime over the fish and salsa.

3. Secure the pressure cooker lid and cook on high pressure for 3 to 4 minutes, depending on the thickness of the fish, then quick release the pressure in the pot and remove the lid.

4. Serve the poached snapper over rice, quinoa, or steamed vegetables. Top with more salsa and chopped cilantro and serve with lime wedges.

Pressure Cooker Tip Most pressure cookers require a minimum amount of liquid to come to pressure properly. In dishes like this one where a high-water-ratio vegetable is used (the tomato salsa), the liquid requirement will be fulfilled by the liquid from the vegetable.

Variation Tip For a Paleo version of the recipe, use water in place of the beer and don't serve with rice.

PER SERVING Calories: 292; Total fat: 3g; Saturated fat: 1g; Cholesterol: 80mg; Carbohydrates: 8g; Fiber: 1g; Protein: 46g

PREP TIME: 10 minutes

COOK TIME: 3 to 4 minutes

TOTAL TIME: 30 minutes,
plus 1 hour to marinate

PRESSURE LEVEL: High
RELEASE: Quick

¼ cup sesame oil

¼ cup soy sauce

¼ cup lime juice

2 tablespoons honey

2 tablespoons fish sauce

1 tablespoon sesame seeds

1 teaspoon grated peeled
fresh ginger

1 teaspoon minced garlic

Grated zest of 1 lime

1 scallion, chopped, plus
more for serving

2 (4- to 6-ounce) skinless or
skin-on salmon fillets

2 teaspoons cornstarch

TO SERVE
- Fresh salad greens
- Shredded red cabbage
- Shredded carrots
- Sliced green bell pepper
- Shelled edamame
- Mandarin orange sections
- Slivered almonds

TERIYAKI SALMON SALAD

PALEO-FRIENDLY

Wild-caught salmon is an excellent source of high-quality protein and heart-healthy omega-3 fatty acids, as well as a number of vitamins and minerals. Combining all those benefits with a delicious teriyaki sauce and serving it on a big green salad? A recipe for delicious.

1. In a gallon-size zip-top bag, combine the sesame oil, soy sauce, lime juice, honey, fish sauce, sesame seeds, ginger, garlic, lime zest, scallion, and salmon. Seal the bag and shake gently. Let the fish marinate in the refrigerator for 1 to 2 hours.

2. Preheat the pressure cooker on sauté mode. Remove the salmon from the marinade and transfer to a plate. When the display reads hot, pour the marinade from the bag into the pot and bring to a simmer. Press cancel.

3. Add the salmon to the pot (skin-side up, if using skin-on fillets). Spoon the marinade over the fish.

4. Secure the lid and cook on high pressure for 4 minutes, then quick release the pressure in the pot and remove the lid. Press cancel.

5. Use a spatula to gently transfer the fish to a clean plate. Remove the skin if necessary. Transfer 2 teaspoons of the warm teriyaki liquid from the pot to a small bowl. Whisk in the cornstarch, then pour it back into the pot. Select sauté and let the liquid simmer, stirring frequently, for 8 to 10 minutes, or until reduced to a glaze-like consistency. →

6. To serve, toss salad greens with shredded cabbage and carrots, sliced bell pepper, edamame, mandarin orange sections, and slivered almonds and divide between two plates. Top each with a salmon fillet.

7. Brush or spoon the teriyaki sauce over the fish and salad.

Ingredient Tip   To get this recipe on the table quickly, substitute bottled teriyaki sauce for the marinade ingredients.

Variation Tip   To make this recipe Paleo, omit the fish sauce and substitute coconut aminos for the soy sauce.

PER SERVING Calories: 608; Total fat: 41g; Saturated fat: 6g; Cholesterol: 78mg; Carbohydrates: 26g; Fiber: 1g; Protein: 39g

PRESSURE LEVEL: High
RELEASE: Quick

2 teaspoons butter, plus more for greasing

1 shallot, chopped

1 celery stalk, chopped

½ cup sliced cremini mushrooms

1 garlic clove, minced

1 cup Chicken Stock (page 167)

1½ cups water

1½ cups egg noodles

Kosher salt

Freshly ground black pepper

2 tablespoons heavy cream

1 tablespoon Dijon mustard

1 tablespoon freshly squeezed lemon juice

1 (5-ounce) can tuna, drained and broken up

½ cup shredded Cheddar cheese

½ cup panko bread crumbs

4 lemon wedges

TUNA CASSEROLE

COMFORT FOOD

This lightened-up classic American comfort food comes together quickly using only fresh ingredients (no condensed soups!) before it is baked to crispy perfection. Try it with fresh tuna if you prefer.

1. Preheat the oven to 325°F. Coat a small casserole dish with butter and set aside.

2. Preheat the pressure cooker on sauté mode. When the display reads hot, add the 2 teaspoons of butter to melt. Add the shallot, celery, and mushrooms and sauté until softened, 3 minutes. Add the garlic and sauté for 1 minute.

3. Add the stock, water, and noodles. Season with salt and pepper.

4. Secure the lid and cook on high pressure for 2 minutes, then quick release the pressure in the pot and remove the lid.

5. Carefully pour the contents of the cooker pot into a colander or fine-mesh strainer to drain the excess liquid, then return the solids to the pot.

6. Stir in the cream, mustard, lemon juice, and tuna and season with salt and pepper. Transfer the mixture to the prepared casserole dish. Top with the shredded cheese and the panko.

7. Bake in the oven for 12 to 15 minutes until the cheese is melted and the panko is lightly browned and crispy. Serve with the lemon wedges.

Variation Tip For a more indulgent version of this casserole, mix 2 ounces of cream cheese into the pot before transferring the tuna mixture to the casserole dish and baking it. Mix the panko with a bit of melted butter to make the topping even crispier.

PER SERVING Calories: 763; Total fat: 25g; Saturated fat: 11g; Cholesterol: 166mg; Carbohydrates: 60g; Fiber: 3g; Protein: 74g

Six

CHICKEN AND TURKEY

Thighs, legs, breasts, or wings? Whatever your favorite part of the bird is, you'll find a recipe for it in this chapter. Admittedly, dark-meat poultry is more pressure cooker–friendly, and you'll find plenty of recipes using those parts; just know that if you're planning on substituting breast meat in a recipe that calls for thigh meat, you'll have to adjust how the whole recipe is cooked. A healthy, juicy chicken breast or turkey tenderloin is possible depending on how you treat it, even straight from the freezer. Refer to your cooker's user manual for specific cooking times when you're experimenting.

Chicken Cacciatore, page 124

Chicken Noodle Soup 111

Pho Ga (Vietnamese Chicken Soup) 112

Chicken-Bacon Stew 113

Bourbon Chicken 114

Indian Butter Chicken 115

Thai Green Curry Chicken and Cauliflower 116

Cranberry Chicken Salad 118

Buffalo Chicken and Cheddar Quesadillas 119

Chipotle Chicken Fajita Lettuce Cups 121

Chicken Alfredo 122

Chicken Cacciatore 124

Chicken Marsala 126

Easy Chicken and Rice 127

Fall-Off-the-Bone Buffalo Wings 128

Turkey, Kale, and Orzo Soup 130

Turkey and Sweet Potato Chili 131

Turkey Potpie 132

Turkey-Stuffed Peppers 134

Turkey Meatball Sub Sandwiches 135

Turkey Breast, Stuffing, and Gravy Dinner 136

PRESSURE LEVEL: High

RELEASE: Natural

1 tablespoon butter

1 small onion, chopped

1 medium carrot, chopped

1 celery stalk, chopped

1 pound skin-on, bone-in chicken pieces

1 teaspoon kosher salt

½ teaspoon freshly ground black pepper

2 thyme sprigs or ½ teaspoon dried thyme

1 teaspoon dried oregano

4 cups Chicken Stock (page 167)

1 cup egg noodles

CHICKEN NOODLE SOUP

30 MINUTES OR LESS | COMFORT FOOD

Chicken noodle soup is the ultimate comfort food. It is synonymous with nostalgic family life throughout the world. Making it in your pressure cooker is almost as good as having your mother or grandmother in the kitchen.

1. Preheat the pressure cooker pot on sauté mode. When the display reads hot, add the butter. Add the onion, carrot, and celery and sauté until softened, 3 to 4 minutes. Press cancel.

2. Add the chicken and sprinkle in the salt, pepper, thyme, and oregano. Add the stock and stir to combine.

3. Secure the lid and cook on high pressure for 7 minutes, then allow the pressure to naturally release for 5 minutes. Open the vent at the top and remove the lid. Press cancel and select sauté.

4. Transfer the chicken to a bowl and add the noodles to the pot.

5. Shred the chicken using two forks, discarding the skin and bones, and add the meat back into the pot. Let simmer uncovered for 5 to 6 minutes, or until the noodles are fully cooked.

Ingredient Tip Out of chicken stock? It's okay to use water instead—the chicken (complete with skin and bones) and vegetables will flavor it enough for the soup to be just as delicious.

PER SERVING Calories: 406; Total fat: 16g; Saturated fat: 7g; Cholesterol: 121mg; Carbohydrates: 29g; Fiber: 3g; Protein: 35g

PRESSURE LEVEL: High
RELEASE: Natural

1 tablespoon oil

1 medium onion, halved

1 (1-inch) piece peeled fresh ginger, cut into ¼-inch slices

1 teaspoon coriander seeds

2 star anise pods

3 whole cloves

1 cinnamon stick

3 skin-on, bone-in chicken thighs or drumsticks

2 tablespoons fish sauce, plus more for seasoning

¼ cup chopped fresh cilantro

½ tablespoon raw sugar

4 cups water

Kosher salt

Freshly ground black pepper

4 ounces rice noodles, prepared according to package directions

TO SERVE

- Bean sprouts
- Sliced scallions
- Chopped fresh cilantro
- Lime wedges
- Jalapeño pepper slices
- Sriracha or sambal sauce, or any other hot sauce you prefer

PHO GA (VIETNAMESE CHICKEN SOUP)

PALEO-FRIENDLY

Pho ga is a Vietnamese noodle soup and one of the most popular street foods throughout the world. The recipe lists lots of ingredients, but the pantry spices are required to make this soup's very unique chicken stock.

1. Preheat the pressure cooker pot on sauté mode. When the display reads hot, add the oil. Add the onion and ginger and cook, without stirring, until charred, 4 to 5 minutes. Add the coriander, star anise, cloves, and cinnamon stick and cook for 1 minute. Add the chicken, 2 tablespoons of fish sauce, the cilantro, sugar, and water. Stir to combine.

2. Secure the lid and cook on high pressure for 15 minutes, then allow the pressure to naturally release for about 10 minutes. Open the vent at the top and remove the lid.

3. Transfer the chicken to a medium bowl. Carefully strain the stock into a large bowl, discarding the solids. Season with salt, pepper, and more fish sauce.

4. Divide the prepared noodles between two bowls. When the chicken is cool enough to handle, pick the meat off the bones and add to the bowls. Pour the stock into the bowls and top with bean sprouts, scallions, chopped cilantro, lime juice (squeezed from the wedges), jalapeño slices, and your favorite hot sauce.

Variation Tip To make this recipe Paleo, substitute maple syrup for the sugar, omit the fish sauce, and serve over zucchini noodles.

PER SERVING Calories: 882; Total fat: 28g; Saturated fat: 5g; Cholesterol: 74mg; Carbohydrates: 123g; Fiber: 8g; Protein: 32g

SERVES 2

PREP TIME: 25 minutes

COOK TIME: 15 minutes

TOTAL TIME: 1 hour

PRESSURE LEVEL: High

RELEASE: Natural

1 tablespoon oil

1 pound skin-on, bone-in chicken thighs and/or drumsticks

Kosher salt

Freshly ground black pepper

5 to 6 slices thick-cut bacon, chopped into ½-inch pieces

1 small onion, diced

2 medium carrots, peeled and chopped

1 tablespoon tomato paste

½ teaspoon dried thyme

1 dried bay leaf

3 garlic cloves, chopped

¼ cup white wine (or stock)

1 cup Chicken Stock (page 167)

1 large potato, cut into 1-inch cubes

2 teaspoons sherry vinegar

CHICKEN-BACON STEW

WORTH THE WAIT

This hearty meal-in-a-bowl is a wonderful way to welcome fall or to warm up on a cold winter day. Crispy bacon, potatoes, and chicken combine in a flavor-packed stew that is done hours before most similar meals. A few dashes of sherry vinegar brightens up the finished dish.

1. Preheat the pressure cooker pot on sauté mode. When the display reads hot, add the oil. Pat the chicken pieces dry with paper towels and season with salt and pepper.

2. In the cooker pot, brown the chicken on all sides, 4 minutes per side. Transfer to a plate and set aside.

3. Add the bacon and cook until it begins to crisp, 2 to 3 minutes. Add the onion, carrots, tomato paste, thyme, and bay leaf and sauté until softened, 3 to 4 minutes. Add the garlic and cook, stirring, for 1 minute.

4. Pour in the wine and deglaze the pot, scraping up the browned bits from the bottom and stirring them into the liquid. Cook for 2 minutes, or until the wine is reduced by half.

5. Add the stock and potato and stir well. Return the browned chicken to the pot.

6. Secure the lid and cook on high pressure for 15 minutes, then allow the pressure to naturally release for about 10 minutes. Open the vent at the top and remove the lid.

7. Remove the bay leaf and discard, then carefully transfer the chicken to a bowl. Remove and discard the skin and bones and shred the meat.

8. Return the chicken meat to the pot to reheat and stir well. Stir in the sherry vinegar. Taste and season with more salt and pepper as needed.

Variation Tip To make this stew even heartier with additional protein, add ½ cup dried lentils and increase the cooking time to 20 minutes.

PER SERVING Calories: 955; Total fat: 55g; Saturated fat: 17g; Cholesterol: 243mg; Carbohydrates: 46g; Fiber: 7g; Protein: 64g

SERVES 2
PREP TIME: 5 minutes
COOK TIME: 15 minutes
TOTAL TIME: 1 hour

PRESSURE LEVEL: High
RELEASE: Natural

1 pound skinless, boneless chicken thighs

½ cup low-sodium soy sauce

½ cup honey

1 tablespoon oil

1 tablespoon ketchup

1 tablespoon apple cider vinegar

1 garlic clove, minced

½ teaspoon ground ginger

½ teaspoon red pepper flakes

Kosher salt

Freshly ground black pepper

½ cup water

1 tablespoon cornstarch

¼ cup bourbon (optional)

1 scallion, chopped

BOURBON CHICKEN

PALEO-FRIENDLY | WORTH THE WAIT

Named after the famed Bourbon Street in New Orleans, this dish is just as spicy, sweet, and sticky as the Deep South. The bourbon is optional, but after the alcohol cooks out, the flavor blends in so well with the honey and soy sauce, you won't want it any other way.

1. Put the chicken in a large zip-top bag with the soy sauce, honey, oil, ketchup, vinegar, garlic, ginger, and red pepper flakes and season with salt and pepper. Seal the bag, massage the liquid into the chicken, and put in the refrigerator to marinate for at least 30 minutes or up to 3 hours.

2. Preheat the pressure cooker on sauté mode. Remove the chicken from the marinade and reserve the marinade. When the display reads hot, brown the chicken in the pot in two batches, 3 to 4 minutes each, transferring to a plate when browned. Deglaze the pot by adding the marinade and scraping up the browned bits from the bottom with a wooden spoon. Add the chicken back to the pot along with ½ cup of water.

3. Secure the lid and cook on high pressure for 7 minutes, then allow the pressure to naturally release for 10 minutes. Open the vent at the top and remove the lid.

4. Return the pot to sauté mode. Place ¼ cup of the cooking liquid in a small bowl. Whisk in the cornstarch until combined, then whisk the slurry back into the pot along with the bourbon (if using). Simmer until the sauce has thickened, then taste and season with salt and pepper as desired. Top with the scallion.

Serving Tip This recipe is best enjoyed over simple white rice or with a batch of Takeout-Style Fried Rice (page 43).

Variation Tip To make the recipe Paleo, substitute coconut aminos for the soy sauce, and omit the ketchup and bourbon.

PER SERVING Calories: 866; Total fat: 24g; Saturated fat: 5g; Cholesterol: 202mg; Carbohydrates: 80g; Fiber: 1g; Protein: 68g

SERVES 2

PREP TIME: 10 minutes

COOK TIME: 5 minutes

TOTAL TIME: 40 minutes

PRESSURE LEVEL: High

RELEASE SETTING: Natural

¼ cup butter

¾ pound skinless, boneless chicken thighs

3 garlic cloves, minced

2 teaspoons grated peeled fresh ginger

1 (14-ounce) can diced tomatoes with their juices, puréed

1 tablespoon tomato paste

2 teaspoons garam masala

1 teaspoon ground cumin

1 teaspoon kosher salt

½ tablespoon paprika

½ teaspoon ground turmeric

¼ teaspoon cayenne pepper

½ cup water

½ cup heavy cream

¼ cup plain yogurt

2 tablespoons chopped fresh cilantro

TO SERVE
- Cooked basmati rice
- Fresh naan bread

INDIAN BUTTER CHICKEN

Butter chicken, or *chicken makhani*, is an extremely flavorful Indian dish. Traditionally, the chicken is grilled in a tandoor oven and takes more than 4 hours to make. Using your electric pressure cooker, you can get this meal on the table in less than an hour. Make it as mild or spicy as you wish by adjusting the cayenne pepper.

1. Preheat the pressure cooker on sauté mode. When the display reads hot, add the butter to melt. Cut the chicken into quarters, add to the pot, and sear for 2 to 3 minutes, or until nicely browned all over. Transfer to a bowl and set aside.

2. Add the garlic and ginger and sauté until softened, 1 minute. Add the tomato purée and tomato paste to the pot and stir.

3. Add the garam masala, cumin, salt, paprika, turmeric, and cayenne pepper. Cook, stirring often, for about 3 to 4 minutes.

4. Add the chicken and water and stir well. Secure the lid and cook on high pressure for 5 minutes, then allow the pressure to naturally release for about 10 minutes. Open the vent at the top and remove the lid. Press cancel.

5. Add the cream, yogurt, and cilantro and stir until well incorporated. Allow the sauce to sit and thicken enough to coat the back of a spoon, 3 to 5 minutes.

6. Serve the butter chicken over cooked basmati rice, with naan bread.

Recipe Tip Not to be confused with *tikka masala*, butter chicken was reportedly developed in the early twentieth century in Delhi as a way to use leftover tandoori chicken. The dried chicken was softened with a creamy, buttery, spiced tomato sauce and repurposed into a new dish.

PER SERVING Calories: 693; Total fat: 48g; Saturated fat: 25g; Cholesterol: 254mg; Carbohydrates: 14g; Fiber: 4g; Protein: 53g

SERVES 2

PREP TIME: 5 minutes

COOK TIME: 25 minutes

TOTAL TIME: 30 minutes

PRESSURE LEVEL: High

RELEASE: Quick

½ tablespoon oil

3 shallots, thinly sliced

1 large garlic clove, crushed

1 (¼-inch) piece peeled fresh ginger, minced

1 cup coconut milk, solids and liquid separated (see Tip)

2 tablespoons green curry paste

2 skinless, boneless chicken breasts, cut into strips

1 teaspoon kosher salt

3 red chiles, stemmed, seeded, and cut into strips

½ cup Chicken Stock (page 167) or water

1 tablespoon fish sauce

1 tablespoon soy sauce, plus more for seasoning (optional)

½ tablespoon packed brown sugar, plus more for seasoning (optional)

Juice of ½ lime

2 cups cauliflower florets

TO SERVE

- Cooked basmati rice
- Minced fresh cilantro
- Minced fresh Thai basil
- Lime wedges
- Roti (Indian flatbread)

THAI GREEN CURRY CHICKEN AND CAULIFLOWER

30 MINUTES OR LESS | LIGHT AND HEALTHY

You wouldn't think green curry would be the hottest of the three curry varieties the Asian continent has given the world. The way it's treated in a given recipe is what kicks up or cools down the heat. This coconut-and-green-chile-based curry has only been in existence since the early 1900s and originally was served with fish as the protein. Instead of the traditional Thai eggplant, the soft yet still crunchy cauliflower florets in this version will please any palate.

1. Preheat the pressure cooker on sauté mode. When the display reads hot, add the oil in the pot until shimmering. Stir in the shallots, garlic, and ginger and cook until the shallots start to soften, 2 to 3 minutes.

2. Stir in the coconut milk solids and curry paste. Cook for 3 to 4 minutes, stirring often, until the curry paste darkens. Add the coconut milk liquid. Stir well.

3. Season the chicken with the salt, add to the pot, and stir to coat with the curry paste. Stir in the red chiles, stock, fish sauce, 1 tablespoon of soy sauce, and ½ tablespoon of brown sugar.

4. Secure the lid and cook on high pressure for 10 minutes, then quick release the pressure in the pot and remove the lid.

5. Select sauté mode. Stir in the lime juice and cauliflower, then simmer for 5 to 6 minutes to let the cauliflower soften and absorb the flavors.

6. Taste the curry for seasoning, adding more soy sauce or brown sugar as desired.

7. Ladle the curry into bowls over cooked rice and garnish with cilantro and basil. Serve with lime wedges and roti.

Ingredient Tip Coconut milk is mostly water and fat, and the solids tend to separate from the liquids in the can. Mixed coconut milk can lose flavor if it's cooked too much. Instead of shaking the can when making curry, keep the cream and water separate and use them as directed in the recipe.

PER SERVING Calories: 587; Total fat: 39g; Saturated fat: 27g; Cholesterol: 73mg; Carbohydrates: 31g; Fiber: 7g; Protein: 35g

SERVES 2

PREP TIME: 10 minutes

COOK TIME: 6 to 10 minutes

TOTAL TIME: 30 minutes

PRESSURE LEVEL: High
RELEASE: Natural/Quick

1 pound skinless, boneless chicken breasts

½ cup water

2 teaspoons kosher salt, plus more for seasoning

½ cup mayonnaise

2 tablespoons diced red onion

1 celery stalk, diced

½ cup chopped dried cranberries

¼ unpeeled organic green apple, shredded

¼ cup chopped walnuts

1 tablespoon freshly squeezed lime juice

Freshly ground black pepper

CRANBERRY CHICKEN SALAD

30 MINUTES OR LESS

Cranberries aren't just for the holidays. This chicken salad is a popular standard, but the addition of juicy, tart grated apple, crunchy walnuts, and dried cranberries makes it extra special. Enjoy it on your favorite sandwich bread, in a wrap, or on a green salad.

1. Put the chicken, water, and 2 teaspoons of salt in the cooker pot. Secure the lid and cook on the poultry setting for 6 minutes. (If using frozen chicken, cook on the poultry setting for 10 minutes.)

2. Allow the pressure to release naturally for 5 minutes, then do a quick release. Transfer the chicken to a cutting board and let rest for 5 to 10 minutes. Shred the meat, transfer to a salad bowl, and mix with ¼ cup of the chicken cooking liquid.

3. Add the mayonnaise and stir to coat well. Add the onion, celery, cranberries, apple, walnuts, and lime juice and season with salt and pepper.

4. Serve immediately, or refrigerate for several hours or overnight.

Variation Tip Thanksgiving got you stuck with leftovers? Shredded turkey breast will be a fine stand-in for chicken in this recipe, and the flavor profile will be perfect for the season.

PER SERVING Calories: 512; Total fat: 32g; Saturated fat: 4g; Cholesterol: 88mg; Carbohydrates: 24g; Fiber: 3g; Protein: 33g

SERVES 2
PREP TIME: 15 minutes
COOK TIME: 6 to 10 minutes
TOTAL TIME: 30 minutes

PRESSURE LEVEL: High
RELEASE: Natural/Quick

2 skinless, boneless
chicken breasts

½ cup water

2 teaspoons kosher salt,
plus more for seasoning

½ cup black beans, rinsed
and drained

⅓ cup canned chopped
tomatoes and chiles, drained

1 cup shredded
Cheddar cheese

⅓ cup Buffalo wing sauce

2 (10-inch) flour tortillas

TO SERVE
- Cooked Spanish rice
- Ranch or blue cheese
  dressing

BUFFALO CHICKEN AND CHEDDAR QUESADILLAS

30 MINUTES OR LESS

Quesadillas are probably the easiest and simplest way to enjoy Mexican food. Combining this south-of-the-border snack with something considerably more Northern—Buffalo chicken—makes for a delicious combination that can be considered a full meal with some ranch or blue cheese dressing on the side.

1. Put the chicken, water, and 2 teaspoons of salt in the cooker pot. Secure the lid and cook on the poultry setting for 6 minutes. (If using frozen chicken, cook on the poultry setting for 10 minutes.)

2. Allow the pressure to release naturally for 5 minutes, then do a quick release. Transfer the chicken to a cutting board and let rest for 5 to 10 minutes. Shred the meat, transfer to a medium bowl, and mix in ¼ cup of the cooking liquid.

3. Heat an indoor grill (or grill pan) to medium and spray it with cooking spray.

4. Add the beans, tomatoes and chiles, cheese, and the Buffalo wing sauce to the bowl with the shredded chicken, season with salt, and stir to combine. →

5. Place a tortilla on a clean work surface. Spread half of the chicken mixture on half of the tortilla and fold gently to close.

6. Place the quesadilla on the prepared grill (or grill pan) and cook for about 4 minutes, turning once, until the cheese is melted and the tortilla is toasted.

7. Repeat with the remaining tortilla and filling, being sure to spray the grill with cooking spray between quesadillas.

8. Cut the cooked quesadillas into thirds with a pizza cutter or large knife. Serve with Spanish rice on the side and salad dressing for dipping.

Variation Tip Not in the mood for Buffalo wing sauce? Leave it out and add taco sauce instead for the best quesadillas you've ever had.

PER SERVING Calories: 616; Total fat: 14g; Saturated fat: 6g; Cholesterol: 85mg; Carbohydrates: 64g; Fiber: 9g; Protein: 57g

SERVES 2

PREP TIME: 15 minutes

COOK TIME: 6 to 10 minutes

TOTAL TIME: 30 minutes

PRESSURE LEVEL: High

RELEASE: Natural/Quick

1 tablespoon oil

¼ red onion, sliced

½ green bell pepper, sliced

2 skinless, boneless chicken breasts

½ cup water

2 canned chipotle chiles in adobo sauce, seeded and minced

Kosher salt

¼ red onion, sliced

¼ cup sour cream

3 tablespoons mayonnaise

½ tablespoon freshly squeezed lime juice

Freshly ground black pepper

TO SERVE
- Bibb or romaine lettuce leaves
- Queso fresco crumbles
- Chopped fresh cilantro

CHIPOTLE CHICKEN FAJITA LETTUCE CUPS

30 MINUTES OR LESS

For a supper that's a little lighter and brighter, lettuce cups are the way to go. Chicken salads are more lunch-appropriate, but this chipotle version, complete with lightly sautéed bell pepper and onion, is perfect for a satisfying evening meal. A bit of cilantro and queso fresco adds flavor and cools the chipotle heat just enough.

1. Preheat the pressure cooker pot on sauté mode. When the display reads hot, add the oil. Add the onion and bell pepper and sauté for 3 to 4 minutes, or until softened. Transfer to a bowl and set aside to cool.

2. Put the chicken, water, and a few teaspoons of the adobo sauce (to taste) in the pot and season with salt. Secure the lid and cook on the poultry setting for 6 minutes. (If using frozen chicken, cook on the poultry setting for 10 minutes.)

3. Allow the cooker to release naturally for 5 minutes, then do a quick release. Transfer the chicken to a cutting board and let rest for 5 to 10 minutes. Cut the chicken into cubes.

4. In a medium bowl, combine the chicken, cooked onion and bell pepper, sour cream, mayonnaise, chipotle chiles, and lime juice. Season with salt and pepper and stir to evenly combine.

5. Serve the fajita filling in Bibb or romaine lettuce leaves, sprinkled with queso fresco and cilantro.

Variation Tip This chicken filling also makes a delicious quesa-dilla. Simply use flour or corn tortillas instead of lettuce wraps and add a bit of salsa and sliced avocado.

PER SERVING Calories: 365; Total fat: 19g; Saturated fat: 7g; Cholesterol: 102mg; Carbohydrates: 14g; Fiber: 3g; Protein: 34g

PRESSURE LEVEL: High
RELEASE: Natural

2 tablespoons butter, divided

2 skinless, boneless chicken breasts, cut into strips

Kosher salt

Freshly ground black pepper

3 garlic cloves, minced

1 cup Chicken Stock (page 167)

4 ounces fettuccine

½ cup heavy cream

½ cup grated Parmesan cheese, plus more for serving

CHICKEN ALFREDO

30 MINUTES OR LESS

This one-pot pressure cooker version of the famous Italian chicken dish tastes just as good as the stove-top version! The chicken and noodles are cooked at the same time, and the cooking liquid quickly becomes a creamy, buttery, cheesy sauce that you might be tempted to slurp up with a straw.

1. Preheat the pressure cooker on sauté mode. When the display reads hot, add 1 tablespoon of butter to the pot to melt. Pat the chicken strips dry with a paper towel. Season with salt and pepper, add to the pot, and brown, undisturbed, for 1 to 2 minutes on each side. Transfer to a plate and set aside.

2. Add the garlic to the pot and sauté until fragrant, about 1 minute. Pour the stock into the pot and deglaze, scraping up the browned bits from the bottom with a wooden spoon and stirring them into the liquid.

3. Break the fettuccine noodles in half and lay them flat in the pot, adding water if needed to submerge them completely. Return the chicken strips to the pot, setting them on top of the noodles.

4. Secure the lid and cook on high pressure for 3 minutes, then allow the pressure to naturally release for about 5 minutes. Open the vent at the top and remove the lid. Press cancel and select sauté.

5. Using tongs, remove the chicken from the pot, transfer to a plate, and set aside. Stir the remaining 1 tablespoon of butter, the heavy cream, and ½ cup of Parmesan cheese into the fettuccine in the pot and cook until warmed through and saucy. Taste and season with salt and pepper as desired. Return the chicken to the pot and stir to coat in the alfredo sauce

6. Divide the chicken alfredo between two plates and serve with additional Parmesan cheese.

Variation Tip Looking for a more eclectic flavor profile? Sauté mushrooms with the chicken and stir a handful of baby spinach leaves and crumbled bacon into the sauce at the end of the cook time.

PER SERVING Calories: 753; Total fat: 44g; Saturated fat: 25g; Cholesterol: 235mg; Carbohydrates: 36g; Fiber: 0g; Protein: 55g

PRESSURE LEVEL: High
RELEASE SETTING: Natural

4 skinless, bone-in chicken thighs

Kosher salt

Freshly ground black pepper

1 tablespoon oil

½ cup diced shallots

½ cup diced green bell pepper

½ cup chopped portobello mushrooms

3 garlic cloves, minced

½ teaspoon herbes de Provence

½ cup white wine (or stock)

1 (14-ounce) can crushed tomatoes with their juices

2 tablespoons tomato paste

1 (6-ounce) can Kalamata or black olives (optional)

Pinch red pepper flakes (optional)

TO SERVE
- Cooked pasta, spaghetti squash, or polenta
- Chopped fresh basil or flat-leaf parsley

CHICKEN CACCIATORE

ONE-POT MEAL | PALEO-FRIENDLY | WORTH THE WAIT

In Italian cuisine, *alla cacciatora* refers to a meal prepared "hunter-style," which is often made with onions, herbs, tomatoes, bell peppers, and sometimes wine. This version is true to its roots: The chicken is braised in the pressure cooker with an assortment of veggies, white wine, and plenty of tomatoes. Toss in some olives at the end for a briny addition.

1. Wash the chicken and pat dry with paper towels, then season with salt and pepper.

2. Preheat the pressure cooker pot on sauté mode. When the display reads hot, add the oil, then add the chicken thighs in a single layer, cooking for 5 minutes on each side, or until browned. Transfer the chicken to a plate and set aside.

3. Add the shallots, bell pepper, and mushrooms and sauté until softened, 4 to 5 minutes. Add the garlic and herbes de Provence and cook for 1 minute, or until fragrant.

4. Pour in the wine and deglaze the pot, scraping up the browned bits from the bottom with a wooden spoon and stirring them into the liquid. Cook until the wine is reduced by half.

5. Set the chicken on top of the contents of the pot, then pour in the tomatoes and their juices and the tomato paste.

6. Secure the lid and cook on high pressure for 12 minutes, then allow the pressure to naturally release, about 10 minutes. Open the vent at the top and remove the lid.

7. Stir in the olives and red pepper flakes (if using). Taste and adjust the seasonings as desired.

8. Serve over pasta, spaghetti squash, or polenta, garnished with basil or parsley.

Ingredient Tip Save money on tomato paste! When you open a new can but don't use it all, divide the rest into tablespoon-size dollops on a piece of wax paper and freeze. When the paste is frozen, slide the paper into a zip-top bag and keep frozen until you're ready to use again, up to 3 months.

Variation Tip For a Paleo version, omit the wine and don't serve with pasta or polenta.

PER SERVING Calories: 569; Total fat: 26g; Saturated fat: 6g; Cholesterol: 115mg; Carbohydrates: 33g; Fiber: 8g; Protein: 40g

SERVES 2
PREP TIME: 10 minutes
COOK TIME: 8 minutes
TOTAL TIME: 40 minutes

PRESSURE LEVEL: High
RELEASE: Quick

2 skinless, boneless chicken breasts

Kosher salt

Freshly ground black pepper

2 tablespoons butter, divided

2 small shallots, diced

1 cup sliced mushrooms

1 large garlic clove, minced

½ cup Marsala wine

¼ cup Chicken Stock (page 167)

2 tablespoons cornstarch

TO SERVE
- Cooked pasta, mashed potatoes, or steamed vegetables

CHICKEN MARSALA

Italian dishes were meant for your electric pressure cooker, including this deliciously savory chicken Marsala. Marsala wine is a worthy addition to your pantry, even if only for cooking. It cuts through the richness of cream or stock, and the alcohol cooks off as your sauce simmers, leaving a wonderful flavor.

1. Season the chicken with salt and pepper. Preheat the pressure cooker on sauté mode. When the display reads hot, add 1 table-spoon of butter to melt. Add the chicken and brown for 2 to 3 minutes on each side. Transfer to a plate and set aside.

2. Add the shallots and mushrooms and sauté until softened, 5 minutes. Add the garlic and cook for 1 minute.

3. Pour in the wine and deglaze the pot, scraping up the browned bits from the bottom with a wooden spoon and stirring them into the liquid. Add the stock and return the chicken to the pot. Season with salt and pepper. Press cancel.

4. Secure the lid and cook on high pressure for 8 minutes, then quick release the pressure in the pot and remove the lid. Press cancel. Transfer the chicken to a plate.

5. Select sauté. Transfer 2 tablespoons of cooking liquid from the pot to a small bowl and stir together with the cornstarch. Return to the pot with the remaining 1 tablespoon of butter, then bring the mixture to a boil and stir until thickened.

6. Return the chicken to the pot and cook for 2 to 3 minutes, tasting and adjusting the seasonings as needed.

7. Serve the chicken and sauce with pasta, mashed potatoes, or steamed vegetables.

PER SERVING Calories: 381; Total fat: 15g; Saturated fat: 8g; Cholesterol: 104mg; Carbohydrates: 14g; Fiber: 1g; Protein: 30g

SERVES 2

PREP TIME: 5 minutes

COOK TIME: 20 minutes

TOTAL TIME: 45 minutes

PRESSURE LEVEL: High

RELEASE: Natural

2 (8-ounce) skin-on, bone-in chicken leg quarters

1 tablespoon ground adobo seasoning, plus more as desired

½ tablespoon oil

½ red onion, diced

2 garlic cloves, minced

¾ cup brown basmati rice

¾ cup Chicken Stock (page 167)

¼ cup chopped fresh cilantro

TO SERVE

- 4 lime wedges (optional)

EASY CHICKEN AND RICE

COMFORT FOOD

This Spanish-influenced chicken and rice dish is a hearty, satisfying paella-like meal everyone will enjoy. Almost a one-pot meal, it has yummy flavors and is ready to eat in less than an hour—what's not to love? The adobo, cilantro, and freshly squeezed lime juice guarantee the rice won't be bland.

1. Generously season the chicken on both sides with 1 tablespoon of adobo seasoning; set aside on a plate.

2. Preheat the pressure cooker pot on sauté mode. When the display reads hot, add the oil. Add the onion and sauté until softened, 3 to 4 minutes. Add the garlic and cook for 1 minute until fragrant.

3. Stir in the rice and stock, scraping up the browned bits from the bottom of the pot with a wooden spoon and stirring them into the liquid. Season with adobo seasoning if you'd like. Press cancel. Place the seasoned chicken on top.

4. Secure the lid and cook on high pressure for 20 minutes, then allow the pressure to naturally release, about 10 minutes. Open the vent at the top and remove the lid. Press cancel.

5. Transfer the chicken to a cutting board and use two forks to shred the meat from the skin and bones (which you should discard). Fluff the cooked rice, then stir in the shredded chicken and cilantro. Serve with the lime wedges (if using).

Variation Tip You can make this dish a little lighter by using white basmati rice and replacing the chicken legs with chicken breasts. Follow the recipe the same way, but instead cook on high pressure for 8 minutes, with a natural release of 10 minutes.

PER SERVING Calories: 585; Total fat: 16g; Saturated fat: 4g; Cholesterol: 134mg; Carbohydrates: 63g; Fiber: 3g; Protein: 45g

PRESSURE LEVEL: High
RELEASE: Quick

1 pound chicken wings
and drumettes

Kosher salt

2 tablespoons unsalted butter

4 cups store-bought
Buffalo wing sauce

1 teaspoon
Worcestershire sauce

2 drops liquid smoke
(optional)

TO SERVE:
- Carrot and celery sticks
- Blue cheese or ranch
  dressing

FALL-OFF-THE-BONE BUFFALO WINGS

5-INGREDIENT | 30 MINUTES OR LESS

Whether you're making them to share with your sweetie or to serve to a crowd on game day, these easy Buffalo wings will delight. Instead of permeating every inch of your house for days with the smell of hot oil, your pressure cooker, combined with your oven broiler, make quick work of this spicy appetizer, leaving you with nothing but finger-lickin'-good, fall-off-the-bone wings and minimal cleanup.

1. Add 1 cup of water to your pressure cooker pot and place a trivet or egg rack inside.

2. Pat the chicken wings and drumettes dry with paper towels. Season with salt, then pile them carefully on top of the trivet.

3. Secure the lid and cook on high pressure for 10 minutes, then quick release the pressure in the pot.

4. Put the butter in a heatproof, microwave-safe bowl and melt in the microwave. Pour the Buffalo sauce into a large bowl and whisk in the melted butter, Worcestershire sauce, and liquid smoke (if using).

5. Remove the lid from the pressure cooker and carefully transfer the wings to an aluminum foil-lined baking sheet. Dry them off with paper towels and toss them in batches in the Buffalo wing sauce. Place in a single layer on the baking sheet.

6. Preheat the oven broiler on high. Broil the wings 8 to 12 minutes, flipping them halfway through the broiling time to ensure even browning.

7. Remove the wings from the oven and immediately toss in the remaining Buffalo wing sauce. Serve with carrot and celery sticks, and blue cheese or ranch dressing for dipping.

Ingredient Tip Buffalo wing sauce is available in different heat levels at the supermarket.

Substitution Tip If extra spicy isn't to your liking, swap out the Buffalo sauce for your favorite barbecue or teriyaki sauce for equally delicious results.

PER SERVING Calories: 761; Total fat: 55g; Saturated fat: 19g; Cholesterol: 221mg; Carbohydrates: 1g; Fiber: 0g; Protein: 61g

SERVES 2

PREP TIME: 10 minutes

COOK TIME: 6 minutes

TOTAL TIME: 30 minutes

PRESSURE LEVEL: High

RELEASE: Natural

2 teaspoons oil

1 small onion, diced

2 carrots, diced

1 celery stalk, diced

2 garlic cloves, minced

1 thyme sprig or ¼ teaspoon dried thyme

1 bay leaf

½ pound chopped turkey breast tenderloin

3 cups low-sodium or unsalted turkey stock or Chicken Stock (page 167), divided

⅓ cup orzo

Kosher salt

Freshly ground black pepper

2 cups chopped kale

1 tablespoon freshly squeezed lemon juice

1 tablespoon chopped fresh parsley

TURKEY, KALE, AND ORZO SOUP

30 MINUTES OR LESS | LIGHT AND HEALTHY | ONE-POT MEAL
PALEO-FRIENDLY

Sometimes you just feel like turkey soup in the summertime. This light and healthy 30-minute meal is a soul-warmer, so crank up the air conditioner and pretend there's a storm a-blowin' outside while you enjoy a bowl.

1. Preheat the pressure cooker pot on sauté mode. When the display reads hot, add the oil. Add the onion, carrots, and celery and sauté until softened, 3 minutes. Add the garlic and cook for 1 minute. Add the thyme, bay leaf, turkey, 2 cups of stock, and the orzo and season with salt and pepper. Stir well.

2. Secure the lid and cook on high pressure for 6 minutes, then allow the pressure to naturally release for about 4 minutes. Open the vent at the top and remove the lid. Press cancel, then select sauté.

3. Discard the bay leaf and thyme sprig. Stir in remaining 1 cup of stock, the kale, lemon juice, and parsley. Taste and season with salt and pepper. Simmer for 2 minutes before serving.

Variation Tip For more of a *zuppa Toscana*-style soup, brown ground turkey instead of chopped tenderloin. You could also replace the orzo with rinsed and drained cannellini beans and add thinly sliced chunks of potato. Just increase the cook time to 8 minutes. For a Paleo version, omit the orzo.

PER SERVING Calories: 363; Total fat: 8g; Saturated fat: 1g; Cholesterol: 45mg; Carbohydrates: 40g; Fiber: 8g; Protein: 36g

SERVES 2

PREP TIME: 10 minutes

COOK TIME: 10 minutes

TOTAL TIME: 30 minutes

PRESSURE LEVEL: High

RELEASE: Natural

½ tablespoon oil

1 small onion, diced

2 garlic cloves, minced

½ pound ground turkey

2 tablespoons tomato paste

1 (14.5-ounce) can diced tomatoes and chiles with their juices

1 (14.5-ounce) can kidney beans, rinsed and drained

1 medium sweet potato, peeled and cubed

½ cup Chicken Stock (page 167)

1 teaspoon chili powder

½ teaspoon cayenne pepper

Kosher salt

Freshly ground black pepper

TO SERVE
- Avocado slices
- Sour cream
- Shredded Cheddar cheese
- Chopped fresh cilantro
- Green Chile Corn Bread (page 55)

TURKEY AND SWEET POTATO CHILI

30 MINUTES OR LESS | ONE-POT MEAL

You'll be making this easy turkey chili on repeat all year long, no matter what month it is. A lighter alternative to beef chili and packed with protein and fiber, it will be on your menu every Sunday come football season. This might even be one recipe you double for leftovers, since the flavors are even better the second day.

1. Preheat the pressure cooker pot on sauté mode. When the display reads hot, add the oil. Add the onion and sauté until softened, 3 minutes. Add the garlic and cook for 1 minute.

2. Add the ground turkey and cook until browned, 3 to 4 minutes. Stir in the tomato paste until combined.

3. Add the tomatoes and chiles and their juices, the beans, sweet potato, stock, chili powder, and cayenne pepper and season with salt and pepper.

4. Secure the lid and cook on high pressure for 10 minutes, then allow the pressure to naturally release, about 5 minutes. Open the vent at the top and remove the lid. Press cancel.

5. Taste and season with more salt and pepper as desired.

6. Serve the chili in bowls with avocado slices, sour cream, shredded cheese, chopped cilantro, and a square of corn bread.

Variation Tip For a fall-forward version of this chili, add ½ cup pumpkin purée and 1 teaspoon pumpkin pie spice to the pot before cooking.

PER SERVING Calories: 515; Total fat: 21g; Saturated fat: 3g; Cholesterol: 116mg; Carbohydrates: 46g; Fiber: 13g; Protein: 43g

SERVES 2

PREP TIME: 25 minutes (plus
30 minutes to thaw)

COOK TIME: 5 minutes

TOTAL TIME: 45 minutes

PRESSURE LEVEL: High

RELEASE: Quick

1 sheet frozen puff pastry

2 teaspoons oil, plus more
for greasing

½ small onion, chopped

1 celery stalk, chopped

1 large potato, peeled
and cubed

1 cup Chicken Stock
(page 167)

1 pound turkey breast cutlets

Kosher salt

Freshly ground black pepper

1½ tablespoons cornstarch

¼ cup whole milk, plus
2 tablespoons

1 cup frozen mixed vegetables

1 egg yolk

TURKEY POTPIE

WORTH THE WAIT

Traditional turkey potpie is baked in a deliciously fattening and buttery piecrust. This pressure cooker version tastes just as good and is not only lighter—substituting the crust for a single layer of equally yummy puff pastry—but also ready to eat in half the time.

1. Thaw the puff pastry sheet for 30 minutes. Preheat the oven to 400°F. Coat a small casserole dish with oil and set aside.

2. Preheat the pressure cooker pot on sauté mode. When the display reads hot, add 2 teaspoons of oil. Add the onion and celery and sauté until softened, 3 to 4 minutes. Add the potato, stock, and turkey cutlets. Season with salt and pepper.

3. Secure the lid and cook on high pressure for 5 minutes, then quick release the pressure in the pot and remove the lid. Press cancel, then select sauté.

4. Transfer the turkey to a cutting board and, when cool enough to handle, cut into cubes.

5. Transfer 2 tablespoons of stock from the pot to a small bowl and whisk in the cornstarch. Mix well, then return the paste to the simmering pot along with ¼ cup of milk and the mixed vegetables. Cook, stirring frequently, until thickened, 3 to 4 minutes.

6. Return the turkey to the pot, taste, and season with salt and pepper.

7. Pour the potpie filling into the prepared casserole dish. Place the puff pastry over the mixture and trim off any excess dough around the rim of the dish. Cut three slits in the center of the puff pastry for steam to escape.

8. In a small bowl, whisk together the egg yolk and remaining 2 tablespoons of milk . Brush the egg mixture onto the dough.

9. Bake the potpie in the oven for 10 to 15 minutes, or until golden brown.

Variation Tip To make this meal even faster, turn it into a stew! Skip the puff pastry, bake some packaged biscuits while the filling cooks, and serve the stew right out of the pressure cooker over the hot biscuits.

PER SERVING Calories: 726; Total fat: 20g; Saturated fat: 6g; Cholesterol: 204mg; Carbohydrates: 67g; Fiber: 9g; Protein: 69g

SERVES 2

PREP TIME: 20 minutes

COOK TIME: 15 minutes

TOTAL TIME: 55 minutes.

PRESSURE LEVEL: High

RELEASE: Natural

2 large bell peppers, stemmed, tops cut off and chopped, and peppers seeded

¼ cup minced onion

2 garlic cloves, minced

½ pound ground turkey

⅓ cup cooked brown rice

1 egg

½ cup Easy Marinara Sauce (page 171), divided

¼ cup grated Parmesan cheese

Kosher salt

Freshly ground black pepper

Pinch cayenne pepper

¼ cup grated mozzarella cheese

Chopped fresh parsley, for garnish

TURKEY-STUFFED PEPPERS

PALEO-FRIENDLY

Stuffed peppers are known around the world by different names, but no matter where you go, they are always a satisfying meal. This juicy turkey-stuffed version is on the lighter side and is likely the easiest you will ever make, all thanks to your pressure cooker. Simply hollow out the peppers, stuff them with the mix, cook, and eat, with no extra pots or utensils to wash.

1. Add ½ cup of water to the pressure cooker pot and place the rack in the bottom.

2. In a large bowl, combine the chopped pepper tops with the onion, garlic, ground turkey, rice, egg, 4 tablespoons of marinara sauce, and the Parmesan cheese and season with salt, black pepper, and the cayenne pepper. Mix thoroughly.

3. Divide the ground turkey mixture between the two peppers. Stand the stuffed peppers upright on the rack, leaning on each other. Top each with the remaining 4 tablespoons of marinara sauce.

4. Secure the cooker lid and cook on high pressure for 15 minutes, then allow the pressure to naturally release for about 10 minutes. Open the vent at the top and remove the lid. Press cancel.

5. Sprinkle the cheese on the two peppers, then loosely place the lid on the cooker and allow the cheese to melt in the residual heat, 2 to 3 minutes. Immediately garnish with the parsley and serve hot.

Variation Tip This recipe is equally delicious with ground beef or pork. Substitute a mix of the two and top with shredded Cheddar instead of mozzarella, and you've got cheeseburger-stuffed peppers. For a Paleo version, omit the cheese and rice.

PER SERVING Calories: 572; Total fat: 24g; Saturated fat: 8g; Cholesterol: 221mg; Carbohydrates: 46g; Fiber: 5g; Protein: 49g

PREP TIME: 25 minutes

COOK TIME: 5 minutes

TOTAL TIME: 1 hour

PRESSURE LEVEL: High

RELEASE: Natural

½ pound ground turkey

2 slices whole grain bread

1 large egg, lightly beaten

2 garlic cloves, minced

½ teaspoon dried oregano

½ teaspoon red pepper flakes

Pinch kosher salt

Pinch freshly ground
black pepper

Oil, for shaping the meatballs

1 cup Chicken Stock
(page 167)

2 cups Easy Marinara Sauce
(page 171)

2 to 3 hoagie rolls

4 to 6 slices provolone cheese

1 cup shredded
mozzarella cheese

TURKEY MEATBALL SUB SANDWICHES

PALEO-FRIENDLY

Cutting back on red meat? You don't have to sacrifice meatballs thanks to your heart-healthy friend ground turkey. Turkey, a much bolder flavor than chicken, is a delicious beef substitute in these saucy, cheesy meatball subs. Pro tip: Double the meatball recipe and freeze half for a quick future dinner.

1. Put the ground turkey in a medium bowl. Dampen the bread with water, gently squeeze out the excess water, then crumble over the turkey. Add the egg, garlic, oregano, red pepper flakes, salt, and pepper. Coat your hands with a bit of oil, mix the meat together well by hand, and roll into tablespoon-size balls, setting them aside on a plate as you work. Refrigerate the meatballs for 20 minutes.

2. Pour the stock and marinara sauce into the pot. Gently place the meatballs on top in an even layer.

3. Secure the lid and cook on high pressure for 5 minutes, then allow the pressure to naturally release, about 10 minutes. Open the vent at the top and remove the lid. Press cancel.

4. Preheat the oven broiler. Cut open the hoagie rolls and set them on a baking sheet. Layer 2 slices of provolone cheese on one side of each roll. Load with the meatballs and cover with marinara sauce, then sprinkle with the mozzarella. Broil until the cheese is melted and the bread is lightly toasted.

Variation Tip To make these meatball subs Paleo and lighter in calories, simply leave out the bread binder and serve over zucchini noodles or spaghetti squash instead of on a sandwich. You can also use the meatballs in the Easy Spaghetti and Meatballs recipe (page 153).

PER SERVING Calories: 1,008; Total fat: 44g; Saturated fat: 17g; Cholesterol: 260mg; Carbohydrates: 95g; Fiber: 16g; Protein: 71g

SERVES 2, TWICE

PREP TIME: 45 minutes

COOK TIME: 20 minutes

TOTAL TIME: 1 hour 30 minutes

PRESSURE LEVEL: High

RELEASE: Natural

1 tablespoon butter

¼ pound Italian sausage, casing removed

1 small onion, chopped

1 celery stalk, chopped

2 tablespoons chopped fresh sage

2 garlic cloves, minced

1 cup crumbled corn bread

1½ teaspoons kosher salt, divided

Freshly ground black pepper

1½ cups Chicken Stock (page 167), divided

1½ to 2 pounds skinless, boneless turkey breast, butterflied and pounded to an even thickness

1 tablespoon oil

1 packet turkey gravy mix

TURKEY BREAST, STUFFING, AND GRAVY DINNER

WORTH THE WAIT

Thanksgiving meals can be a hassle to make for just two people, but a little effort and some delicious flavors can create this convenient and beautiful turkey roulade—esque meal. Skinless, boneless turkey breast is pounded flat, rolled with corn bread stuffing, then cooked for 20 minutes in the pressure cooker. The cooking liquid becomes an easy gravy, and the best part? There are still leftovers!

1. Preheat the pressure cooker pot on sauté mode. When the display reads hot, add the butter. Add the sausage and cook until it begins to brown, 2 to 3 minutes. Add the onion, celery, and sage and sauté until softened, 3 to 4 minutes. Add the garlic and cook for 1 minute. Press cancel.

2. Transfer the sausage mixture to a large bowl and add the crumbled corn bread, 1 teaspoon of salt, and a pinch of black pepper. Mix well with a fork, then add ½ cup of stock. Stir until well combined.

3. Lay the butterflied turkey breast on a cutting board and season with the remaining ½ teaspoon of salt and some pepper. Spread the sausage stuffing in the middle of the turkey breast, leaving a 1-inch border on the two long edges and the edge farthest from you on the cutting board.

4. Grab the edge of the turkey that's closest to you and to roll it tightly. When the turkey is rolled up, use a length of kitchen twine to tie it closed, then tuck in the sides.

5. Press sauté on the pressure cooker. When the display reads hot, add the oil to the pot, then add the rolled-up turkey breast and brown on all sides, 8 to 10 minutes. Pour in the remaining 1 cup of stock.

6. Secure the lid and cook on high pressure for 20 minutes. At the end of the cooking time, press cancel. Allow the pressure to naturally release, 15 to 20 minutes, then open the vent at the top and remove the lid.

7. Carefully transfer the turkey roast to a serving platter and let rest before cutting in slices. Press sauté and add the pouch of turkey gravy mix to the liquid in the cooker pot, whisking until smooth. Simmer for 4 to 5 minutes, until thickened, then serve over the stuffed turkey breast.

Serving Tip Make it an entire Thanksgiving dinner by pairing this recipe with Loaded "Baked" Sweet Potatoes (page 49), Holiday Cranberry Sauce (page 180), Hot Honey Maple Carrots (page 53), and Balsamic Brown Sugar Brussels Sprouts (page 52). Serve Mini Crustless Pumpkin Pies (page 198) for dessert!

PER SERVING Calories: 945; Total fat: 22g; Saturated fat: 6g; Cholesterol: 54mg; Carbohydrates: 31g; Fiber: 1g; Protein: 154g

Seven
PORK AND BEEF

Your pressure cooker will really show off its skills when cooking tough cuts of meat from the shoulder and leg—which you'll find an abundance of in these recipes. Pot roasts and pulled pork that normally take hours are easily made in less time than it takes to watch a movie, and the end results are just as tender and flavorful. To seal in those precious juices, browning your roasts is key, but if your cooker comes with a nonstick pot instead of a stainless steel one, you might be tempted to skip that step. Don't. Fire up a cast-iron skillet and make quick work of it, then proceed as the recipe directs.

Tonkotsu Ramen, page 142

Dublin Coddle 141

Tonkotsu Ramen 142

Pork Chops with Mushroom Gravy 144

Pork with Sauerkraut 145

Quick Smoky Bourbon Barbecue Ribs 146

Southern Barbecue Pulled Pork Sandwiches 147

Carnitas Tacos with Avocado Crema 149

Kalua Pork Rice Bowls 151

Easy Spaghetti and Meatballs 153

Easy Beef Enchiladas 154

Quick Texas Chili con Carne 156

Red Wine—Braised Boneless Short Ribs and Gravy 158

Beef Pot Roast and Potatoes 160

Beef Ragù with Pappardelle 161

Beef and Broccoli 163

PRESSURE LEVEL: High
RELEASE: Natural

1 teaspoon oil

½ pound uncooked thick-cut bacon, chopped

½ pound fully cooked kielbasa sausage, cut into 2-inch pieces

1 onion, chopped

2 garlic cloves, minced

1 bay leaf

½ teaspoon dried tarragon

Kosher salt

Freshly ground black pepper

2 medium potatoes, quartered and thickly sliced

2 carrots, peeled and chopped

1 cup apple cider

1 teaspoon ham bouillon powder

¼ cup chopped fresh parsley

DUBLIN CODDLE

30 MINUTES OR LESS | PALEO-FRIENDLY

If you're looking for a meal to pair with that pint of Guinness, this is it. An Irish dish often made to use up leftovers, coddle commonly consists of sliced bangers (sausages) and rashers (bacon) with chunks of potatoes, onions, and other root veggies, so feel free to empty the fridge on this one.

1. Preheat the pressure cooker pot on sauté mode. When the display reads hot, add the oil. Add the bacon and kielbasa and sauté until crisp and brown, 3 to 5 minutes. Transfer to a plate and set aside.

2. Add the onion to the rendered bacon fat in the pot and sauté until softened, 3 to 4 minutes. Add the garlic, bay leaf, and tarragon and sauté for 1 minute. Season with salt and pepper.

3. Add the potatoes and carrots, then return the bacon and sausage to the pot. Stir in the apple cider and ham bouillon powder.

4. Secure the lid and cook on high pressure for 12 minutes, then allow the pressure to naturally release for 5 minutes. Open the vent at the top and remove the lid. Press cancel.

5. Discard the bay leaf. Taste and season with more salt and pepper if needed. Divide between serving bowls and garnish with the parsley.

Substitution Tip To make this recipe Paleo, use sweet potatoes instead of white potatoes, and be sure to use uncured bacon and fresh kielbasa instead of the processed variety.

PER SERVING Calories: 695; Total fat: 36g; Saturated fat: 11g; Cholesterol: 104mg; Carbohydrates: 66g; Fiber: 8g; Protein: 31g

SERVES 2, TWICE
PREP TIME: 25 minutes
COOK TIME: 90 minutes
TOTAL TIME: 2 hours 45 minutes

PRESSURE LEVEL: High
RELEASE: Natural

1 pound pork spare ribs, cut into 2-inch pieces

½ pound chicken wings

1 tablespoon oil

1 large onion, cut into thick slices

2 garlic cloves, smashed

1 (2-inch) piece peeled fresh ginger

Soy sauce, for seasoning

6 ounces Japanese ramen noodles, cooked according to package directions

TO SERVE

- Sliced chashu pork belly or thickly sliced cooked bacon
- Shiitake mushrooms
- Scallions
- Bean sprouts
- Sliced nori (seaweed)
- Canned bamboo shoots
- Soft-boiled eggs
- Sesame seeds
- Spicy sesame oil

TONKOTSU RAMEN

PALEO-FRIENDLY | WORTH THE WAIT

Thick, creamy, and rich, Japanese tonkotsu broth takes an entire day to make and involves lots of boiling and skimming. But by using your pressure cooker, you can make this delicious, comforting soup in just a few hours, and it is guaranteed to satisfy. Once the broth is made, building the soup bowls goes quickly, so have your other ingredients ready to go when that pressure-release valve drops.

1. Bring 3 cups of water to a boil in a large saucepan on the stove. While the water comes to a boil, put the ribs and wings inside the pot of the pressure cooker. Select sauté. Carefully pour the boiling water into the pot. Allow the meat to simmer for 10 minutes with the lid loosely covering the pot.

2. Press cancel. Carefully drain the water from the ribs and wings, transfer them to a large bowl of cold water, and remove any fat. Rinse the cooker pot, dry it thoroughly, and return to the cooker.

3. Select sauté and add the oil when the display reads hot. Add the onion and brown for 8 to 10 minutes. Press cancel. Add the garlic and ginger, then add the ribs and wings. Fill the pot with water to the ¾ fill line or until everything is submerged. Secure the lid and cook on high for 90 minutes, then allow the pressure to naturally release, about 20 minutes. Place a kitchen towel over the pressure release valve, then turn it to venting. Remove the lid.

4. Using a fine-mesh strainer, strain the stock into a large bowl; reserve the ribs and wings for another use and discard the other solids. Skim any surface oil off the stock, if desired. Season the stock with soy sauce.

5. Divide the ramen between two soup bowls. Pour the stock over the noodles, then serve with the toppings of your choice from the "to serve" list above.

Variation Tip If you're looking for a clearer, more traditional preparation of the broth, skip the wings and ribs and make it with pork trotters instead. Have your butcher cut them into 1-inch rounds for easier cooking. For a Paleo version, substitute coconut aminos for the soy sauce and omit the ramen noodles.

PER SERVING Calories: 913; Total fat: 48g; Saturated fat: 14g; Cholesterol: 386mg; Carbohydrates: 70g; Fiber: 10g; Protein: 50g

SERVES 2

PREP TIME: 10 minutes

COOK TIME: 8 minutes

TOTAL TIME: 40 minutes

PRESSURE LEVEL: High

RELEASE: Natural

1 tablespoon oil

2 bone-in, medium-cut
pork chops

Kosher salt

Freshly ground black pepper

½ small onion, sliced

4 ounces cremini
mushrooms, sliced

2 garlic cloves, minced

Splash of dry white wine

1 cup Chicken Stock
(page 167)

1 tablespoon cornstarch

¾ cup sour cream

1 tablespoon butter

TO SERVE
- Mashed potatoes
- Steamed vegetables
- Chopped fresh parsley

PORK CHOPS WITH MUSHROOM GRAVY

When tender pork chops are required to cheer you up after a tough weekday, this is your go-to recipe. A creamy mushroom gravy pumps up the pork flavors and begs for a pile of mashed potatoes on the plate.

1. Preheat the pressure cooker pot on sauté mode. When the display reads hot, add the oil. Season the pork chops generously with salt and pepper, sear on both sides, and transfer to a plate.

2. Add the onion, mushrooms, and garlic and sauté until softened, 3 minutes. Pour in the white wine and deglaze the pot, scraping up any browned bits from the bottom with a wooden spoon and stirring them into the liquid.

3. Add the stock and stir. Set the seared pork chops in the pot. Secure the lid and cook on high pressure for 8 minutes, then allow the pressure to naturally release, about 10 minutes. Open the vent at the top and remove the lid. Press cancel, then select sauté.

4. Transfer the pork chops to a plate. Remove 1 tablespoon of cooking liquid from the pot and put in a small bowl with the cornstarch. Whisk well then return the mixture to the pot and whisk in the sour cream and butter until combined. Simmer to thicken, 4 to 5 minutes. Season with more salt and pepper if desired. Serve with mashed potatoes and steamed vegetables, and garnish with parsley.

Recipe Tip This can be a great pot-in-pot recipe! If you'd like to pair these pork chops with mashed potatoes, wash and chop 1 pound of potatoes and place them in a steamer basket set on a trivet in the cooker pot on top of the pork chops. Cook as directed in the recipe, then remove the potatoes and mash them in a separate bowl.

PER SERVING Calories: 522; Total fat: 38g; Saturated fat: 18g; Cholesterol: 110mg; Carbohydrates: 17g; Fiber: 1g; Protein: 29g

SERVES 2

PREP TIME: 5 minutes

COOK TIME: 30 minutes

TOTAL TIME: 45 minutes

PRESSURE LEVEL: High

RELEASE: Natural

2 tablespoons butter or oil

½ pound pork (such as roast or loin), cut into 1-inch chunks

Kosher salt

Freshly ground black pepper

¼ cup beer or stock

½ onion, thinly sliced

16 ounces jarred sauerkraut with its juices (see Tip)

½ apple, sliced (optional)

¼ pound fully cooked kielbasa sausage, sliced into ½-inch rounds (optional)

TO SERVE

- Mashed potatoes

PORK WITH SAUERKRAUT

COMFORT FOOD | ONE-POT MEAL

This simple recipe is traditionally served on New Year's Eve in Germany, it is believed to bring blessings and wealth for the new year. My Nana made this meal often, but every December 31st was extra special, as we would sit around the dinner table and wish each other as much luck and money as there were shreds of cabbage in the sauerkraut. While you might not get a winning lottery ticket from eating this meal, you will definitely find both your belly and your heart full, which are blessings in themselves.

1. Preheat the pressure cooker pot on sauté mode. When the display reads hot, add the butter to melt. Season the pork with salt and pepper, add to the pot, and sear for 3 minutes, browning the chunks on all sides.

2. Stir in the beer and deglaze the pot, scraping up any browned bits from the bottom with a wooden spoon and stirring them into the liquid. Add the onion and sauté, stirring often, for 2 to 3 minutes, or until the liquid is reduced by half.

3. Press the cancel button. Layer the sauerkraut and its juices and the apple (if using) on top of the pork and onion.

4. Secure the lid and cook on high pressure for 15 minutes, then allow the pressure to naturally release for 10 minutes. Open the vent at the top and remove the lid.

5. Add the kielbasa (if using) and stir the contents of the pot. Close the lid and let the kielbasa warm up in the mixture for 5 to 10 minutes.

6. Serve over a bed of warm mashed potatoes.

Ingredient Tip A shredded head of green cabbage, a couple of tablespoons of kosher salt, and a few pinches of caraway seeds are all that stand between you and homemade sauerkraut goodness.

PER SERVING Calories: 689; Total fat: 44g; Saturated fat: 21g; Cholesterol: 148mg; Carbohydrates: 25g; Fiber: 9g; Protein: 46g

SERVES 2

PREP TIME: 5 minutes

COOK TIME: 25 minutes

TOTAL TIME: 55 minutes
(including baking time)

PRESSURE LEVEL: High

RELEASE: Natural

1 rack baby back ribs

Kosher salt

Freshly ground black pepper

¼ cup barbecue meat rub
(optional)

1 cup Beef Stock (page 168)
or water

1 tablespoon liquid smoke
(optional)

¼ cup bourbon

1 cup Classic Barbecue Sauce
(page 173)

QUICK SMOKY BOURBON BARBECUE RIBS

COMFORT FOOD

Baby back ribs in under an hour?! It's possible! You don't have to fire up your grill or smoker to enjoy a rack of succulent ribs. Your pressure cooker will do it for you in record time, and the results are just as saucy, tender, and delicious.

1. Remove the membrane from the back of the ribs and cut the rack into four equal pieces. Season generously with salt, pepper, and your favorite barbecue meat rub (if using).

2. Put the ribs in the pressure cooker pot. Add the beef stock and liquid smoke (if using). Secure the lid and cook on high pressure for 25 minutes, then allow the pressure to naturally release, about 10 minutes. Open the vent at the top and remove the lid.

3. Preheat the oven to 450°F. Line a baking pan with aluminum foil.

4. In a small bowl, mix the bourbon and barbecue sauce, whisking to combine.

5. Transfer the cooked ribs to the prepared baking pan. Brush the bourbon-barbecue sauce all over the ribs, including the bones. Bake for 6 minutes on each side, or until the sauce caramelizes.

6. Remove from the oven. Brush the remaining sauce on the ribs before serving.

Ingredient Tip Bottled barbecue sauce is great for this recipe, but a homemade version like the one in this book (page 173) will make the ribs extra tasty.

PER SERVING Calories: 780; Total fat: 37g; Saturated fat: 14g; Cholesterol: 162mg; Carbohydrates: 55g; Fiber: 1g; Protein: 43g

SERVES 2, TWICE

PREP TIME: 15 minutes

COOK TIME: 45 minutes

TOTAL TIME: 1 hour 20 minutes

PRESSURE LEVEL: High

RELEASE: Natural

½ tablespoon packed light brown sugar

½ teaspoon paprika

½ teaspoon kosher salt

½ teaspoon ground mustard

¼ teaspoon ground cumin

¼ teaspoon freshly ground black pepper

1 pound boneless pork shoulder roast

1 teaspoon oil

½ cup Chicken Stock (page 167)

2 cups Classic Barbecue Sauce (page 173), divided

TO SERVE

- Hamburger buns or portobello mushroom caps
- More barbecue sauce
- Coleslaw

SOUTHERN BARBECUE PULLED PORK SANDWICHES

PALEO-FRIENDLY | WORTH THE WAIT

This super-tender pulled pork recipe is almost as good as that slow-smoked stuff you get at your favorite local barbecue joint! This one is even easier to make. There's no messing around with a giant smoker; just toss the ingredients into your pressure cooker and go about your day. Dinner is ready when you are, and it's packed with smoky-sweet barbecue flavors.

1. In a small bowl, combine the brown sugar, paprika, salt, mustard, cumin, and pepper and stir well to combine. Rub the mixture all over the pork roast.

2. Preheat the pressure cooker pot on sauté mode. When the display reads hot, add the oil. Add the pork and brown on both sides, 2 to 3 minutes per side. Press cancel.

3. Add the stock and 1 cup of barbecue sauce and stir to combine.

4. Secure the lid and cook on high pressure for 45 minutes, then allow the pressure to naturally release, about 15 minutes. Open the vent at the top and remove the lid. Press cancel and select sauté. →

5. Transfer the pork to a large bowl. Stir the contents of the pot and allow to simmer, uncovered, for 10 to 12 minutes, or until thickened and reduced. During cooking, use a spoon to remove any fat that rises to the top. Taste and adjust the seasonings as necessary.

6. Meanwhile, shred the pork with two forks. Return the meat to the pot, stir, and warm through.

7. Serve on hamburger buns or portobello mushroom caps with additional barbecue sauce and coleslaw.

Variation Tip To make this recipe Paleo and gluten-free, use maple syrup in place of the brown sugar, omit the barbecue sauce, and serve the pork on large portobello mushroom caps instead of buns.

PER SERVING Calories: 988; Total fat: 48g; Saturated fat: 17g; Cholesterol: 306mg; Carbohydrates: 47g; Fiber: 1g; Protein: 86g

SERVES 2, GENEROUSLY
PREP TIME: 15 minutes
COOK TIME: 30 minutes
TOTAL TIME: 1 hour 30 minutes,
including marinating and
broiling times

PRESSURE LEVEL: High
RELEASE: Natural

FOR THE CARNITAS
1 pound boneless pork
shoulder roast, cut into
2-inch chunks

Kosher salt

Freshly ground black pepper

1 cup Chicken Stock
(page 167)

½ cup freshly squeezed
orange juice

Juice of 1 lime

1 cup sliced onion

2 garlic cloves, crushed

½ teaspoon ground cumin

FOR THE AVOCADO CREMA
1 medium avocado, halved and
pitted, and cubed

½ cup coarsely chopped fresh
cilantro

¼ cup sour cream

Juice of 1 lime

½ teaspoon kosher salt

TO SERVE
- Corn or flour tortillas
- Fresh salsa
- Shredded Cheddar or
  Jack cheese
- Fresh chopped cilantro

CARNITAS TACOS WITH AVOCADO CREMA

WORTH THE WAIT

Pulled pork isn't only made for barbecue, which this citrusy carnitas recipe proves. Inspired by a favorite Chipotle meal, these tacos will make any day of the week Taco Tuesday. Serve them up however you like, with salsas, cheeses, and a side of rice. Just don't skip the refreshing avocado crema!

TO MAKE THE CARNITAS

1. Place the pork shoulder meat in the pressure cooker pot. Season generously with salt and pepper. Add the stock, orange juice, lime juice, onion, garlic, and cumin. Mix well and let the pork marinate for 20 minutes.

2. Secure the lid and cook on high pressure for 30 minutes, then allow the pressure to naturally release, about 10 minutes. Open the vent at the top and remove the lid. Press cancel.

3. Preheat the oven broiler. Line a baking sheet with aluminum foil.

4. Transfer the pork to a plate. Carefully strain the juices from the pot through a fine-mesh sieve into a bowl, reserving the cooked onions. Use two forks to shred the meat, discarding any extra fat. Place the pork and onion in a single layer on the prepared baking sheet.

5. Broil for 4 to 5 minutes, or until the edges are crispy, then flip the meat, spoon on some of the reserved liquid if necessary, and broil for another 4 to 5 minutes. $\longrightarrow$

TO MAKE THE AVOCADO CREMA

1. Scoop the avocado from the skin into the bowl of a food processor fitted with the blade attachment (or into a blender) and add the cilantro, sour cream, lime juice, and salt. Process until smooth, stopping to scrape down the side of the bowl with a rubber spatula as needed.

2. Transfer the crema to a small bowl. Cover with plastic wrap and store in the refrigerator for up to 2 hours if not using immediately.

TO SERVE

Spoon the carnitas into warmed tortillas and top with salsa, shredded cheese, chopped fresh cilantro, and the avocado crema.

Variation Tip Skip the tortillas and have a build-a-taco-bowl bar for dinner! Make the pork as instructed. Provide rice, cooked beans, a variety of salsas, shredded cheese, shredded lettuce, and—of course—the avocado crema.

PER SERVING Calories: 1,015; Total fat: 60g; Saturated fat: 20g; Cholesterol: 331mg; Carbohydrates: 22g; Fiber: 7g; Protein: 95g

SERVES 2, GENEROUSLY

PREP TIME: 10 minutes

COOK TIME: 94 minutes

TOTAL TIME: 2 hours 30 minutes

PRESSURE LEVEL: High

RELEASE: Natural (for the pork);
Quick (for the cabbage)

2 uncooked bacon slices

¾ pound boneless pork
shoulder roast

2 garlic cloves, peeled
and halved

1½ teaspoons red Hawaiian
sea salt

1 cup water

½ red cabbage, cored and cut
into thirds

TO SERVE

• Cooked rice

KALUA PORK RICE BOWLS

5-INGREDIENT | WORTH THE WAIT

Kalua pork is a taste of the islands—pure salty and savory goodness that can be used in all kinds of dishes. In the case of this recipe, pairing it with some simple steamed rice and braised cabbage highlights the delicious umami flavor of the red Hawaiian sea salt that cures the pork as it cooks.

1. Preheat the pressure cooker pot on sauté mode. When the display reads hot, add the bacon and cook until both sides are browned but not crispy, about 5 minutes.

2. While the bacon is cooking, prepare the pork. Place the roast on a cutting board and use a sharp knife to make four slits in it. Tuck half of a garlic clove into each slit. Rub the sea salt evenly over the meat.

3. Move the bacon to the side of the pot, add the pork, and sear it on both sides in the bacon grease, about 3 minutes per side. Add the water and deglaze the pot, scraping up any browned bits from the bottom with a wooden spoon and making sure the bacon and pork do not stick to the pot.

4. Secure the lid and cook on high for 90 minutes. When the cook time is up, press cancel and allow the pressure to naturally release for about 15 minutes, then open the vent at the top and remove the lid. $\longrightarrow$

5. Transfer the pork to a large bowl and let rest for 5 minutes. Taste the cooking liquid and add more water or season with more salt if desired. Reserve ¼ cup of the cooking liquid and set aside.

6. Add the cabbage to the pot. Secure the lid and cook on high pressure for 4 minutes. Quick release the pressure in the pot, then remove the lid.

7. While the cabbage is cooking, use two forks to shred the pork, adding the reserved liquid to keep it moistened.

8. Serve the pork over rice, with the cabbage on the side.

Recipe Tip Kalua pork is a Hawaiian traditional meal often served at luaus. Cooking it is a long process, which involves wrapping a whole pig in banana leaves, then burying it in a fire pit lined with hot stones, where it smokes for hours until tender and juicy. Serving it with a side of steamed cabbage is common, but if you're not a fan, opt for steamed rice and macaroni salad.

Ingredient Tip Red Hawaiian sea salt, the traditional seasoning for native Hawaiian dishes, can be found in specialty markets and online.

PER SERVING Calories: 944; Total fat: 47g; Saturated fat: 15g; Cholesterol: 402mg; Carbohydrates: 8g; Fiber: 2g; Protein: 116g

SERVES 2, GENEROUSLY

PREP TIME: 20 minutes

COOK TIME: 15 minutes

TOTAL TIME: 1 hour 15 minutes

PRESSURE LEVEL: High

RELEASE: Quick

¼ pound ground beef

¼ pound ground pork

2 slices white bread

¼ cup grated
Parmesan cheese

1 large egg

1 garlic clove, minced

½ teaspoon dried oregano

½ tablespoon dried parsley

Pinch kosher salt

Pinch freshly ground
black pepper

Oil, for shaping the meatballs

3 cups Easy Marinara Sauce
(page 171), divided

6 ounces spaghetti

1 cup Beef Stock (page 168)

TO SERVE
- Grated Parmesan cheese
- Garlic bread

EASY SPAGHETTI AND MEATBALLS

ONE-POT MEAL | WORTH THE WAIT

This saucy spaghetti dinner is made entirely in one pot, including the noodles! The homemade meatballs in the recipe come together quickly. Making them in advance cuts the prep time, so you can have this meal ready in about 30 minutes!

1. Put the ground beef and pork in a medium bowl. Dampen the bread with water, gently squeeze the excess water out, then crumble over the meat. Add the cheese, egg, garlic, oregano, parsley, salt, and pepper. Coat your hands with a bit of the oil, mix the meat together well by hand, and roll into tablespoon-size balls, setting them aside on a plate as you work. Refrigerate for 20 minutes.

2. Pour half of the marinara sauce into the pot. Gently place the meatballs on top in an even layer and cover with another thin layer of sauce. Break the spaghetti in half and lay on top of the meatballs. Pour the remaining sauce on top, then add the beef stock.

3. Secure the lid and cook on high pressure for 15 minutes, then quick release the pressure in the pot and remove the lid.

4. Stir the contents of the pot, breaking apart any noodles stuck together. Divide the spaghetti and meatballs between two bowls or plates and serve with grated Parmesan and garlic bread.

Ingredient Tip Not a fan of white bread? Try using sourdough, grain, or rye bread as a filler in the meatballs instead for different textures and flavors.

PER SERVING Calories: 920; Total fat: 27g; Saturated fat: 10g; Cholesterol: 275mg; Carbohydrates: 105g; Fiber: 10g; Protein: 63g

SERVES 2, GENEROUSLY
PREP TIME: 30 minutes
COOK TIME: 60 minutes
TOTAL TIME: 1 hour 45 minutes

PRESSURE LEVEL: High
RELEASE: Natural

1 tablespoon oil, plus more for greasing

1 pound beef roast

Kosher salt

Freshly ground black pepper

1 small onion, chopped

1 cup Beef Stock (page 168)

½ cup tomato salsa

1 tablespoon red wine vinegar

½ tablespoon ground cumin

1 (10-ounce) can enchilada sauce, divided

6 (6-inch) corn or flour tortillas

1 cup shredded sharp Cheddar cheese

TO SERVE
- Sour cream
- Guacamole
- Salsa
- Chopped fresh cilantro

EASY BEEF ENCHILADAS

PALEO-FRIENDLY | WORTH THE WAIT

These enchiladas, filled with flavorful shredded beef and gooey cheese, are perfect for satisfying that Mexican food craving. Though enchiladas are traditionally made with corn tortillas, you could also use flour tortillas for equally delicious results. Just don't forget to load on the sauce and extra cheese.

1. Preheat the pressure cooker pot on sauté mode. When the display reads hot, add 1 tablespoon of oil. Season the beef with salt and pepper, then sear it on all sides, 8 to 10 minutes.

2. To the pot, add the onion, stock, salsa, vinegar, and cumin. Secure the lid and cook on high pressure for 60 minutes, then allow the pressure to naturally release, about 10 minutes. Open the vent at the top and remove the lid. Press cancel.

3. Preheat the oven to 350°F. Coat an 8-by-8-inch baking dish with oil.

4. Remove the roast from the pot and transfer to a large bowl, discarding the liquid. Use two forks to shred the roast. Add ¼ cup of the enchilada sauce to the meat and toss to combine. Taste and adjust the seasonings if desired.

5. Spread half of the remaining enchilada sauce (about ½ cup) on the bottom of the prepared baking dish.

6. Lay the tortillas out on a cutting board. Fill each tortilla with ⅓ cup of the shredded beef mixture and 1 tablespoon of cheese. Roll up and place seam-side down in the baking dish. Pour the remaining enchilada sauce (about ½ cup) over the top of the enchiladas and sprinkle with the remaining cheese.

7. Bake for 20 minutes, or until the cheese is bubbly. Transfer to a cooling rack and let rest for 5 to 10 minutes before serving with sour cream, guacamole, salsa, and chopped cilantro.

Variation Tip These enchiladas are also delicious when stuffed with carnitas pork or shredded chicken and green chiles. If you're in the mood for ground beef but forgot to thaw it out, cook it quickly from frozen in your pressure cooker. Add 1 cup of water to your cooker pot and put the frozen ground beef on a trivet. Cook on high for 20 minutes and perform a quick release at the end of the cook time. Drain the liquid and grease and follow the rest of the recipe as written, using the ground beef. To make this dish Paleo, omit the tortillas and dairy.

PER SERVING Calories: 646; Total fat: 30g; Saturated fat: 13g; Cholesterol: 175mg; Carbohydrates: 32g; Fiber: 6g; Protein: 61g

SERVES 2, TWICE
PREP TIME: 25 minutes
COOK TIME: 15 minutes
TOTAL TIME: 1 hour

PRESSURE LEVEL: High
RELEASE: Natural

1 tablespoon oil, plus
2 teaspoons

1 pound beef chuck roast, cut
in half, fat trimmed

Kosher salt

Freshly ground black pepper

1 small onion, diced

3 garlic cloves, minced

2 cups Adobo Barbacoa Sauce
(page 175)

1 (14.5-ounce) can diced
tomatoes with their juices

1 (6-ounce) can green chiles

Red pepper flakes

1 tablespoon fish sauce

1 tablespoon apple
cider vinegar

2 tablespoons masa harina or
cornmeal

TO SERVE
- Chopped fresh cilantro
- Chopped scallions
- Grated cheese
- Sliced avocado

QUICK TEXAS CHILI CON CARNE

ONE-POT MEAL | PALEO-FRIENDLY | WORTH THE WAIT

Real Texas chili con carne is made with beef, chiles, and not a whole lot else. This version has been Texan-approved, plus it's done in a quarter of the time and is still the real deal despite the nontraditional addition of tomato. The tender beef falls apart in your mouth, and the heat is variable based on your tastes. The flavor intensifies and develops the second day, so don't be afraid to make the recipe ahead to enjoy for lunch tomorrow!

1. Preheat the pressure cooker pot on sauté mode. Once hot, add 1 tablespoon of oil. Season the beef roast generously with salt and pepper and sear on all sides, 5 to 10 minutes. Transfer to a cutting board and set aside.

2. Heat the remaining 2 teaspoons of oil in the pot, then add the onion and garlic and sauté until softened, 3 minutes. Add the adobo sauce, tomatoes and their juices, and the green chiles. Cut the seared beef into 1- to 2-inch chunks and transfer to the pot. Bring to a simmer, then season with salt and pepper.

3. Secure the lid and cook on high pressure for 15 minutes, then allow the pressure to naturally release, about 10 minutes. Open the vent at the top and remove the lid. Press cancel, then select sauté.

4. Stir in the fish sauce, vinegar, and masa harina. Simmer until thickened to your desired consistency, about 5 minutes. Taste and adjust the seasonings, if necessary. Serve with chopped cilantro, chopped scallions, grated cheese, and sliced avocado.

Ingredient Tip Masa harina is the recommended thickener in this recipe, though cornmeal will work just fine as a substitute. If you do decide to buy a bag of masa, go ahead: It's the main ingredient in homemade tortillas, and fresh tortillas made with masa are so delicious (and would be great to serve with this meal).

Variation Tip For a Paleo version of this recipe, use tomato paste in place of the masa harina (or cornmeal) and do not serve the chili with cheese.

PER SERVING Calories: 1,172; Total fat: 62g; Saturated fat: 20g; Cholesterol: 360mg; Carbohydrates: 42g; Fiber: 7g; Protein: 111g

PRESSURE LEVEL: High

RELEASE: Natural

2 tablespoons oil, divided

1 pound boneless beef
short ribs

Kosher salt

Freshly ground black pepper

½ onion, chopped

1 whole carrot, peeled
and chopped

1 celery stalk, chopped

2 garlic cloves, minced

1 cup dry red wine, divided

1 cup Beef Stock (page 168)

1 rosemary sprig

¼ cup water

2 tablespoons cornstarch

TO SERVE
- Mashed potatoes, pasta,
  or polenta

RED WINE–BRAISED BONELESS SHORT RIBS AND GRAVY

PALEO-FRIENDLY | WORTH THE WAIT

These short ribs are melt-in-your-mouth luxurious comfort food, swimming in a rich red wine gravy. Your electric pressure cooker cuts the "braising" time in half, putting this savory meal on your table in record time.

1. Preheat the pressure cooker pot on sauté mode. When the display reads hot, add 1 tablespoon of oil. Season the short ribs with salt and pepper, place them in a single layer in the pot, and sear on both sides for 6 to 7 minutes.

2. Transfer the ribs to a plate and set aside. Heat the remaining 1 tablespoon of oil in the pot and add the onion, carrot, celery, and garlic, allowing them to sweat for about 5 minutes, or until softened. Season with salt and pepper.

3. Deglaze the pot with ½ cup of wine, scraping up the browned bits from the bottom with a wooden spoon and stirring them into the liquid, for 2 to 3 minutes. Return the short ribs to the pot.

4. Add the remaining ½ cup of wine, the stock, and the rosemary. Secure the lid and cook on high pressure for 35 minutes, then allow the pressure to naturally release, about 10 minutes. Open the vent at the top and remove the lid. Press cancel.

5. Transfer the meat to a cutting board and let rest. Using a large, shallow spoon, skim any fat from the surface of the liquid in the pot.

6. In a small bowl, whisk together the water and cornstarch. Press sauté and let the liquid in the pot heat for 2 to 3 minutes. Whisk in the cornstarch mixture and let the liquid boil until it thickens, 4 to 5 minutes. Add the ribs back to the pot and reheat in the gravy.

7. Serve the short ribs and gravy over mashed potatoes, pasta, or polenta.

Ingredient Tip If you can only find bone-in short ribs, or just prefer them, this recipe will work exactly the same way and will taste just as delicious. Simply add 15 minutes to your cook time.

Variation Tip To make the dish Paleo, omit the cornstarch and don't serve with potatoes, pasta, or polenta.

PER SERVING Calories: 766; Total fat: 35g; Saturated fat: 10g; Cholesterol: 206mg; Carbohydrates: 19g; Fiber: 2g; Protein: 69g

PRESSURE LEVEL: High
RELEASE: Natural

1 tablespoon oil

1½ pounds lean beef shoulder roast, trimmed

Kosher salt

Freshly ground black pepper

1 medium onion, chopped

3 garlic cloves, crushed

2 large carrots, peeled and chopped

12 ounces fingerling potatoes

2 cups Beef Stock (page 168)

1 tablespoon Worcestershire sauce

1 tablespoon cornstarch

Fresh thyme, for garnish

BEEF POT ROAST AND POTATOES

ONE-POT MEAL | PALEO-FRIENDLY | WORTH THE WAIT

Pot roast brings back nostalgic memories of Mom and Grandma's Sunday dinners, filling the house for hours with wonderful smells. The only thing you'll be missing by making it in your pressure cooker is the late-evening sore arm from scrubbing the roasting pan clean.

1. Preheat the pressure cooker pot on sauté mode. When the display reads hot, add the oil. Season the roast with salt and pepper and use tongs to lower it into the pot. Sear on all sides, 3 to 4 minutes each side. Press cancel.

2. Arrange the onion, garlic, carrots, and potatoes around the roast. Pour in the stock and add the Worcestershire sauce.

3. Secure the lid and cook on high pressure for 60 minutes, then allow the pressure to naturally release, about 10 minutes. Open the vent at the top and remove the lid. Press cancel.

4. Transfer the roast and vegetables to a serving platter. Let rest while you make the gravy. Strain the beef stock into a bowl, discarding the fat solids. Return all but 2 tablespoons of the stock to the pot and select sauté. Whisk the cornstarch into the reserved stock in the bowl, then stir the slurry into the pot and bring to a simmer, stirring often, for 5 minutes, or until thickened. Taste and season with more salt, pepper, or Worcestershire sauce if desired. Pour the gravy into a gravy boat.

5. Serve the pot roast and veggies with the gravy and garnish with fresh thyme.

Recipe Tip Tough cuts of meat like shoulder and chuck roasts are perfect for electric pressure cookers, which tenderize the fibrous, marbled meat faster and more efficiently than oven heat.

Variation Tip To make this dish Paleo, omit the cornstarch, potatoes, and Worcestershire sauce.

PER SERVING Calories: 891; Total fat: 30g; Saturated fat: 8g; Cholesterol: 228mg; Carbohydrates: 48g; Fiber: 1g; Protein: 101g

SERVES **2**

PREP TIME: 5 minutes

COOK TIME: 1 hour

TOTAL TIME: 1 hour 15 minutes

PRESSURE LEVEL: High

RELEASE: Natural

2 tablespoons oil, plus more if needed

½ pound beef chuck roast, cut into 4 equal pieces

Kosher salt

Freshly ground black pepper

1 small onion, diced

1 carrot, diced

1 celery stalk, diced

3 garlic cloves, smashed

½ cup dry red wine

1 (14.5-ounce) can diced tomatoes with their juices

1 tablespoon tomato paste

½ cup Beef Stock (page 168)

2 thyme sprigs or ¼ teaspoon dried thyme

1 rosemary sprig, chopped, or ½ teaspoon dried rosemary

1 bay leaf

6 ounces pappardelle, boiled until al dente

TO SERVE

• Grated Parmesan cheese

• Chopped fresh parsley

BEEF RAGÙ WITH PAPPARDELLE

WORTH THE WAIT

Luscious, comforting, and filling, this shredded beef dish might make you question why you ever ate spaghetti with regular meat sauce. Making it in your electric pressure cooker slashes the cook time in half, bringing you that much closer to juicy tomato, savory garlic, and big, fat pappardelle noodles covered in delicious sauce.

1. Preheat the pressure cooker pot on sauté mode. When the display reads hot, add 2 tablespoons of oil and heat until shimmering. Season the beef with salt and pepper. When the oil is hot, add the beef to the pot and sear for 3 minutes, turning to brown on all sides. Transfer the beef to a plate and set aside.

2. Heat more oil in the pot, if needed, add the onion, carrot, and celery, and cook for 4 to 5 minutes, stirring frequently, until the vegetables begin to soften. Add the garlic and cook for 1 minute. Stir in the wine and deglaze the pot, scraping up the browned bits from the bottom with a wooden spoon and stirring them into the liquid. Cook until the wine is reduced by half, about 2 minutes, then press cancel.

3. Return the beef to the pot and stir in the tomatoes with their juices, the tomato paste, beef stock, thyme, rosemary, and bay leaf and season with salt and pepper.

4. Secure the lid and cook on high pressure for 30 minutes, then allow the pressure to naturally release, about 10 minutes. Open the vent at the top, remove the lid, and return the cooker to sauté mode. →

5. Using two forks, shred the beef in the pot. Let the sauce cook down for 10 to 15 minutes, stirring occasionally, until thickened. In the last 3 to 5 minutes, stir in the al dente pasta.

6. Discard the bay leaf. Divide the meat and pasta between two bowls. Top with grated Parmesan cheese and chopped parsley.

Recipe Tip Though pronounced the same way, ragù should not be confused with ragout. Ragù is an Italian pasta sauce made with ground or minced meat, vegetables, and tomatoes. Ragout is a slow-cooked French–style stew made with meat and vegetables, often eaten with polenta or couscous.

PER SERVING Calories: 1,213; Total fat: 34g; Saturated fat: 9g; Cholesterol: 502mg; Carbohydrates: 132g; Fiber: 12g; Protein: 84g

PRESSURE LEVEL: High
RELEASE: Quick

2 teaspoons sesame oil

12 ounces thinly sliced uncooked beef roast

Freshly ground black pepper

½ small onion, chopped

3 garlic cloves, minced

½ cup Beef Stock (page 168)

¼ cup low-sodium soy sauce

2 tablespoons packed brown sugar

Pinch red pepper flakes (optional)

1 tablespoon cornstarch

8 ounces fresh broccoli florets

TO SERVE

- Cooked white or brown rice, or Takeout-Style Fried Rice (page 43)
- Sesame seeds

BEEF AND BROCCOLI

30 MINUTES OR LESS | LIGHT AND HEALTHY | PALEO-FRIENDLY

Skip the Chinese buffet and make a tasty—and healthy—beef and broccoli dinner at home! Feel free to adjust the sweet-to-salt balance to your liking and leave out the red pepper flakes altogether if you're not looking for heat.

1. Preheat the pressure cooker pot on sauté mode. When the display reads hot, add the sesame oil. Season the beef with black pepper, add to the pot, and brown on all sides, about 1 minute per side. Transfer to a plate and set aside. Add the onion and garlic to the pot and sauté until softened, 2 minutes.

2. Add the stock and deglaze the pot, scraping up the browned bits from the bottom with a wooden spoon and stirring them into the liquid. Stir in the soy sauce, brown sugar, and red pepper flakes (if using). Stir until the sugar is dissolved, then return the beef to the pot with any juices from the plate.

3. Secure the lid and cook on high pressure for 10 minutes, then quick release the pressure in the pot and remove the lid. Press cancel and select sauté.

4. Transfer about 2 tablespoons of liquid from the pot to a small bowl. Whisk it together with the cornstarch, then add back to the pot along with the broccoli. Loosely cover with the lid and let simmer for 3 to 4 minutes, or until the sauce is thick and the broccoli is softened. Taste and adjust the seasonings as desired.

5. Serve the beef and broccoli over a scoop of rice and sprinkle with sesame seeds.

Recipe Tip Save yourself even more time by using the pot-in-pot method to cook the rice at the same time as the beef! Just combine 1 cup salted water and 1 cup rice in a metal bowl, place it on a trivet, and let it go.

Variation Tip To make this dish Paleo, omit the soy sauce, brown sugar, cornstarch, and rice.

PER SERVING Calories: 506; Total fat: 16g; Saturated fat: 5g; Cholesterol: 152mg; Carbohydrates: 31g; Fiber: 4g; Protein: 59g

Eight
KITCHEN STAPLES

From stocks to sauces to yogurt, you'll find yourself using the recipes in this chapter often. A variety of easy stocks and broths will enhance all of the soup recipes, and since the pressure cooker relies on liquid, they'll also add layers of flavor to any other meal that calls for water. The sauces range from a classic marinara to a versatile spicy chipotle chile–based adobo blend to two very different but equally popular barbecue sauces. Sweet sauces and yogurt elevate your breakfasts and desserts.

Citrus Marmalade, page 181

Chicken Stock 167

Beef Stock 168

Bone Broth 169

Vegetable Stock 170

Easy Marinara Sauce 171

Red Garden Salsa 172

Classic Barbecue Sauce 173

Carolina Mustard Barbecue Sauce 174

Adobo Barbacoa Sauce 175

Greek Yogurt 176

Homestyle Applesauce 178

Apple Butter 179

Holiday Cranberry Sauce 180

Citrus Marmalade 181

Strawberry Compote 183

MAKES 1 QUART
PREP TIME: 5 minutes
COOK TIME: 1 hour
TOTAL TIME: 1 hour 30 minutes

PRESSURE LEVEL: High
RELEASE: Natural

2 pounds chicken bones and parts

1 large garlic clove, smashed (optional)

¼ teaspoon kosher salt (optional)

8 cups water

CHICKEN STOCK

5-INGREDIENT | PALEO | WORTH THE WAIT

Chicken stock is as ubiquitous as water in my kitchen. More often than not, it's from a carton, but when I save up enough bones from chicken dinner nights, a batch of stock isn't far behind. This recipe is more bone broth-ish, in that it lacks any sort of vegetable, but it is no less nutritious or useful than its counterpart.

1. Add the chicken bones and parts and the garlic (if using) to the pressure cooker pot and add the salt (if using). Pour in the water, making sure the chicken is completely submerged.

2. Secure the lid and cook on high for 60 minutes, then allow the pressure to naturally release, about 15 minutes. Open the vent at the top and remove the lid. Press cancel.

3. Over a large bowl, carefully strain the stock through a fine-mesh strainer. Let cool, then pour into clean jars, leaving about ½ inch headroom, and refrigerate for several hours or overnight. Remove the layer of fat that forms on the top, if desired.

4. Store in the refrigerator for up to 4 days or in the freezer for 6 to 12 months.

Ingredient Tip This is the single best way to recycle leftover chicken parts, skin, meat, and bones: Dedicate a one-gallon zip-top freezer bag to storing leftover parts, adding to it until you have enough for a chicken stock recipe. If you'd like a more vegetable-forward stock, feel free to add scraps of onion, carrot, and celery stalks to the pot before cooking.

PER SERVING (1 CUP) Calories: 55; Total fat: 3g; Saturated fat: 1g; Cholesterol: 0mg; Carbohydrates: 8g; Fiber: 0g; Protein: 6g

MAKES 1 QUART

PREP TIME: 10 minutes

COOK TIME: 1 hour 15 minutes

TOTAL TIME: 2 hours

PRESSURE LEVEL: High

RELEASE: Natural

1 tablespoon oil

2 pounds meaty beef bones

¼ teaspoon kosher salt
(optional)

8 cups water

BEEF STOCK

5-INGREDIENT | PALEO | WORTH THE WAIT

A richer, more robust stock, beef stock rounds out the heartiest of cold-weather meals. If there were a list of the top-10 uses for an electric pressure cooker, broths and stocks would be at the top. The technique infuses massive flavor in a much shorter time than traditional preparation. Searing the bones is optional, but roasting them in the oven before loading into the cooker introduces an even deeper flavor.

1. Preheat the pressure cooker pot on sauté mode. When the display reads hot, add the oil. Working in batches to prevent overcrowding, add the beef bones in a single layer and sear on each side. Sprinkle with the salt (if using).

2. Pour in the water, ensuring that the bones are completely submerged with 1 inch to spare.

3. Secure the lid and cook on high pressure for 75 minutes, then allow the pressure to naturally release, about 15 minutes. Open the vent at the top and remove the lid. Press cancel.

4. Over a large bowl, carefully strain the stock through a fine-mesh strainer. Let cool, pour into clean jars, leaving about ½ inch headroom, and refrigerate for several hours or overnight. Remove the layer of fat that forms on the top, if desired.

5. Store in the refrigerator for up to 4 days or in the freezer for 6 to 12 months.

Ingredient Tip Make your dinner for two that much easier: Before freezing the stock, divide it into 1-cup portions and pour into small zip-top freezer bags. Pull out the amount you need for the recipe you're making and thaw in the refrigerator.

PER SERVING (1 CUP) Calories: 54; Total fat: 1g; Saturated fat: 0g; Cholesterol: 0mg; Carbohydrates: 0g; Fiber: 0g; Protein: 4g

MAKES 1 QUART
PREP TIME: 10 minutes
COOK TIME: 1 hour 30 minutes
TOTAL TIME: 2 hours 30 minutes

PRESSURE LEVEL: High
RELEASE: Natural

1 tablespoon oil

2 pounds meaty bones (beef, pork, chicken)

½ teaspoon kosher salt (optional)

1 large onion, quartered

1 celery stalk, cut into large chunks

2 carrots, cut into large chunks

2 to 3 thyme or parsley sprigs

2 teaspoons apple cider vinegar

8 cups water

BONE BROTH

PALEO | WORTH THE WAIT

Warming, soothing, nutritious bone broth is an oldie but a goodie. Essentially a riff on every other kind of stock, it's enjoying a newfound place in the spotlight as a natural remedy and overall health booster. Instead of spending a ton of money on it at the grocery store or from a takeout place, make it at home with all the meat bone scraps you save from the week. It's frugal, too!

1. Preheat the pressure cooker pot on sauté mode. When the display reads hot, add the oil. Working in batches to prevent overcrowding, add the bones in a single layer and sear on both sides. Sprinkle the bones with the salt (if using).

2. Add the onion, celery, carrots, and thyme to the pot. Pour in the vinegar and water, ensuring that everything is completely submerged.

3. Secure the lid and cook on high pressure for 90 minutes, then allow the pressure to naturally release, about 15 minutes. Open the vent at the top and remove the lid. Press cancel.

4. Over a large bowl, carefully strain the stock through a fine-mesh strainer. Let cool, then pour into jars, leaving about ½ inch headroom, and refrigerate for several hours or overnight. Remove the layer of fat that forms on top, if desired.

5. Store in the refrigerator for up to 4 days or in the freezer for 6 to 12 months.

Variation Tip Thanksgiving or Christmas come and gone? Throw your leftover turkey and ham bones and parts in the freezer and prepare for that New Year's detox!

PER SERVING (1 CUP) Calories: 65; Total fat: 3g; Saturated fat: 0g; Cholesterol: 0mg; Carbohydrates: 1g; Fiber: 0g; Protein: 4g

MAKE 1 QUART
PREP TIME: 5 minutes
COOK TIME: 1 hour
TOTAL TIME: 1 hour 30 minutes

PRESSURE LEVEL: High
RELEASE: Natural

2 onions, quartered

2 celery stalks, cut into large chunks

2 carrots, peeled and cut into large chunks

8 ounces portobello mushrooms, halved

4 large garlic cloves, smashed

1 small bunch fresh herbs (parsley, thyme, rosemary, sage, oregano), tied into a bouquet

¼ teaspoon kosher salt (optional)

8 cups water

VEGETABLE STOCK

LIGHT AND HEALTHY | PALEO | VEGAN | VEGETARIAN | WORTH THE WAIT

For all the meatless Monday and vegetarian recipes you'll ever make, this veggie stock adds more layers of flavor than you might imagine. Grab extra veggies at the farmers' market, save your carrot and celery tops—however you do it, make this stock happen.

1. To the pressure cooker pot, add the onions, celery, carrots, mushrooms, garlic, herbs, and salt (if using). Pour in the water, ensuring that the everything is completely submerged.

2. Secure the lid and cook on high pressure for 60 minutes, then allow the pressure to naturally release, about 15 minutes. Open the vent at the top and remove the lid. Press cancel.

3. Over a large bowl, carefully strain the stock through a fine-mesh strainer. Let cool, then pour into clean jars, leaving about ½ inch headroom. Refrigerate for several hours or overnight.

4. Store in the refrigerator for up to 4 days or in the freezer for 6 to 12 months.

Variation Tip Vegetable stock is a great way to clean out your crisper drawer. As long as your stock includes the trinity (onion, celery, carrots), feel free to add any good vegetable scraps you have on hand, like fennel, leeks, green onions, or potatoes.

PER SERVING (1 CUP) Calories: 42; Total fat: 0g; Saturated fat: 0g; Cholesterol: 0mg; Carbohydrates: 4g; Fiber: 0g; Protein: 0g

MAKES 1 QUART
PREP TIME: 5 minutes
COOK TIME: 10 minutes
TOTAL TIME: 30 minutes

PRESSURE LEVEL: High
RELEASE: Quick

2 tablespoons oil

1 medium onion, grated

3 garlic cloves,
coarsely chopped

1 (28-ounce) can or carton
whole or crushed tomatoes

2 oregano sprigs or
½ teaspoon dried oregano

1 teaspoon kosher salt, plus
more for seasoning

Freshly ground black pepper

Pinch granulated or raw sugar
(optional)

EASY MARINARA SAUCE

30 MINUTES OR LESS | 5-INGREDIENT | PALEO-FRIENDLY | VEGAN
VEGETARIAN

You don't have to be Italian to make a good marinara.
You also don't have to cook it over the stove for hours.
Try this recipe and forget that the prepared jarred stuff
even exists. This sauce is versatile and perfect for all
your pastas and pizza. Just make sure it begins with
high-quality tomatoes like the famous San Marzano
variety.

1. Preheat the pressure cooker pot on sauté mode. When the
display reads hot, add the oil. Add the onion and sauté until
softened, 2 minutes. Add the garlic and cook for 1 minute.

2. Add the tomatoes, oregano, and salt and stir to combine.

3. Secure the cooker lid and cook on high pressure for 10 minutes, then quick release the pressure in the pot and remove the
lid. Press cancel.

4. Stir and taste, seasoning with salt and pepper as desired. Add
a pinch of sugar to balance the acidity of the tomatoes, if desired.

5. Store in clean lidded jars in the refrigerator for up to 4 days or
freeze for up to 6 months.

Variation Tip For a twist on the classic, add freshly chopped
basil after cooking. If you're looking for a bit of heat, sauté a diced
jalapeño with the onion, or toss in a pinch of red pepper flakes.
For a Paleo recipe, omit the granulated sugar.

PER SERVING (1 CUP) Calories: 94; Total fat: 7g; Saturated fat: 1g; Cholesterol: 0mg;
Carbohydrates: 7g; Fiber: 2g; Protein: 1g

MAKES 5 CUPS

PREP TIME: 5 minutes

COOK TIME: 10 minutes

TOTAL TIME: 30 minutes

PRESSURE LEVEL: High

RELEASE: Natural

2 cups diced fresh tomatoes

1 medium red onion, diced

1 green bell pepper, stemmed, seeded, and diced

1 jalapeño pepper, stemmed, seeded, and diced

2 canned chipotle chiles in adobo sauce (optional)

3 garlic cloves, minced

1 (8-ounce) can tomato sauce

1 tablespoon apple cider vinegar

3 teaspoons ground cumin

3 teaspoons kosher salt

RED GARDEN SALSA

30 MINUTES OR LESS | PALEO | VEGAN | VEGETARIAN

It might surprise you how great it is to have homemade salsa on hand. Not only is it a perfect chip dipper, but this fresh, bright kitchen staple is also excellent on tacos, salads, and egg-based breakfast dishes. It also makes a wonderful substitute when you're out of canned tomatoes.

1. To the pot of the pressure cooker, add the tomatoes, onion, bell pepper, jalapeño, chipotles (if using), garlic, and tomato sauce.

2. Secure the lid and cook on high pressure for 10 minutes, then allow the pressure to naturally release, about 10 minutes. Open the vent at the top and remove the lid. Press cancel.

3. Stir the vinegar, cumin, and salt into the pot. Taste and adjust the seasonings if necessary. Transfer 3 cups of the salsa to a bowl, then use an immersion or countertop blender to purée the rest of the salsa until mostly smooth. Return the reserved salsa to the pot.

4. Store in a covered jar in the refrigerator for up to 4 days or in the freezer for 3 to 4 months.

Variation Tip If you don't have fresh tomatoes on hand, using a 14-ounce can of diced tomatoes will work in a pinch. You can also adjust the heat levels in this salsa by using more, fewer, or different chiles, depending on your taste.

PER SERVING (½ CUP) Calories: 30; Total fat: 1g; Saturated fat: Og; Cholesterol: Omg; Carbohydrates: 6g; Fiber: 2g; Protein: 1g

MAKES ABOUT 4 CUPS
PREP TIME: 5 minutes
COOK TIME: 10 minutes
TOTAL TIME: 30 minutes

PRESSURE LEVEL: High
RELEASE: Natural

1 tablespoon oil

1 small onion,
roughly chopped

3 garlic cloves, minced

1 cup tomato sauce

½ cup ketchup

¼ cup apple cider vinegar

¼ cup honey

2 tablespoons molasses

½ tablespoon kosher salt

¼ teaspoon freshly ground
black pepper

1 teaspoon liquid smoke
(optional)

Pinch of cayenne pepper
(optional)

CLASSIC BARBECUE SAUCE

30 MINUTES OR LESS | PALEO-FRIENDLY | VEGAN | VEGETARIAN

Grilled and smoked meats are always better slathered in sticky, tangy, finger-lickin'-good barbecue sauce. Making your own is easy and satisfying, especially when the rave reviews from your dinner companions come rolling in. The flavors intensify after a day or two, so don't be afraid to make a lot and keep it in the fridge—you'll be putting it on everything.

1. Preheat the pressure cooker pot on sauté mode. When the display reads hot, add the oil. Add the onion and sauté until softened, 3 to 4 minutes. Add the garlic and cook for 1 minute.

2. Add the tomato sauce, ketchup, vinegar, honey, molasses, salt, pepper, and the liquid smoke and cayenne pepper (if using), scraping up any browned bits from the bottom with a wooden spoon and stirring them into the sauce.

3. Secure the lid and cook on high pressure for 10 minutes, then allow the pressure to naturally release, about 10 minutes. Open the vent at the top and remove the lid. Press cancel.

4. Using an immersion or countertop blender, purée the sauce until smooth. Taste and adjust the seasonings, adding more salt, vinegar, honey, liquid smoke, or cayenne pepper as desired. If you'd like to thicken the sauce, select sauté and simmer with the lid off, stirring frequently, until it reaches your desired consistency.

5. Store in an airtight jar in the refrigerator for up to 12 days or in the freezer (leave ½ inch headroom in the jar for expansion from freezing) for up to 6 months.

Ingredient Tip Liquid smoke and cayenne pepper are optional in this recipe but add a depth of flavor that lends itself well to pressure-cooked meats that are normally smoked.

Variation Tip To make this recipe Paleo, omit the ketchup and molasses.

PER SERVING (½ CUP) Calories: 91; Total fat: 2g; Saturated fat: 0.3g; Cholesterol: 0mg; Carbohydrates: 19g; Fiber: 1g; Protein: 1g

MAKE ABOUT 3 CUPS
PREP TIME: 5 minutes
COOK TIME: 5 minutes
TOTAL TIME: 15 minutes

PRESSURE LEVEL: High
RELEASE: Natural

2 cups yellow mustard

⅔ cup apple cider vinegar

½ cup honey

½ cup amber beer or water

2 tablespoons ketchup

2 teaspoons garlic powder

2 teaspoons onion powder

2 teaspoons kosher salt

Pinch freshly ground
black pepper

2 tablespoons butter

½ teaspoon cayenne pepper
(optional)

CAROLINA MUSTARD BARBECUE SAUCE

30 MINUTES OR LESS | COMFORT FOOD | PALEO-FRIENDLY
VEGAN | VEGETARIAN

The United States has no shortage of food competition events, including one for barbecue sauce. Unlike the standard sweet ketchup-based sauce that is loved by the Northern regions, the German-settled Carolinas love their vinegar-based varieties. This mustard-heavy recipe is enjoyable on just about anything, but especially pulled pork and brisket.

1. Put the mustard, vinegar, honey, beer, ketchup, garlic powder, onion powder, salt, pepper, butter, and cayenne pepper (if using) in the pressure cooker pot and stir well. Secure the lid and cook on high pressure for 5 minutes, then allow the pressure to naturally release, about 5 minutes. Open the vent at the top and remove the lid. Press cancel.

2. Using an immersion or countertop blender, purée the sauce until smooth. Taste and adjust the seasonings, adding more salt, vinegar, or honey as desired. If you'd like to thicken the sauce, select sauté and simmer with the lid off, stirring often, until it reaches your desired consistency. When cool, pour into clean jars, leaving about ½ inch headroom.

3. Cover and store in the refrigerator for up to 12 days or in the freezer for up to 6 months.

Variation Tip This recipe is versatile and can easily be adapted to your tastes. Parts of the Carolinas lean heavier on the vinegar, while some favor the honey. Experiment with the blend until you find one you love. For this recipe to be Paleo, omit the beer, ketchup, and butter.

PER SERVING (½ CUP) Calories: 200; Total fat: 7g; Saturated fat: 3g; Cholesterol: 10mg; Carbohydrates: 31g; Fiber: 3g; Protein: 4g

MAKES ABOUT **2 CUPS**
PREP TIME: **10** minutes
COOK TIME: **5** minutes
TOTAL TIME: **15** minutes

PRESSURE LEVEL: None
RELEASE: None

2 large dried guajillo chiles, stemmed and seeded

1½ cups hot water

2 teaspoons oil

½ onion, sliced

5 garlic cloves, smashed

2 teaspoons kosher salt, divided

¼ cup white wine

¼ cup Vegetable Stock (page 170)

2 to 3 canned chipotle chiles in adobo sauce

1 tablespoon apple cider vinegar

1 teaspoon ground cumin

½ teaspoon dried oregano

½ teaspoon paprika

¼ teaspoon sugar or honey

ADOBO BARBACOA SAUCE

30 MINUTES OR LESS | PALEO-FRIENDLY | VEGAN | VEGETARIAN

This spicy chile-based sauce was originally developed solely to be the main flavor component of the Barbacoa Bella Burrito Bowls (page 78). It found its new home as a solo sauce, a move that boded well for my culinary development. Keep a jar of this in your fridge when you want to add smoky heat to your dinner.

1. Place the guajillo chiles in a shallow bowl and cover with the hot water for 15 minutes to rehydrate.

2. Meanwhile, preheat the pressure cooker pot on sauté mode. When the display reads hot, add the oil to the pot and heat until shimmering. Add the onion, garlic, and 1½ teaspoons of salt and sauté until the onion is browned and softened, about 5 minutes.

3. Stir in the wine and deglaze the pot, scraping up the browned bits from the bottom with a wooden spoon and stirring them into the liquid. Add the stock and simmer until reduced by half, 3 to 4 minutes.

4. Carefully transfer the contents of the pot to a blender, along with the rehydrated chiles and ½ cup of their soaking liquid, the chipotles chiles, vinegar, cumin, oregano, paprika, sugar, and the remaining ½ teaspoon of salt. Blend until smooth. When cool, transfer to clean airtight jars, leaving about ½ inch headroom.

5. Store in the refrigerator for up to 12 days or in the freezer for up to 6 months.

Cooking Tip This sauce is a delicious addition to many recipes in the book, and it can be used to add flavor to soups and stews, other sauces, and even as a delicious barbecue-style sauce for baked chicken.

Variation Tip To make the recipe Paleo, omit the wine and sugar.

PER SERVING (½ CUP) Calories: 63; Total fat: 3g; Saturated fat: 0g; Cholesterol: 0mg; Carbohydrates: 7g; Fiber: 2g; Protein: 1g

MAKES 4 CUPS

PREP TIME: 5 minutes

COOK TIME: 9 hours

TOTAL TIME: 24 hours

PRESSURE LEVEL: None

RELEASE SETTING: None

½ gallon whole milk

2 tablespoons yogurt starter (purchased Greek yogurt with active bacterial cultures)

1 tablespoon vanilla extract (optional)

GREEK YOGURT

LIGHT AND HEALTHY | VEGETARIAN | WORTH THE WAIT

Why buy single-serve cartons of Greek yogurt at the store when you can easily make a fresh batch at home? Whether you're mixing it into your morning oatmeal, blending it into a smoothie, using it as a base for French onion dip, or eating it plain with a bit of honey and crunchy granola as a post-workout snack, you'll never regret the time spent patiently waiting for your pressure cooker timer to go off!

1. Pour the milk into the cooker pot. Secure the lid and follow the directions in your pressure cooker manual to use the yogurt function to boil the milk to at least 180°F. Open the lid (yogurt-making does not require pressure, so no need to wait) after 35 to 40 minutes and stir the milk, then use a kitchen thermometer to check the temperature in a few spots to ensure it's over 180°F. Return the cooker to the yogurt function if necessary until it reaches at least 180°F.

2. When the milk reaches temperature, remove the pot from the cooker and place it on a cooling rack. Allow the milk to cool to 110°F, stirring occasionally to blend in any hot spots. Alternatively, you can cool it faster (in about 5 minutes) by filling your kitchen sink with cold tap water and partially submerging the pot in it, stirring frequently.

3. When the milk has reached 110°F (remove the pot from the water and dry it off thoroughly if you used the quick-cooling method), transfer ½ cup milk from the pot into a bowl and whisk the yogurt starter in. Return this mixture to the pot and stir gently. Stir in the vanilla (if using).

4. Return the pot to the pressure cooker. Secure the lid and follow the directions in your pressure cooker manual to use the yogurt function to incubate the yogurt. The default time is 8 hours, but if you prefer to make the Greek yogurt more tart, set the time to 9 or 10 hours instead. At 6 hours, it will be set enough for you to taste-test.

5. When the incubation period has counted down, remove the lid and strain the whey from the yogurt. Options for doing this include either using a Greek yogurt maker; a nut milk bag hung from a cabinet knob and set over a large bowl; or a fine-mesh strainer lined with cheesecloth, set over a large bowl.

6. Allow the yogurt to strain for 3 to 12 hours until it reaches the desired consistency. You can also let it strain in the refrigerator.

7. Place the finished yogurt in large glass jars or single-serve jars with lids. Refrigerate for up to 14 days.

Cooking Tip If your yogurt gets too thick, whisk in some whey (the liquid you drained off in Step 5) to thin it out to the desired consistency.

PER SERVING (½ CUP) Calories: 168; Total fat: 8g; Saturated fat: 5g; Cholesterol: 25mg; Carbohydrates: 12g; Fiber: 0g; Protein: 10g

MAKES ABOUT 6 CUPS

PREP TIME: 10 minutes

COOK TIME: 7 minutes

TOTAL TIME: 30 minutes

PRESSURE LEVEL: High

RELEASE: Natural

¼ cup water

4 pounds unpeeled organic apples, cored and roughly chopped

1 tablespoon ground cinnamon

1 teaspoon vanilla extract

¼ teaspoon kosher salt

¼ teaspoon nutmeg (optional)

HOMESTYLE APPLESAUCE

5-INGREDIENT | 30 MINUTES OR LESS | PALEO | VEGAN | VEGETARIAN

Any apples can be used in this recipe, depending on the season, but using both organic Honeycrisp and Granny Smith will yield a perfect mix of sweet and tart. Not only is this applesauce nutritious and delicious on its own, it's also incredibly versatile! Try it on yogurt, ice cream, or waffles, or use it in place of oil in your favorite baked goods.

1. Add the water to your pressure cooker pot, then add the apples, cinnamon, vanilla, salt, and nutmeg (if using). Secure the lid and cook on high for 7 minutes, then allow the pressure to naturally release, about 5 minutes. Open the vent at the top and remove the lid. Press cancel.

2. Using an immersion blender, or in batches using a countertop blender, carefully blend the applesauce to the desired texture. It will thicken more when it cools. Spoon into clean glass jars, leaving about ½ inch headroom.

3. Store in the refrigerator for up to 10 days or in the freezer for 8 to 10 months.

Ingredient Tip Apples are considered one of the Dirty Dozen (see the Dirty Dozen™ and Clean Fifteen™ charts on page 218); nonorganic varieties often have elevated levels of pesticides. This recipe calls for unpeeled organic apples, so there's no concern, but whichever kind of apples you use, always be sure to wash them thoroughly first. Almost all the dietary fiber in apples is found in the skin, and since the sauce is blended after it is cooked, you end up with a perfectly smooth (or chunky), nutritious applesauce.

PER SERVING (½ CUP) Calories: 41; Total fat: 0g; Saturated fat: 0g; Cholesterol: 0mg; Carbohydrates: 11g; Fiber: 2g; Protein: 0g

MAKES ABOUT 3 CUPS

PREP TIME: 10 minutes

COOK TIME: 7 minutes

TOTAL TIME: 1 hour 30 minutes

PRESSURE LEVEL: High

RELEASE: Natural

¼ cup water

4 pounds unpeeled organic sweet apples, cored and roughly chopped

2 tablespoons packed brown sugar

2 teaspoons ground cinnamon

½ teaspoon ground nutmeg

Pinch kosher salt

2 tablespoons freshly squeezed lemon juice

APPLE BUTTER

5-INGREDIENT | PALEO-FRIENDLY | VEGAN | VEGETARIAN WORTH THE WAIT

Apple butter is the older, more mature sister of apple-sauce. It's a spread worthy of humble toast, fluffy biscuits, and hearty waffles. Using your pressure cooker to cook it down keeps your ingredient list short. You won't find any sugar substitute in the homemade kind, but you will find all of the comforting autumn vibes apple butter is known for.

1. Add the water to your pressure cooker pot, then add the apples, brown sugar, cinnamon, nutmeg, salt, and lemon juice. Secure the lid and cook on high pressure for 7 minutes, then allow the pressure to naturally release, about 20 minutes. Open the vent at the top and remove the lid. Press cancel.

2. Using an immersion blender, or in batches using a countertop blender, blend the apples to the desired texture. Taste and adjust seasonings and spices as desired.

3. Select sauté and loosely cover the cooker with the lid. Let the apple butter simmer for 30 to 60 minutes, stirring occasionally, until it's thickened and browned to the desired color. Spoon into glass jars, leaving about ½ inch headroom, and store in the refrigerator for up to 10 days or in the freezer for 8 to 10 months.

Ingredient Tip Depending on your taste and the variety of apples you use, you can leave out the brown sugar completely for a Paleo apple butter that's to die for.

PER SERVING (¼ CUP) Calories: 46; Total fat: 0g; Saturated fat: 0g; Cholesterol: 0mg; Carbohydrates: 12g; Fiber: 2g; Protein: 0g

MAKES ABOUT 2 CUPS
PREP TIME: 5 minutes
COOK TIME: 3 minutes
TOTAL TIME: 15 minutes

PRESSURE LEVEL: High
RELEASE: Natural

12 ounces fresh or frozen cranberries, rinsed and picked over

Grated zest and juice of 1 large orange (about ¼ cup of juice)

2 tablespoons honey

½ teaspoon ground cinnamon (optional)

Pinch kosher salt

HOLIDAY CRANBERRY SAUCE

5-INGREDIENT | 30 MINUTES OR LESS | PALEO | VEGETARIAN

The holidays just aren't complete without a bowl of cranberry sauce on the table. This homemade one is tart and sweet and kissed with plenty of orange—a far cry from the shapely canned slices you may remember from your childhood. A bit of cinnamon adds another layer of flavor to the final product.

1. Put the cranberries, orange zest and juice, honey, cinnamon (if using), and salt in the pot of the pressure cooker and stir to combine. Secure the lid and cook on high pressure for 3 minutes, then allow the pressure to naturally release, about 5 minutes. Open the vent at the top and remove the lid. Press cancel.

2. Stir and break up the cranberries with a wooden spoon. Taste and adjust the flavors as desired, perhaps adding a touch more honey or salt. If using frozen berries results in extra liquid, select sauté and simmer uncovered until the sauce thickens. Spoon into clean glass jars, leaving about ½ inch headroom.

3. Store in the refrigerator for up to 3 weeks or in the freezer for up to 6 months.

Serving Tip Cranberry sauce is a natural side for a turkey dinner, but it's also delicious served with simple pork tenderloin or roast beef.

PER SERVING (⅓ CUP) Calories: 67; Total fat: 0g; Saturated fat: 0g; Cholesterol: 0mg; Carbohydrates: 15g; Fiber: 3g; Protein: 0g

PRESSURE LEVEL: High
RELEASE: Natural

1 cup water

1 pound assorted citrus fruits

½ pound sugar, plus more as desired

CITRUS MARMALADE

5-INGREDIENT | 30 MINUTES OR LESS | VEGAN | VEGETARIAN

Marmalade, is a lovely, sophisticated breakfast spread for toast, warm croissants, pancakes, or crêpes. Standard orange marmalade, or *confiture d'orange*, is delicious, but try using other citrus types in this recipe. The flavors are fantastic, and the multicolored peels in the finished product look like edible stained glass in their jars.

1. Add the water to the pot of your pressure cooker.

2. Wash the citrus fruits, scrubbing to remove any waxy coating on the skin. Dry thoroughly. Use a mandoline or very sharp knife to thinly slice the fruit. Stack the slices and quarter them, then place in the pot along with any juices on the cutting board. Add ½ pound of sugar and stir to dissolve.

3. Secure the lid and cook on high pressure for 10 minutes, then allow the pressure to naturally release, about 10 minutes. Open the vent at the top and remove the lid. Press cancel, then select sauté.

Bring the marmalade to a simmer and cook, stirring frequently to avoid scorching, until it reaches 212°F. It will be very thin. Once it comes to temperature, press cancel. →

4. Let the marmalade cool for about 5 minutes. For marmalade without peel in it, firmly press it through a fine-mesh sieve to separate the jelly from the peel and discard the peel.

5. Spoon the marmalade into clean jars, leaving about ½ inch headroom. Store in the refrigerator for up to 10 days or in the freezer for up to 8 months.

Cooking Tip A candy thermometer is a great tool to have for recipes like these, but any kitchen thermometer that measures over 250°F will do. This marmalade can be easily canned with your pressure cooker, using the classic water bath method.

PER SERVING (¼ CUP) Calories: 89; Total fat: 0g; Saturated fat: 0g; Cholesterol: 0mg; Carbohydrates: 23g; Fiber: 1g; Protein: 0g

MAKES ABOUT 2 CUPS

PREP TIME: 5 minutes

COOK TIME: 1 minute

TOTAL TIME: 20 minutes

PRESSURE LEVEL: High

RELEASE: Natural

1 pound fresh strawberries, hulled

Grated zest and juice of ½ lemon (about 2 tablespoons juice)

2 tablespoons honey

Pinch kosher salt

Sugar (optional)

STRAWBERRY COMPOTE

5-INGREDIENT | 30 MINUTES OR LESS | PALEO-FRIENDLY | VEGETARIAN

Remember that time you bought a flat of strawberries at the farmers' market and a week later, they started to shrivel? You should have made them into compote. Strawberries get sweeter as they ripen off the vine, and even after they're past the point of enjoyment as a fruit, they can turn into a delicious, saucy compote for ice cream sundaes or an impressive stack of pancakes.

1. Add the strawberries, lemon zest and juice, honey, and salt to the cooker pot and stir well to combine. Secure the lid and cook on high pressure for 1 minute, then allow the pressure to naturally release, about 10 minutes. Open the vent at the top and remove the lid. Press cancel.

2. Stir and break up the strawberries with a wooden spoon. Taste and adjust the flavors as desired, adding sugar or a touch more honey if desired.

3. Spoon the compote into clean jars, leaving about ½ inch headroom. Store in the refrigerator for up to 12 days or in the freezer for 8 to 10 months.

Variation Tip This is a great basic recipe for any kind of fruit compote. Just replace the strawberries with whatever fruit you have on hand (blueberries, peaches, diced apples, etc.). You might have to adjust the sugar levels, depending on the type of fruit and its ripeness. For a Paleo version, omit the sugar.

PER SERVING (⅓ CUP) Calories: 47; Total fat: 0g; Saturated fat: 0g; Cholesterol: 0mg; Carbohydrates: 12g; Fiber: 2g; Protein: 1g

Nine
DESSERTS AND SWEET TREATS

One of the hardest things about watching what you eat comes in the form of a big, decadent chocolate cake. Once it's baked and sitting on the counter, the temptation to nibble is irresistible. But there is a solution to this problem: small-batch recipes made in your electric pressure cooker. Some of the recipes in this chapter (Crème Brûlée, Sticky Toffee Puddings, and Mini Bananas Foster Cheesecakes) are individually sized, made in 1-cup ramekins or small springform pans, vessels you'll use repeatedly when baking for two. Some of the recipes, like the Pineapple Upside-Down Cake and Tangy Key Lime Pie, are made in 7-inch pans, yielding more slices for when you can afford to consume calories a little more freely. Keep in mind when making these recipes that "baking" in a pressure cooker will result in considerably denser, heavier cakes than traditional oven baking. Your pressure cooker will, however, out-bake anything egg- or custard-based by miles, and in a much shorter time.

Mini White Chocolate—Cherry Bundt Cakes, page 203

Sticky Toffee Puddings 187

Coconut-Almond Rice Pudding 188

Crème Brûlée 189

Flan 191

Stout-Poached Pears 193

Peach Dumplings 194

Pineapple Upside-Down Cake 195

Tangy Key Lime Pie 197

Mini Crustless Pumpkin Pies 198

Cannoli Cheesecake 199

Mini Bananas Foster Cheesecakes 201

Mini White Chocolate—Cherry Bundt Cakes 203

Chocolate-Hazelnut Lava Cakes 205

Flourless Chocolate-Espresso Cake 206

Chocolate Peanut Butter Brownies 208

PREP TIME: 10 minutes

COOK TIME: 25 minutes

TOTAL TIME: 45 minutes

PRESSURE LEVEL: High
RELEASE: Quick

1½ tablespoons unsalted butter, at room temperature, plus more for greasing

¼ cup medjool dates, pitted and chopped

¼ cup boiling water

½ cup all-purpose flour

1 egg

½ teaspoon baking soda

Pinch kosher salt

1 tablespoon molasses

3 tablespoons packed brown sugar

3 tablespoons turbinado sugar

½ teaspoon vanilla extract

TO SERVE
• Caramel or toffee sauce

STICKY TOFFEE PUDDINGS

VEGETARIAN

Dense and moist sticky toffee pudding, sweetened with dates, actually has to be made in two parts: a cake and a sauce. If you're a baking whiz, an easy homemade toffee sauce will be a breeze. If not, a jar of the store-bought sauce will reign just as supreme on this classic British dessert.

1. Add 1 cup of water to your pressure cooker pot and place the trivet in the bottom. Butter two (1-cup) ramekins and set aside.

2. In a small bowl, combine the dates and boiling water to soften, 5 minutes. Mix and let cool. (Do not discard the water.)

3. Combine the flour, egg, baking soda, salt, molasses, brown sugar, turbinado sugar, and vanilla extract in a food processor or blender and pulse until just combined. Add the softened dates and ¼ cup of their soaking water and pulse until almost smooth.

4. Divide the batter evenly between the two prepared ramekins. Cover each with a piece of buttered foil, sealing well. Set the ramekins on the trivet in the pot, placing a third empty ramekin inside with them to ensure they don't jostle during cooking.

5. Secure the lid and cook on high pressure for 25 minutes, then quick release the pressure in the pot and remove the lid. Carefully remove the ramekins from the inner pot and put them on a cooling rack.

6. Remove the foil, turn the puddings out onto dessert plates, and serve warm with caramel or toffee sauce.

Serving Tip These puddings actually taste even better the day after they're cooked, as the flavors meld and deepen overnight. Cook them the day before serving, cover with plastic wrap, and refrigerate. When ready to serve, reheat to warm.

PER SERVING Calories: 413: Total fat: 11g; Saturated fat: 6g; Cholesterol: 105mg; Carbohydrates: 75g; Fiber: 3g; Protein: 7g

SERVES 2

PREP TIME: 5 minutes

COOK TIME: 12 minutes

TOTAL TIME: 30 minutes

PRESSURE LEVEL: High

RELEASE: Natural

1 tablespoon butter

½ cup Arborio rice

1 cup coconut milk, divided

¼ cup water

¼ cup sugar

½ teaspoon almond extract

¼ teaspoon ground cinnamon

Pinch kosher salt

TO SERVE

• Toasted sliced almonds

• Shredded coconut

COCONUT-ALMOND RICE PUDDING

30 MINUTES OR LESS | VEGETARIAN

This recipe is close to my heart and was inspired by a Norwegian Christmas Eve tradition. Before feasting on *fiskeboller* (fish balls) and potatoes with gravy, families must eat through a big pot of rice pudding until someone finds a single boiled almond, signifying a year of good luck. While coconut milk isn't traditionally used in the pudding, it adds a creaminess that is irresistible.

1. Preheat the pressure cooker pot on sauté mode. When the display reads hot, add the butter to melt. Add the rice and toast for 1 minute, stirring. Add ½ cup of coconut milk, the water, sugar, almond extract, cinnamon, and salt. Simmer for 1 to 2 minutes to dissolve the sugar.

2. Secure the lid and cook on high pressure for 12 minutes, then allow the pressure to naturally release, about 10 minutes. Open the vent at the top and remove the lid. Press cancel, then select sauté.

3. Stir the pudding and add the remaining ½ cup of coconut milk, stirring until the desired texture is reached. Divide between two bowls and garnish with toasted almonds and shredded coconut.

Variation Tip To reduce the calorie count but keep the coconut flavor, leave out the coconut milk and use coconut water instead.

PER SERVING Calories: 596; Total fat: 35g; Saturated fat: 29g; Cholesterol: 15mg; Carbohydrates: 70g; Fiber: 4g; Protein: 6g

PREP TIME: 5 minutes
COOK TIME: 10 minutes
TOTAL TIME: 30 minutes,
plus 2 hours to chill

PRESSURE LEVEL: High
RELEASE: Natural

2 egg yolks, lightly beaten

6 tablespoons sugar, divided

Pinch kosher salt

⅔ cup heavy cream

1 teaspoon vanilla extract

CRÈME BRÛLÉE

5-INGREDIENT | PALEO-FRIENDLY | VEGETARIAN | WORTH THE WAIT

Who knew burnt cream could taste so decadent? The rich custard in this crème brûlée comes together in 5 minutes, and it cooks in only twice the time. A handy-dandy kitchen torch makes the brûlée-ing easy, or, if you don't have one, your oven broiler will do the job. Make this Paleo and dairy-free by skipping the heavy cream and sugar and using coconut cream and coconut sugar instead.

1. Add 1 cup of water to your pressure cooker pot and place the trivet in the bottom.

2. In a medium bowl, whisk together the egg yolks, 4 tablespoons of sugar, and the salt. Add the cream and vanilla and whisk until well blended.

3. Divide the mixture between two (1-cup) ramekins and cover with foil. Set the ramekins on the trivet, placing a third empty ramekin next to them to ensure they don't jostle during cooking.

4. Secure the lid and cook on high pressure for 9 minutes, then allow the pressure to naturally release, about 10 minutes. Open the vent at the top and remove the lid. →

5. Using tongs, remove the ramekins from the pressure cooker, transfer to a heatproof surface, and let cool to room temperature. Cover with plastic wrap and refrigerate for at least 2 hours or up to 2 days.

6. When ready to serve, sprinkle the entire surface of each custard with 1 tablespoon of sugar. Caramelize the sugar with a kitchen torch or broil in the oven for 2 to 3 minutes, watching carefully, until the sugar is melted and browned.

Variation Tip This crème brûlée recipe is incredibly adaptable. Turn it into Spanish *crema catalana* by simmering the ⅔ cup of heavy cream with ¼ teaspoon of ground cinnamon and ½ tea-spoon of grated orange or lemon zest. When the mixture cools to room temperature, whisk it into the egg yolks, sugar, and salt, then follow the rest of the recipe as written, adding a sprinkle of nutmeg to the tops before torching.

PER SERVING Calories: 333; Total fat: 19g; Saturated fat: 11g; Cholesterol: 265mg; Carbohydrates: 38g; Fiber: 0g; Protein: 4g

SERVES 2
PREP TIME: 15 minutes
COOK TIME: 9 minutes
TOTAL TIME: 35 minutes,
plus 4 hours to chill

PRESSURE LEVEL: High
RELEASE SETTING: Natural

4 tablespoons raw
sugar, divided

3 tablespoons orange juice,
plus 2 teaspoons

½ cup heavy cream

1 teaspoon grated orange zest,
plus two pieces for garnish

½ teaspoon vanilla extract

Pinch kosher salt

1 egg

FLAN

VEGETARIAN | WORTH THE WAIT

Egg-based desserts are such a perfect fit for your pressure cooker, it would be a crime not to include a recipe for a traditional Mexican flan. This *flan de naranja* version is intensely flavored with refreshing orange and is loved throughout the Hispanic world for its citrusy flavor.

1. Add 1 cup of water to your pressure cooker pot and place the trivet in the bottom.

2. In a small saucepan set over medium heat on the stove top, heat 2 tablespoons of sugar and 2 teaspoons of orange juice. Cook, stirring constantly, until reduced and thickened, 3 to 4 minutes. Swirl the pan occasionally until the mixture takes on a dark golden brown color. Carefully pour the caramel liquid evenly into two (1-cup) ramekins, tilting the ramekins to coat the bottoms completely. Set aside.

3. In a clean small saucepan, heat the remaining 3 tablespoons of orange juice, the cream, and grated orange zest over medium heat. Add the remaining 2 tablespoons of sugar, the vanilla, and salt and stir until the sugar has fully dissolved. Remove from the heat.

4. In a medium bowl, beat the egg lightly. Temper it slowly by whisking in a little of the hot cream mixture at a time. Continue to whisk until all of the cream mixture is incorporated with the egg. $\longrightarrow$

5. Pour the egg-cream mixture through a fine-mesh strainer into the caramel-filled ramekins. Cover the ramekins with foil, set them on the trivet, and place a third empty ramekin next to them to ensure that they don't jostle during cooking.

6. Secure the pressure cooker lid and cook on high pressure for 9 minutes, then allow the pressure to naturally release, about 10 minutes. Open the vent at the top and remove the lid.

7. Using tongs, remove the ramekins from the pressure cooker, transfer to a heatproof surface, and let cool to room temperature. Cover with plastic wrap and refrigerate for at least 4 hours or up to 2 days. When ready to serve, run a small, sharp knife around the edges of the ramekins and invert the flan onto a plate. The melted caramel in the bottom of the ramekins will flow over the flan. Garnish each flan with a twist of orange.

Cooking Tip If you're a major fan of flan and are dying for a larger version to enjoy more than once, simply double this recipe and cook it in a medium metal bowl or 7-inch flan or cake pan. Increase the cook time to 15 minutes and allow a full natural release. Let it cool in the pan for 20 minutes, then cover with plastic wrap and refrigerate overnight for best results.

PER SERVING Calories: 246; Total fat: 14g; Saturated fat: 8g; Cholesterol: 134mg; Carbohydrates: 28g; Fiber: 0g; Protein: 4g

PRESSURE LEVEL: High

RELEASE: Quick

3 peeled (stem on) firm Bartlett pears

1½ cups (1 bottle) stout beer

1 vanilla bean, split lengthwise and seeds scraped

½ cup packed brown sugar

TO SERVE

- Whipped cream
- Chocolate sauce

STOUT-POACHED PEARS

5-INGREDIENT | 30 MINUTES OR LESS | LIGHT AND HEALTHY
VEGAN | VEGETARIAN

Simple yet elegant, poached pears will be a welcome dessert after a satisfying dinner. A belly full of a hearty meal can easily make room for such a light dessert, and you will have an easier time digesting poached fruit. While pears are normally poached in wine, this stout-flavored version is only mildly sweetened and picks up hints of rich chocolate from the beer.

1. Slice a thin layer from the bottom of each pear so they can stand upright. Using a melon baller, scoop out the seeds and core from the bottom.

2. In the pressure cooker pot, stir together the beer, vanilla bean and seeds, and brown sugar. Place the pears upright in the pot.

3. Secure the lid and cook on high pressure for 9 minutes, then quick release the pressure in the pot and remove the lid. Press cancel.

4. Using tongs, carefully remove the pears by their stems and transfer to a plate. Set aside. Select sauté and simmer the liquid in the pot until reduced by half.

5. Strain the liquid into a bowl through a fine-mesh sieve, then pour over the pears. Serve at room temperature or chilled, plain or with whipped cream and a drizzle of chocolate sauce.

Serving Tip To enhance the flavors of the pears, serve them with a dollop of mascarpone cheese and light drizzles of Irish cream liqueur and chocolate syrup or ganache.

PER SERVING Calories: 402; Total fat: 0.4g; Saturated fat: 0g; Cholesterol: 0mg; Carbohydrates: 90g; Fiber: 10g; Protein: 2g

SERVES 2

PREP TIME: 5 minutes

COOK TIME: 10 minutes

TOTAL TIME: 30 minutes

PRESSURE LEVEL: High

RELEASE: Natural

1 (4-ounce) can crescent rolls

1 large peach, cut into
4 wedges

¼ cup packed brown sugar,
plus 1 tablespoon

2 tablespoons butter

½ teaspoon vanilla extract

½ teaspoon ground cinnamon

Pinch ground cardamom

½ cup white wine or rosé

TO SERVE

- Vanilla ice cream
- Mint sprigs (optional)

PEACH DUMPLINGS

5-INGREDIENT | 30 MINUTES OR LESS | ONE-POT MEAL | VEGETARIAN

Apples always get top billing when it comes to dumpling desserts, but sweet summer peaches deserve their time to shine. Canned crescent rolls, available at your local grocery store, serve as the dumpling pastry in this easy, five-ingredient recipe, hugging the peach slices in a buttery, sugary pool of your favorite white wine or rosé. Move over, peach cobbler!

1. Preheat the pressure cooker pot on sauté mode.

2. Remove the crescent rolls from the can and roll them out flat on a cutting board. Sprinkle 1 tablespoon of brown sugar over the surface of the four triangles of dough. Roll each peach wedge up in a crescent roll.

3. Add the butter to the cooker pot and press cancel. Add the remaining ¼ cup of brown sugar, the vanilla, cinnamon, and cardamom and stir until dissolved and combined.

4. Place the peach dumplings upright and side by side in the pot. Pour the wine around them.

5. Secure the cooker lid and cook on high pressure for 10 minutes, then allow the pressure to naturally release, about 10 minutes. Open the vent at the top and remove the lid. Press cancel.

6. Let the dumplings cool for 5 to 8 minutes, then transfer to serving bowls and place a scoop of vanilla ice cream on the side. Drizzle the sweet wine sauce on top and garnish each with a sprig of mint (if desired).

PER SERVING Calories: 510; Total fat: 24g; Saturated fat: 10g; Cholesterol: 31mg; Carbohydrates: 58g; Fiber: 2g; Protein: 5g

MAKES 4 SLICES

PREP TIME: 10 minutes

COOK TIME: 20 minutes

TOTAL TIME: 50 minutes

PRESSURE LEVEL: High

RELEASE SETTING: Natural

6 tablespoons butter, at room temperature, divided

⅓ cup packed brown sugar

4 slices fresh or canned pineapple

4 pitted maraschino cherries, stems removed

¾ cup all-purpose flour

1 teaspoon baking powder

¼ teaspoon ground cinnamon

Pinch ground nutmeg

Pinch kosher salt

½ cup granulated sugar

1 egg, at room temperature

½ teaspoon vanilla extract

3 teaspoons dark rum

¼ cup pineapple juice

PINEAPPLE UPSIDE-DOWN CAKE

VEGETARIAN

If upside-down cake and bread pudding had a baby, this would be it. Instead of the usual fluffy cake you'd expect, this version is fairly dense and moist, and absolutely jammed full of pineapple flavor. Some rum and spices pump up the Caribbean vibes.

1. Add 1 cup of water to the pressure cooker pot and place the trivet in the bottom.

2. In a small microwave-safe bowl, melt 3 tablespoons of butter in the microwave. Pour into a 7-inch cake pan, tipping it to distribute the butter evenly across the bottom. Sprinkle the brown sugar on top of the butter, then place the pineapple slices on top of the brown sugar, slightly overlapping them if necessary to fit. Place the cherries in the holes in the pineapple slices. Set the cake pan aside.

3. In a medium bowl, whisk together the flour, baking powder, cinnamon, nutmeg, and salt.

4. In another medium bowl, using an electric hand mixer on medium speed, cream the remaining 3 tablespoons of butter and the granulated sugar until light and fluffy. Add the egg, vanilla, and rum, beating just until incorporated; scrape down the sides of the bowl as needed.

5. Add the flour mixture to the butter mixture in two batches, alternating with the pineapple juice. Beat until just blended (don't worry if the batter looks a bit curdled—that's normal). →

6. Pour the batter over the pineapple slices in the pan, spreading it in an even layer. Cover the pan with a paper towel and then with a piece of aluminum foil. Prepare a foil sling (see page 4), center the pan on it, and lower the pan into the pressure cooker pot. Arrange the sling ends across the pan.

7. Secure the cooker lid and cook on high pressure for 20 minutes, then allow the pressure to naturally release, 15 to 20 minutes. Open the vent at the top and remove the lid.

8. Remove the foil and paper towel from the cake and let cool in the cooker for 10 minutes. Using the sling tails, carefully transfer the cake to a cooling rack.

9. Cut the cake into slices and serve warm or at room temperature.

Variation Tip This upside-down cake recipe would be great with any kind of fruit. Instead of the pineapple/maraschino combination, try using sliced apples, sliced or halved plums tossed with cinnamon, peach slices tossed with ginger, or cranberries and orange zest for a holiday flavor treat.

PER SERVING (1 SLICE) Calories: 451; Total fat: 19g; Saturated fat: 11g; Cholesterol: 87mg; Carbohydrates: 67g; Fiber: 1g; Protein: 4g

MAKES 4 SLICES

PREP TIME: 15 minutes

COOK TIME: 15 minutes

TOTAL TIME: 45 minutes, plus 4 hours to chill

PRESSURE LEVEL: High

RELEASE: Natural

2 tablespoons unsalted butter, melted, plus more for greasing

½ cup graham cracker crumbs (from about 4 crackers)

½ teaspoon sugar

2 egg yolks

½ can (7 ounces) sweetened condensed milk

½ cup freshly squeezed Key lime juice

1 tablespoon grated Key lime zest

¼ cup sour cream

TO SERVE

- Whipped cream
- Toasted almonds
- Key lime slices

TANGY KEY LIME PIE

VEGETARIAN | WORTH THE WAIT

This tart and tangy tropical pie is a pure taste of sunshine! A compact list of ingredients and a quick cooking time make it even more irresistible. If the idea of juicing so many tiny Key limes gets you down, bottled lime juice works wonderfully.

1. Add 1 cup of water to the pressure cooker pot and place the trivet in the bottom. Coat one 6-inch or two 4-inch springform pans with butter.

2. In a medium bowl, combine the graham cracker crumbs, 2 tablespoons of butter, and the sugar. Press the crumb mixture evenly into the bottom and up the side of the pan (if using two pans, divide the crumb mixture evenly between them). Refrigerate the crust while you make the filling.

3. In a medium bowl, beat the egg yolks until they thicken and turn pale yellow, 2 to 3 minutes. Gradually beat in the condensed milk until thickened. Slowly add the lime juice and zest and beat until smooth. Stir in the sour cream.

4. Pour the batter into the prepared springform pan(s). Cover the top of the pan(s) with aluminum foil. For each pan, prepare a foil sling (see page 4), center the pan on it, and lower into the pressure cooker pot. Arrange the sling ends across the pan.

5. Secure the lid and cook on high pressure for 15 minutes, then allow the pressure to naturally release, about 10 minutes. Open the vent at the top and remove the lid.

6. Using the foil sling ends, carefully transfer the pan(s) to a cooling rack. Remove the foil. When the pie is cool, cover with plastic wrap and refrigerate for at least 4 hours until set. Serve with whipped cream, toasted almonds, and Key lime slices.

Serving Tip For a traditional Bahamian version, top the finished pie with a fluffy egg-white-and-sugar meringue instead of whipped cream.

PER SERVING (1 SLICE) Calories: 322; Total fat: 16g; Saturated fat: 9g; Cholesterol: 143mg; Carbohydrates: 39g; Fiber: 1g; Protein: 7g

SERVES 2

PREP TIME: 5 minutes

COOK TIME: 10 minutes

TOTAL TIME: 30 minutes

PRESSURE LEVEL: High

RELEASE: Natural

Butter, at room temperature, for greasing

½ cup pumpkin purée

3 tablespoons packed brown sugar

1 teaspoon cornstarch

Pinch kosher salt

½ teaspoon pumpkin pie spice

1 egg, lightly beaten

¼ cup plus 2 tablespoons heavy cream

TO SERVE
- Whipped cream
- Crumbled gingersnap cookies

MINI CRUSTLESS PUMPKIN PIES

30 MINUTES OR LESS | LIGHT AND HEALTHY | VEGETARIAN

The lack of crust keeps these single-serve pumpkin pies gluten-free and on the lighter side, but the pumpkin pie flavor comes through as strongly as in the slices enjoyed on Thanksgiving Day.

1. Add 1 cup of water to your pressure cooker pot and place the trivet in the bottom. Butter two 1-cup ramekins.

2. In a medium bowl, whisk together the pumpkin, brown sugar, cornstarch, salt, pumpkin pie spice, and egg. Add the cream and stir to combine.

3. Divide the pumpkin mixture between the prepared ramekins. Set the ramekins on the trivet, placing a third empty ramekin next to them to ensure that they don't jostle during cooking.

4. Secure the cooker lid and cook on high pressure for 10 minutes, then allow the pressure to naturally release, about 10 minutes. Open the vent at the top and remove the lid.

5. Using tongs, remove the ramekins from the cooker, transfer to a heatproof surface, and let cool for 5 to 10 minutes before serving with a dollop of whipped cream and crumbled gingersnap cookies, if you're looking for some crunch. The pie can also be refrigerated for up to 2 days; let cool completely first and cover with plastic wrap.

Ingredient Tip Want to make these from homemade pumpkin purée? Cut a 2-pound sugar (pie) pumpkin in half, then scoop out and discard (or roast!) the seeds. Place ½ cup of water, a trivet, and the pumpkin halves in your pressure cooker pot and cook on high for 15 minutes, using a quick release at the end of cooking. When the pumpkin is cool enough to handle, scoop out the flesh and purée in a blender until smooth. Use it as you would the canned pumpkin and freeze any extra in a large zip-top bag for up to 3 months.

PER SERVING Calories: 269; Total fat: 19g; Saturated fat: 11g; Cholesterol: 154mg; Carbohydrates: 21g; Fiber: 2g; Protein: 5g

YIELDS 4 SLICES

PREP TIME: 15 minutes

COOK TIME: 25 minutes

TOTAL TIME: 1 hour,
plus 3 hours to chill

PRESSURE LEVEL: High

RELEASE: Natural

2 tablespoons unsalted butter,
melted, plus more at room
temperature, for greasing

4 anise biscotti

⅛ teaspoon kosher salt

10 ounces ricotta cheese, at
room temperature

4 ounces mascarpone cheese,
at room temperature

½ cup sugar

2 tablespoons flour

2 teaspoons vanilla extract

½ teaspoon ground cinnamon

2 eggs, at room temperature

½ cup mini semisweet
chocolate chips

TO SERVE
- Whipped cream
- Crushed pistachios
- Pitted Amarena cherries

CANNOLI CHEESECAKE

VEGETARIAN | WORTH THE WAIT

Combining the flavors of a cannoli with the decadence of a thick slice of cheesecake, this recipe is a must-try for Italian dessert lovers. Unlike a regular cheesecake, this one is made with a combination of ricotta and mascarpone, making it lighter in calories and fat but still offering that delicious flavor.

1. Add 1 cup of water to the pressure cooker pot and place the trivet in the bottom. Coat a 7-inch springform pan with butter.

2. In a food processor or blender, pulse the biscotti to fine crumbs. Add the melted butter and the salt and pulse until the mixture has the texture of wet sand. Press the crumb mixture into the bottom of the prepared pan to form a crust.

3. In a stand mixer fitted with the paddle attachment (or in a tall bowl using a hand mixer), beat the ricotta, mascarpone, sugar, and flour on low speed until smooth, about 3 minutes, scraping down the side of the bowl occasionally with a rubber spatula. Add the vanilla and cinnamon and continue beating on low speed.

4. Add the eggs one at a time, beating on low speed after each addition until well combined. Scrape down the side of the bowl. Fold in the chocolate chips.

5. Pour the batter into the crust in the springform pan. Gently tap the pan on the counter to release any air bubbles. Cover the pan with a paper towel and then with a piece of aluminum foil. Prepare a foil sling (see page 4), center the pan on it, and lower it into the cooker pot. Arrange the sling ends across the pan. →

6. Secure the cooker lid and cook on high pressure for 25 minutes, then allow the pressure to naturally release, about 10 minutes. Open the vent at the top and remove the lid.

7. Using the sling ends, lift the cheesecake out of the cooker and transfer to a cooling rack. Remove the foil and paper towel. Let cool for about 30 minutes. Refrigerate for 3 to 4 hours before serving. Serve with whipped cream, pistachios, and cherries (if desired).

Ingredient Tip You can switch up the crust ingredients if you have no biscotti (or don't care for them). For a more authentic cannoli flavor, crush about 6 cannoli shells and combine them with the melted butter. Graham crackers will also work well, with cinnamon and chocolate varieties being your top flavor contenders.

PER SERVING (1 SLICE) Calories: 531; Total fat: 25g; Saturated fat: 15g; Cholesterol: 59mg; Carbohydrates: 66g; Fiber: 3g; Protein: 17g

SERVES 2, GENEROUSLY

PREP TIME: 20 minutes

COOK TIME: 21 minutes

TOTAL TIME: 1 hour 5 minutes,
plus 4 hours to chill

PRESSURE LEVEL: High
RELEASE: Natural (for the
cheesecakes); Quick (for the
bananas Foster)

FOR THE CHEESECAKES

2 tablespoons butter, melted,
plus more at room temperature
for greasing

1 cup vanilla wafers, crushed

1 (8-ounce) package cream
cheese, at room temperature

¼ cup granulated sugar

2 tablespoons sour cream

2 teaspoons vanilla extract

Pinch kosher salt

1 egg

¼ cup mashed ripe banana

FOR THE BANANAS FOSTER

¼ cup butter, at room
temperature

¼ cup water

¼ cup dark rum

½ cup packed brown sugar

½ teaspoon ground cinnamon

½ teaspoon vanilla extract

2 slightly green medium
bananas, peeled and cut into
thick slices

MINI BANANAS FOSTER CHEESECAKES

VEGETARIAN

Caramelized bananas and a warm, rich rum sauce make a mildly banana-flavored cheesecake sing in this indulgent just-for-two treat. This New Orleans-inspired dessert is a lovely ending to a Mardi Gras feast of Seafood Gumbo (page 90) and is perfectly prepared in two parts in your pressure cooker.

TO MAKE THE CHEESECAKES

1. Add 1 cup of water to the pressure cooker pot and place the trivet in the bottom. Line two 4-inch springform pans with small circles of parchment paper (use the bottom of one of the pans as a guide for cutting them out) and butter the pans and the paper. Set aside.

2. In a medium bowl, mix the crushed vanilla wafers and melted butter with a fork until well combined. Divide evenly between the two pans and press firmly into the bottoms and up the sides to make a crust.

3. In a medium bowl, using a hand mixer, beat the cream cheese and granulated sugar together until smooth. Add the sour cream, vanilla, and salt and beat well, then beat in the egg until just combined. Gently stir in the banana.

4. Divide the mixture between the two crusts. Gently tap each pan on the counter to release any air bubbles. Cover each pan with foil and place on top of the trivet in the pressure cooker.

5. Secure the cooker lid and cook the cheesecakes on high pressure for 13 minutes, then allow the pressure to naturally release. Open the vent at the top and remove the lid.

6. Using tongs, carefully remove the cheesecakes from the pressure cooker, transfer to a cooling rack, and let cool to room temperature, 30 to 40 minutes. Cover with plastic wrap and chill in the refrigerator for at least 4 hours or up to 2 days. ⟶

TO MAKE THE BANANAS FOSTER

1. Preheat the pressure cooker pot on sauté mode. Once hot, combine the butter, water, rum, brown sugar, cinnamon, and vanilla in the pot, mixing until well combined and the sugar is mostly dissolved. Add the bananas and toss to coat in the sauce.

2. Secure the cooker lid and cook on high pressure for 8 minutes, then quick release the pressure in the pot and remove the lid. Remove the pot from the cooker and pour the bananas foster into a heatproof medium bowl. Cover and refrigerate until ready to serve.

3. When ready to serve, remove the chilled cheesecakes from the springform pans (being sure to remove the parchment from the bottom) and transfer to serving plates. Reheat the bananas Foster in the microwave just until saucy. Top each cheesecake with your desired amount of the warmed bananas Foster.

Variation Tip Looking for a different flavor combo? Skip the bananas Foster and instead top the banana cheesecakes with a scoop of Strawberry Compote (page 183) and a dollop of whipped cream.

PER SERVING Calories: 1,281; Total fat: 74g; Saturated fat: 44g; Cholesterol: 304mg; Carbohydrates: 129g; Fiber: 5g; Protein: 16g

SERVES 2
PREP TIME: 15 minutes
COOK TIME: 25 minutes
TOTAL TIME: 1 hour, plus
45 minutes to cool

PRESSURE LEVEL: High
RELEASE: Quick

5 tablespoons butter, at room temperature, plus more for greasing

½ cup all-purpose flour, plus 1 tablespoon

½ teaspoon baking powder

⅛ teaspoon baking soda

Pinch kosher salt

⅓ cup sugar

1 egg, at room temperature

1 teaspoon vanilla extract

¼ teaspoon almond extract

2 ounces white chocolate, melted and cooled, divided

¼ cup sour cream

1 ounce drained chopped Maraschino cherries, plus a few whole ones for garnish

MINI WHITE CHOCOLATE–CHERRY BUNDT CAKES

VEGETARIAN | WORTH THE WAIT

The perfect little bite to enjoy with a cup of afternoon tea, these Bundt cakes are considerably denser than an oven-baked cake (steaming instead of baking in dry heat adds moisture) but are no less delicious. The cake base is a blend of simple vanilla, almond, and white chocolate flavors, and the juicy maraschino cherries are a lovely surprise.

1. Add 1 cup of water to your pressure cooker pot and place the trivet in the bottom. Butter two mini Bundt cake pans and set aside.

2. In a medium bowl, whisk together ½ cup of flour, the baking powder, baking soda, and salt.

3. In another medium bowl, using an electric hand mixer, cream the 5 tablespoons of butter and the sugar on medium speed until light and fluffy, about 2 minutes. Beat in the egg, vanilla, and almond extract just until incorporated. Slowly beat in half of the melted white chocolate, scraping down the side of the bowl with a rubber spatula as needed.

4. Beat the flour mixture into the butter mixture in two batches, alternating with the sour cream, just until combined. Toss the chopped cherries with the remaining 1 tablespoon of flour, then fold gently into the batter. Pour the batter into the two prepared pans and cover with aluminum foil. Place the pans on the trivet in the pot. →

5. Secure the lid and cook on high pressure for 25 minutes, then quick release the pressure in the pot and remove the lid. Carefully transfer the Bundt pans from the pot to a rack and let cool for 10 minutes

6. Remove the Bundt cakes from the pans and let cool completely on the rack, 30 to 45 minutes. Serve on dessert plates, drizzled with the remaining melted white chocolate and garnished with whole Maraschino cherries.

Cooking Tip Don't own a set of mini Bundt pans? Just pour the batter into two 4-inch springform pans. The cakes may be a bit flatter, but they will be just as tasty.

PER SERVING Calories: 750; Total fat: 45g; Saturated fat: 27g; Cholesterol: 171mg; Carbohydrates: 81g; Fiber: 1g; Protein: 9g

SERVES 2

PREP TIME: 10 minutes
COOK TIME: 9 minutes
TOTAL TIME: 30 minutes

PRESSURE LEVEL: High
RELEASE: Quick

Butter, at room temperature, for greasing

2 ounces bittersweet chocolate, chopped

1 egg

1 egg yolk

2 tablespoons granulated sugar

¼ cup hazelnut spread

3 tablespoons all-purpose flour

Pinch kosher salt

TO SERVE:
- Powdered sugar
- Vanilla ice cream
- Whipped cream
- Chopped toasted hazelnuts
- Sliced strawberries

CHOCOLATE-HAZELNUT LAVA CAKES

5-INGREDIENT | 30 MINUTES OR LESS | VEGETARIAN

Flourless cake meets soufflé in these ultrarich and decadent individual-size lava cakes. Once flipped onto a serving plate, the little cakes might not win any beauty contests (pressure cooking can cause uneven rising), but the gooey chocolate and hazelnut goodness will not disappoint.

1. Add 1 cup of water to your pressure cooker pot and place the trivet in the bottom. Butter two 1-cup ramekins; set aside.

2. Put the chocolate in a microwave-safe bowl and microwave in 30-second bursts, stirring with a rubber spatula at the end of each one, until melted and smooth. (Alternatively, set the bowl over a double boiler.) Let cool.

3. In a medium bowl, whisk the egg and egg yolk until smooth. Add the granulated sugar and whisk well. Add the hazelnut spread and cooled chocolate and mix with a rubber spatula until smooth. Gently fold in the flour and salt until no streaks remain.

4. Spoon the batter into the prepared ramekins, dividing it evenly. Set the ramekins on the trivet in the pot, placing a third empty ramekin inside with them to ensure they don't jostle during cooking. Secure the cooker lid and cook on high pressure for 9 minutes, then quick release the pressure in the pot and remove the lid. Using tongs, carefully remove the ramekins from the pot and transfer to a rack to cool for 5 minutes.

5. When ready to serve (warm), turn the cakes out onto individual serving plates and dust with powdered sugar. Serve with a scoop of high-quality vanilla ice cream, whipped cream, toasted hazelnuts, and sliced strawberries.

Variation Tip If you'd rather not use hazelnut spread (which stands in for the butter in this recipe), substitute an equal amount of butter instead. The results will be slightly less rich but just as tasty.

PER SERVING Calories: 711; Total fat: 38g; Saturated fat: 16g; Cholesterol: 193mg; Carbohydrates: 80g; Fiber: 3g; Protein: 14g

PRESSURE LEVEL: High

RELEASE: Quick

1 cup (2 sticks) unsalted butter, cubed, plus more for greasing

1 pound bittersweet chocolate, finely chopped

8 eggs, whites and yolks separated

2 tablespoons espresso powder

Pinch kosher salt

TO SERVE
- Powdered sugar
- Dulce de leche

FLOURLESS CHOCOLATE-ESPRESSO CAKE

5-INGREDIENT | COMFORT FOOD | WORTH THE WAIT

Some days just call for a slice of decadence, and this supremely rich dessert will not disappoint. The electric pressure cooker is the ideal vessel to produce a perfectly fudgy flourless cake, which will please both chocolate devotees and gluten-free fans. Serve it with a scoop of your favorite high-quality vanilla ice cream for a real treat.

1. Place a round of parchment paper on the bottom of a 7-inch cake pan. Grease the pan and paper with butter. Set aside.

2. Put the chocolate and butter in a microwave-safe medium bowl and microwave in 30-second bursts, stirring with a rubber spatula at the end of each one, until melted and smooth. (Alternatively, set the bowl over a double boiler.)

3. When the chocolate is melted, add the egg yolks and espresso powder to the bowl and stir to combine.

4. In another medium bowl, using an electric hand mixer, beat the egg whites on high speed until soft peaks form.

5. Gently fold the egg whites into the chocolate mixture until fully combined.

6. Pour the batter into the prepared pan, then cover it with aluminum foil.

7. Add 1 cup of water to the pressure cooker pot and place the trivet in the bottom.

8. Prepare a foil sling (see page 4), center the pan on it, and lower it into the pressure cooker. Arrange the sling ends across the cake pan.

9. Secure the lid and cook on high pressure for 35 minutes, then quick release the pressure from the pot. Carefully remove the lid, then remove the cake from the cooker using the foil sling ends and transfer to a rack to cool completely.

10. Remove the cake from the pan and transfer to a serving plate. When ready to serve, dust with powdered sugar and drizzle with dulce de leche, then cut into slices.

Substitution Tip Not a fan of coffee? Substitute the espresso powder with a few teaspoons of vanilla or almond extract to enhance the chocolate flavor.

PER SERVING (1 SLICE) Calories: 760; Total fat: 59g; Saturated fat: 37g; Cholesterol: 317mg; Carbohydrates: 45g; Fiber: 3g; Protein: 14g

MAKES 4 BROWNIES

PREP TIME: 10 minutes

COOK TIME: 25 minutes

TOTAL TIME: 1 hour

PRESSURE LEVEL: High

RELEASE: Natural

3 tablespoons unsalted butter, plus more for greasing

¼ cup semisweet chocolate chips, divided

½ cup sugar

¼ cup unsweetened cocoa powder

1 tablespoon water

½ teaspoon vanilla extract

1 egg, lightly beaten

½ cup all-purpose flour

¼ teaspoon baking powder

Pinch kosher salt

2 to 3 tablespoons natural peanut butter, at room temperature

TO SERVE:
- Vanilla ice cream
- Whipped cream

CHOCOLATE PEANUT BUTTER BROWNIES

PALEO-FRIENDLY | WORTH THE WAIT

Fudgy and moist, these peanut butter-swirled brownies aren't meant for casual snacking, and as a matter of fact, they'd prove difficult to eat all by themselves. These brownies were made for the *à la mode* treatment, served in a bowl with ice cream and freshly whipped cream . . . and maybe with a large glass of milk on the side.

1. Add 1 cup water to your pressure cooker pot and place the trivet in the bottom. Coat a small loaf pan or a 7-inch cake pan with butter and set aside.

2. Place 3 tablespoons of butter and ⅛ cup of chocolate chips in a microwave-safe bowl and microwave on high for 1 to 2 minutes, stirring every 30 seconds, until the chocolate is smooth. Stir in the sugar and cocoa powder until well combined. Add the water, vanilla, and egg and stir to mix well. Fold in the flour, baking powder, and salt and stir until combined. Spread the batter evenly in the prepared pan.

3. Drop the peanut butter by the spoonful onto the chocolate batter and use a butter knife to swirl it in just a bit. Sprinkle the remaining ⅛ cup of chocolate chips on top. Prepare a foil sling (see page 4), center the pan on it, and lower it into the pressure cooker pot. Tuck the sling ends around the outside edges of the brownie pan.

4. Secure the cooker lid and cook on high pressure for 25 minutes, then allow the pressure to naturally release, about 10 minutes. Open the vent at the top and remove the lid. Using the foil sling ends, remove the brownies from the cooker, transfer to a cooling rack, and let cool completely.

5. To serve, cut the brownies into 4 large squares and, using a wide spatula, transfer 2 squares to dessert bowls. Top with high-quality vanilla ice cream and whipped cream. The remaining two brownies can be wrapped in plastic and kept at room temperature to use for another dessert.

Substitution Tip Paleo brownies are possible, and equally delicious! Simply substitute ghee for the butter, use cassava flour instead of all-purpose flour, and sweeten the batter with maple syrup or maple sugar instead of granulated sugar. Instead of peanut butter, swirl in almond or cashew butter.

PER SERVING (1 BROWNIE) Calories: 404; Total fat: 21g; Saturated fat: 10g; Cholesterol: 69mg; Carbohydrates: 51g; Fiber: 4g; Protein: 8g

Appendix A ELECTRIC PRESSURE COOKING TIME CHARTS

The following charts provide approximate cook times for a variety of foods used in a 6-quart electric pressure cooker like the Instant Pot. Larger electric pressure cookers may need a little extra time to cook. To begin, you may want to cook for a minute or two less than the times listed; you can always simmer foods at natural pressure to finish cooking.

Keep in mind that these times are for the foods partially submerged in water (or broth) or steamed, and for the foods cooked alone. The cooking times for the same foods when they are part of a recipe may differ because of additional ingredients or cooking liquids, or a different release method than the one listed here.

For any foods labeled with "natural" release, allow at least 15 minutes of natural pressure release before quick releasing any remaining pressure.

Beans and Legumes

When cooking beans, if you have a pound or more, it's best to use low pressure and increase the cooking time by a minute or two (with larger amounts, there's more chance for foaming at high pressure). If you have less than a pound, high pressure is fine. A little oil in the cooking liquid will reduce foaming.

Unless a shorter release time is indicated, let the beans release naturally for at least 15 minutes, after which any remaining pressure can be quick released.

	Minutes Under Pressure UNSOAKED	Minutes Under Pressure SOAKED IN SALTED WATER	Pressure	Release
Black beans	22	10	High	Natural
	25	12	Low	
Black-eyed peas	12	5	High	Natural for 8 minutes, then quick
	15	7	Low	
Cannellini beans	25	8	High	Natural
	28	10	Low	
Chickpeas (garbanzo beans)	18	3	High	Natural for 3 minutes, then quick
	20	4	Low	
Kidney beans	25	8	High	Natural
	28	10	Low	
Lentils	10	not recommended	High	Quick
Navy beans	18	8	High	Natural
	20	10	Low	
Pinto beans	25	10	High	Natural
	28	12	Low	
Split peas (unsoaked)	5 (firm peas) to 8 (soft peas)	not recommended	High	Natural
Lima beans	15	4	High	Natural for 5 minutes, then quick
	18	5	Low	
Soy beans, fresh (edamame)	1	not recommended	High	Quick
Soybeans, dried	25	12	High	Natural
	28	14	Low	

Grains

To prevent foaming, it's best to rinse these grains thoroughly before cooking or to include a small amount of butter or oil with the cooking liquid. Unless a shorter release time is indicated, let the grains release naturally for at least 15 minutes, after which any remaining pressure can be quick released.

	Liquid Per 1 Cup of Grain	Minutes Under Pressure	Pressure	Release
Arborio (or other medium-grain) rice	1½ cups	6	High	Quick
Barley, pearled	2½ cups	10	High	Natural
Brown rice, medium-grain	1½ cups	6 to 8	High	Natural
Brown rice, long-grain	1½ cups	13	High	Natural for 10 minutes, then quick
Buckwheat	1¾ cups	2 to 4	High	Natural
Farro, whole-grain	3 cups	22 to 24	High	Natural
Farro, pearled	2 cups	6 to 8	High	Natural
Oats, rolled	3 cups	3 to 4	High	Quick
Oats, steel-cut	4 cups	12	High	Natural
Quinoa	2 cups	2	High	Quick
Wheat berries	2 cups	30	High	Natural for 10 minutes, then quick
White rice, long-grain	1½ cups	3	High	Quick
Wild rice	2½ cups	18 to 20	High	Natural

Meat

Except as noted, these times are for braised meats—that is, meats that are seared before pressure cooking and partially submerged in liquid. Unless a shorter release time is indicated, let the meat release naturally for at least 15 minutes, after which any remaining pressure can be quick released.

	Minutes Under Pressure	Pressure	Release
Beef, shoulder (chuck) roast (2 lb.)	35	High	Natural
Beef, shoulder (chuck), 2" chunks	20	High	Natural for 10 minutes
Beef, bone-in short ribs	40	High	Natural
Beef, flat iron steak, cut into ½" strips	1	Low	Quick
Beef, sirloin steak, cut into ½" strips	1	Low	Quick
Lamb, shoulder, 2" chunks	35	High	Natural
Lamb, shanks	40	High	Natural
Pork, shoulder roast (2 lb.)	25	High	Natural
Pork, shoulder, 2" chunks	20	High	Natural
Pork, tenderloin	4	Low	Quick
Pork, back ribs (steamed)	30	High	Quick
Pork, spare ribs (steamed)	20	High	Quick
Pork, smoked sausage, ½" slices	20	High	Quick

Poultry

Except as noted, these times are for poultry that is partially submerged in liquid. Unless otherwise indicated, let the poultry release naturally for at least 15 minutes, then do a quick release.

	Minutes Under Pressure	Pressure	Release
Chicken breast, bone-in (steamed)	8	Low	Natural for 5 minutes
Chicken breast, boneless (steamed)	5	Low	Natural for 8 minutes
Chicken thigh, bone-in	15	High	Natural for 10 minutes
Chicken thigh, boneless	8	High	Natural for 10 minutes
Chicken thigh, boneless, 1" to 2" pieces	5	High	Quick
Chicken, whole (seared on all sides)	12 to 14	Low	Natural for 8 minutes
Duck quarters, bone-in	35	High	Quick
Turkey breast, tenderloin (12 oz.) (steamed)	5	Low	Natural for 8 minutes
Turkey thigh, bone-in	30	High	Natural

Fish and Seafood

All times are for steamed fish and shellfish.

	Minutes Under Pressure	Pressure	Release
Clams	2	High	Quick
Mussels	1	High	Quick
Salmon, fresh (1" thick)	5	Low	Quick
Halibut, fresh (1" thick)	3	High	Quick
Tilapia or cod, fresh	1	Low	Quick
Tilapia or cod, frozen	3	Low	Quick
Large shrimp, frozen	1	Low	Quick

Vegetables

The cooking method for all of the following vegetables is steaming; if the vegetables are cooked in liquid, the times may vary. Green vegetables will be crisp-tender; root vegetables will be soft. Unless a shorter release time is indicated, let the vegetables release naturally for at least 15 minutes, after which any remaining pressure can be quick released.

	Prep	Minutes Under Pressure	Pressure	Release
Acorn squash	Halved	9	High	Quick
Artichokes, large	Whole	15	High	Quick
Beets	Quartered if large; halved if small	9	High	Natural
Broccoli	Cut into florets	1	Low	Quick
Brussels sprouts	Halved	2	High	Quick
Butternut squash	Peeled, cut into ½" chunks	8	High	Quick
Cabbage	Sliced	5	High	Quick
Carrots	Cut into ½" to 1" slices	2	High	Quick
Cauliflower	Whole	6	High	Quick
Cauliflower	Cut into florets	1	Low	Quick
Green beans	Cut in half or thirds	1	Low	Quick
Potatoes, large Russet (for mashing)	Quartered	8	High	Natural for 8 minutes, then quick
Potatoes, red	Whole if less than 1½" across, halved if larger	4	High	Quick
Spaghetti squash	Halved lengthwise	7	High	Quick
Sweet potatoes	Halved lengthwise	8	High	Natural

THE DIRTY DOZEN™ AND THE CLEAN FIFTEEN™

A nonprofit environmental watchdog organization called Environmental Working Group (EWG) looks at data supplied by the US Department of Agriculture (USDA) and the Food and Drug Administration (FDA) about pesticide residues. Each year it compiles a list of the best and worst pesticide loads found in commercial crops. You can use these lists to decide which fruits and vegetables to buy organic to minimize your exposure to pesticides and which produce is considered safe enough to buy conventionally. This does not mean the items on the "clean" list are pesticide-free, though, so wash these fruits and vegetables thoroughly.

These lists change every year, so make sure you look up the most recent one before you fill your shopping cart. You'll find the most recent lists, as well as a guide to pesticides in produce, at EWG.org/FoodNews.

DIRTY DOZEN™

Apples	Nectarines	*In addition to the Dirty Dozen, the EWG added two types of produce contaminated with highly toxic organophosphate insecticides:*
Celery	Peaches	
Cherries	Spinach	
Cherry tomatoes	Strawberries	Kale/Collard greens
Cucumbers	Sweet bell peppers	Hot peppers
Grapes	Tomatoes	

CLEAN FIFTEEN™

Asparagus	Eggplant	Onions
Avocados	Grapefruit	Papayas
Cabbage	Honeydew melon	Pineapples
Cantaloupe	Kiwis	Sweet corn
Cauliflower	Mangos	Sweet peas (frozen)

Appendix C **MEASUREMENTS AND CONVERSIONS**

VOLUME EQUIVALENTS (LIQUID)

US STANDARD	US STANDARD (OUNCES)	METRIC (APPROXIMATE)
2 tablespoons	1 fl. oz.	30 mL
¼ cup	2 fl. oz.	60 mL
½ cup	4 fl. oz.	120 mL
1 cup	8 fl. oz.	240 mL
1½ cups	12 fl. oz.	355 mL
2 cups or 1 pint	16 fl. oz.	475 mL
4 cups or 1 quart	32 fl. oz.	1 L
1 gallon	128 fl. oz.	4 L

OVEN TEMPERATURES

FAHRENHEIT	CELSIUS (APPROXIMATE)
250°F	120°C
300°F	150°C
325°F	165°C
350°F	180°C
375°F	190°C
400°F	200°C
425°F	220°C
450°F	230°C

VOLUME EQUIVALENTS (DRY)

US STANDARD	METRIC (APPROXIMATE)
⅛ teaspoon	0.5 mL
¼ teaspoon	1 mL
½ teaspoon	2 mL
¾ teaspoon	4 mL
1 teaspoon	5 mL
1 tablespoon	15 mL
¼ cup	59 mL
⅓ cup	79 mL
½ cup	118 mL
⅔ cup	156 mL
¾ cup	177 mL
1 cup	235 mL
2 cups or 1 pint	475 mL
3 cups	700 mL
4 cups or 1 quart	1 L

WEIGHT EQUIVALENTS

US STANDARD	METRIC (APPROXIMATE)
½ ounce	15 g
1 ounce	30 g
2 ounces	60 g
4 ounces	115 g
8 ounces	225 g
12 ounces	340 g
16 ounces or 1 pound	455 g

RECIPE TITLE INDEX

A

Adobo Barbacoa Sauce, 175
Apple Butter, 179
Arugula and Feta Frittata, 24

B

Baked Apples with Coconut Muesli, 36
Balsamic Brown Sugar Brussels Sprouts, 52
Barbacoa Bella Burrito Bowls, 78
Beef and Broccoli, 163
Beef Pot Roast and Potatoes, 160
Beef Ragù with Pappardelle, 161—162
Beef Stock, 168
Biscuits with Sausage Gravy, 30
Blueberries and Cream Clafouti, 32
Bone Broth, 169
Bourbon Chicken, 114
Broccoli-Cheddar Scalloped Potatoes, 47
Buffalo Chicken and Cheddar
    Quesadillas, 119—120
Butternut Squash and Broccoli
    Rabe Lasagna, 73—74

C

Cacio e Pepe Spaghetti Squash, 41—42
Cajun Shrimp Boil, 89
California Fish Tacos, 102—103
Cannoli Cheesecake, 199—200
Carnitas Tacos with Avocado Crema, 149—150
Carolina Mustard Barbecue Sauce, 174
Cheesy Broccoli and Cauliflower Soup, 62
Chicken Alfredo, 122—123
Chicken-Bacon Stew, 113
Chicken Cacciatore, 124—125
Chicken Marsala, 126
Chicken Noodle Soup, 111
Chicken Stock, 167
Chinese Vegetable Stir-Fry with
    Brown Rice, 68—69
Chipotle Chicken Fajita Lettuce Cups, 121
Chocolate Chip Banana Bread, 35

Chocolate-Covered-Strawberry
    Breakfast Quinoa, 37
Chocolate-Hazelnut Lava Cakes, 205
Chocolate Peanut Butter Brownies, 208—209
Cilantro-Lime Cauliflower Rice, 50
Cioppino, 91—92
Citrus Marmalade, 181—182
Clam Chowder, 93—94
Classic Barbecue Sauce, 173
Coconut-Almond Rice Pudding, 188
Cranberry Chicken Salad, 118
Creamy Buttered Mashed Potatoes, 46
Creamy Four-Cheese Macaroni and Cheese, 45
Crème Brûlée, 189—190

D

Deviled Egg Salad Sandwiches, 72
Dublin Coddle, 141

E

Easy Beef Enchiladas, 154—155
Easy Chicken and Rice, 127
Easy Marinara Sauce, 171
Easy Spaghetti and Meatballs, 153
Eggs and Smoked Sausage Bake, 26

F

Fall-Off-the-Bone Buffalo Wings, 128—129
Flan, 191—192
Flea Market Kettle Corn, 57
Flourless Chocolate-Espresso Cake, 206—207
French Toast Casserole, 28

G

Greek Yogurt, 176—177
Green Chile Corn Bread, 55—56

H

Holiday Cranberry Sauce, 180
Homestyle Applesauce, 178
Hot Honey Maple Carrots, 53

I

Indian Butter Chicken, 115

K

Kalua Pork Rice Bowls, 151—152

L

Lightened-Up Southern-Style
Potato Salad, 48
Loaded "Baked" Sweet Potatoes, 49

M

Maple-Pecan Steel-Cut Oatmeal, 31
Mexican Street Corn (On the Cob), 54
Mini Bananas Foster
Cheesecakes, 201—202
Mini Crustless Pumpkin Pies, 198
Mini White Chocolate-Cherry
Bundt Cakes, 203—204
Mushroom Risotto, 44
Mussels Fra Diavolo with Linguine, 96—97

P

Peach Dumplings, 194
Penne alla Vodka, 75
Perfect Lobster Tails with
Lemon-Butter Sauce, 98—99
Pho Ga (Vietnamese Chicken Soup), 112
Pineapple Upside-Down Cake, 195—196
Pork Chops with Mushroom Gravy, 144
Pork with Sauerkraut, 145

Q

Quick Shrimp Scampi, 87
Quick Smoky Bourbon Barbecue Ribs, 146
Quick Texas Chili con Carne, 156—157

R

Raspberry-Almond Breakfast Cake, 33—34
Ratatouille, 66—67
Red Garden Salsa, 172
Red Wine-Braised Boneless Short Ribs and
Gravy, 158—159
Refried Bean and Cheese Burritos, 70—71

S

Salsa-Poached Red Snapper, 104
Savory Oatmeal with Eggs and Chorizo, 21
Seafood Coconut Curry, 95
Seafood Gumbo, 90
Shakshuka, 25
Shrimp and Grits, 85—86
Shrimp Paella, 88
Southern Barbecue Pulled Pork
Sandwiches, 147—148
Southern Beans and Greens, 51
Southwestern Hash, 29
Steamed Cod and Vegetables, 100—101
Sticky Toffee Puddings, 187
Stout-Poached Pears, 193
Strawberry Compote, 183
Stuffed Acorn Squash, 79—80
Sweet Potato Lentil Soup, 64

T

Takeout-Style Fried Rice, 43
Tangy Key Lime Pie, 197
Teriyaki Salmon Salad, 105—106
Thai Green Curry Chicken and
Cauliflower, 116—117
Tomato-Basil Bisque, 61
Tomato-Basil Eggs en Cocotte, 22—23
Tonkotsu Ramen, 142—143
Tuna Casserole, 107
Turkey, Kale, and Orzo Soup, 130
Turkey and Sweet Potato Chili, 131
Turkey and Sweet Potato Egg Breakfast Cups, 27
Turkey Breast, Stuffing, and
Gravy Dinner, 136—137
Turkey Meatball Sub Sandwiches, 135
Turkey Potpie, 132—133
Turkey-Stuffed Peppers, 134
Tuscan Bean and Kale Soup, 63

V

Vegan Sloppy Joes, 81
Vegetable Shepherd's Pie, 76—77
Vegetable Stock, 170
Vegetarian Quinoa Chili Verde, 65

INDEX

A

Apples
Apple Butter, 179
Baked Apples with Coconut Muesli, 36
Cranberry Chicken Salad, 118
Homestyle Applesauce, 178
Pork with Sauerkraut, 145
Arugula
Arugula and Feta Frittata, 24
Avocados
California Fish Tacos, 102—103
Carnitas Tacos with Avocado Crema, 149—150

B

Bacon
Balsamic Brown Sugar Brussels Sprouts, 52
Chicken-Bacon Stew, 113
Clam Chowder, 93—94
Dublin Coddle, 141
Kalua Pork Rice Bowls, 151—152
Shrimp and Grits, 85—86
Bananas
Chocolate Chip Banana Bread, 35
Mini Bananas Foster Cheesecakes, 201—202
Basil
Mussels Fra Diavolo with Linguine, 96—97
Penne alla Vodka, 75
Ratatouille, 66—67
Tomato-Basil Bisque, 61
Tomato-Basil Eggs en Cocotte, 22—23
Beans, 12
Barbacoa Bella Burrito Bowls, 78
Buffalo Chicken and Cheddar
Quesadillas, 119—120
electric pressure cooking time chart, 212
Refried Bean and Cheese Burritos, 70—71
Southern Beans and Greens, 51
Turkey and Sweet Potato Chili, 131
Tuscan Bean and Kale Soup, 63
Vegetarian Quinoa Chili Verde, 65

Beef
Beef and Broccoli, 163
Beef Pot Roast and Potatoes, 160
Beef Ragù with Pappardelle, 161—162
Beef Stock, 168
Bone Broth, 169
Easy Beef Enchiladas, 154—155
Easy Spaghetti and Meatballs, 153
electric pressure cooking time chart, 214
Quick Texas Chili con Carne, 156—157
Red Wine-Braised Boneless Short Ribs and
Gravy, 158—159
Beer
Carolina Mustard Barbecue Sauce, 174
Pork with Sauerkraut, 145
Salsa-Poached Red Snapper, 104
Stout-Poached Pears, 193
Bell peppers
Chicken Cacciatore, 124—125
Chipotle Chicken Fajita Lettuce Cups, 121
Ratatouille, 66—67
Red Garden Salsa, 172
Seafood Gumbo, 90
Shakshuka, 25
Shrimp and Grits, 85—86
Southwestern Hash, 29
Turkey-Stuffed Peppers, 134
Vegan Sloppy Joes, 81
Berries
Blueberries and Cream Clafouti, 32
Chocolate-Covered-Strawberry Breakfast
Quinoa, 37
Cranberry Chicken Salad, 118
Holiday Cranberry Sauce, 180
Raspberry-Almond Breakfast Cake, 33—34
Strawberry Compote, 183
Stuffed Acorn Squash, 79—80
Bourbon
Bourbon Chicken, 114
Quick Smoky Bourbon Barbecue Ribs, 146

Bread
    Deviled Egg Salad Sandwiches, 72
    Easy Spaghetti and Meatballs, 153
    French Toast Casserole, 28
    Turkey Meatball Sub Sandwiches, 135
Broccoli
    Beef and Broccoli, 163
    Broccoli-Cheddar Scalloped Potatoes, 47
    Cheesy Broccoli and Cauliflower Soup, 62
    Chinese Vegetable Stir-Fry with
        Brown Rice, 68—69
    electric pressure cooking time chart, 217
Broccoli rabe
    Butternut Squash and Broccoli Rabe
        Lasagna, 73—74
Broths and stocks, 11, 15
    Beef Stock, 168
    Bone Broth, 169
    Chicken Stock, 167
    Vegetable Stock, 170
Browning function, 4
Brussels sprouts
    Balsamic Brown Sugar Brussels Sprouts, 52
    electric pressure cooking time chart, 217
    Steamed Cod and Vegetables, 100—101
Buttermilk
    Green Chile Corn Bread, 55—56
    Raspberry-Almond Breakfast Cake, 33—34

C
Cabbage
    electric pressure cooking time chart, 217
    Kalua Pork Rice Bowls, 151—152
Carrots
    Beef Pot Roast and Potatoes, 160
    Beef Ragù with Pappardelle, 161—162
    Bone Broth, 169
    Cheesy Broccoli and Cauliflower Soup, 62
    Chicken-Bacon Stew, 113
    Chicken Noodle Soup, 111
    Chinese Vegetable Stir-Fry with
        Brown Rice, 68—69
    Dublin Coddle, 141
    electric pressure cooking time chart, 217

Hot Honey Maple Carrots, 53
    Red Wine-Braised Boneless Short Ribs and
        Gravy, 158—159
    Sweet Potato Lentil Soup, 64
    Takeout-Style Fried Rice, 43
    Tomato-Basil Bisque, 61
    Turkey, Kale, and Orzo Soup, 130
    Tuscan Bean and Kale Soup, 63
    Vegan Sloppy Joes, 81
    Vegetable Stock, 170
Cauliflower
    Cheesy Broccoli and Cauliflower Soup, 62
    Cilantro-Lime Cauliflower Rice, 50
    electric pressure cooking time chart, 217
    Thai Green Curry Chicken and
        Cauliflower, 116—117
Celery
    Beef Ragù with Pappardelle, 161—162
    Bone Broth, 169
    Chicken Noodle Soup, 111
    Cranberry Chicken Salad, 118
    Deviled Egg Salad Sandwiches, 72
    Lightened-Up Southern-Style
        Potato Salad, 48
    Red Wine-Braised Boneless Short Ribs and
        Gravy, 158—159
    Seafood Gumbo, 90
    Shrimp and Grits, 85—86
    Stuffed Acorn Squash, 79—80
    Sweet Potato Lentil Soup, 64
    Tomato-Basil Bisque, 61
    Tuna Casserole, 107
    Turkey, Kale, and Orzo Soup, 130
    Turkey Breast, Stuffing, and Gravy
        Dinner, 136—137
    Turkey Potpie, 132—133
    Vegetable Stock, 170
Cheese, 13. See also Cream cheese; Mascarpone
        cheese; Ricotta cheese
    Arugula and Feta Frittata, 24
    Barbacoa Bella Burrito Bowls, 78
    Broccoli-Cheddar Scalloped Potatoes, 47
    Buffalo Chicken and Cheddar
        Quesadillas, 119—120

Cheese, 13. (*Continued*)
  Butternut Squash and Broccoli
    Rabe Lasagna, 73—74
  Cacio e Pepe Spaghetti Squash, 41—42
  Cheesy Broccoli and Cauliflower Soup, 62
  Chicken Alfredo, 122—123
  Creamy Four-Cheese Macaroni and
    Cheese, 45
  Easy Beef Enchiladas, 154—155
  Easy Spaghetti and Meatballs, 153
  Eggs and Smoked Sausage Bake, 26
  Mexican Street Corn (On the Cob), 54
  Mushroom Risotto, 44
  Penne alla Vodka, 75
  Refried Bean and Cheese Burritos, 70—71
  Shrimp and Grits, 85—86
  Southwestern Hash, 29
  Tomato-Basil Bisque, 61
  Tomato-Basil Eggs en Cocotte, 22—23
  Tuna Casserole, 107
  Turkey and Sweet Potato Egg
    Breakfast Cups, 27
  Turkey Meatball Sub Sandwiches, 135
  Turkey-Stuffed Peppers, 134
  Tuscan Bean and Kale Soup, 63
  Vegetable Shepherd's Pie, 76—77
Chicken
  Bone Broth, 169
  Bourbon Chicken, 114
  Buffalo Chicken and Cheddar
    Quesadillas, 119—120
  Chicken Alfredo, 122—123
  Chicken-Bacon Stew, 113
  Chicken Cacciatore, 124—125
  Chicken Marsala, 126
  Chicken Noodle Soup, 111
  Chicken Stock, 167
  Chipotle Chicken Fajita Lettuce Cups, 121
  Cranberry Chicken Salad, 118
  Easy Chicken and Rice, 127
  electric pressure cooking time chart, 215
  Fall-Off-the-Bone Buffalo Wings, 128—129
  Indian Butter Chicken, 115
  Pho Ga (Vietnamese Chicken Soup), 112

Thai Green Curry Chicken and
    Cauliflower, 116—117
  Tonkotsu Ramen, 142—143
Chickpeas
  electric pressure cooking time chart, 212
  Stuffed Acorn Squash, 79—80
Chocolate. *See also* Cocoa powder;
    White chocolate
  Cannoli Cheesecake, 199—200
  Chocolate Chip Banana Bread, 35
  Chocolate-Hazelnut Lava Cakes, 205
  Chocolate Peanut Butter Brownies, 208—209
  Flourless Chocolate-Espresso
    Cake, 206—207
Cilantro
  Carnitas Tacos with Avocado Crema, 149—150
  Cilantro-Lime Cauliflower Rice, 50
  Easy Chicken and Rice, 127
  Indian Butter Chicken, 115
  Mexican Street Corn (On the Cob), 54
  Pho Ga (Vietnamese Chicken Soup), 112
  Seafood Coconut Curry, 95
  Vegetarian Quinoa Chili Verde, 65
Cocoa powder
  Chocolate-Covered-Strawberry Breakfast
    Quinoa, 37
  Chocolate Peanut Butter Brownies, 208—209
Coconut milk
  Chocolate-Covered-Strawberry Breakfast
    Quinoa, 37
  Coconut-Almond Rice Pudding, 188
  Seafood Coconut Curry, 95
  Thai Green Curry Chicken and
    Cauliflower, 116—117
Comfort Food, 16
  Biscuits with Sausage Gravy, 30
  Carolina Mustard Barbecue Sauce, 174
  Chicken Noodle Soup, 111
  Creamy Buttered Mashed Potatoes, 46
  Creamy Four-Cheese Macaroni and
    Cheese, 45
  Easy Chicken and Rice, 127
  Flourless Chocolate-Espresso
    Cake, 206—207

Lightened-Up Southern-Style
    Potato Salad, 48
Loaded "Baked" Sweet Potatoes, 49
Mushroom Risotto, 44
Pork with Sauerkraut, 145
Quick Smoky Bourbon Barbecue Ribs, 146
Southern Beans and Greens, 51
Tuna Casserole, 107
Corn
    Cajun Shrimp Boil, 89
    Green Chile Corn Bread, 55—56
    Mexican Street Corn (On the Cob), 54
    Southwestern Hash, 29
Cream
    Blueberries and Cream Clafouti, 32
    Chicken Alfredo, 122—123
    Clam Chowder, 93—94
    Crème Brûlée, 189—190
    Flan, 191—192
    Indian Butter Chicken, 115
    Mini Crustless Pumpkin Pies, 198
    Penne alla Vodka, 75
    Shrimp and Grits, 85—86
    Tomato-Basil Bisque, 61
    Tomato-Basil Eggs en Cocotte, 22—23
    Tuna Casserole, 107
Cream cheese
    Creamy Buttered Mashed Potatoes, 46
    Creamy Four-Cheese Macaroni and
        Cheese, 45
    Mini Bananas Foster Cheesecakes, 201—202

D
Dates
    Sticky Toffee Puddings, 187

E
Egg noodles
    Chicken Noodle Soup, 111
    Tuna Casserole, 107
Eggplants
    Ratatouille, 66—67
Eggs, 12
    Arugula and Feta Frittata, 24

Blueberries and Cream Clafouti, 32
Cannoli Cheesecake, 199—200
Chocolate Chip Banana Bread, 35
Chocolate-Hazelnut Lava Cakes, 205
Chocolate Peanut Butter Brownies, 208—209
Crème Brûlée, 189—190
Deviled Egg Salad Sandwiches, 72
Easy Spaghetti and Meatballs, 153
Eggs and Smoked Sausage Bake, 26
Flan, 191—192
Flourless Chocolate-Espresso
    Cake, 206—207
French Toast Casserole, 28
Green Chile Corn Bread, 55—56
Lightened-Up Southern-Style
    Potato Salad, 48
Mini Bananas Foster Cheesecakes, 201—202
Mini Crustless Pumpkin Pies, 198
Mini White Chocolate-Cherry Bundt
    Cakes, 203—204
Pineapple Upside-Down Cake, 195—196
pressure cooking, 15
Raspberry-Almond Breakfast Cake, 33—34
Savory Oatmeal with Eggs and Chorizo, 21
Shakshuka, 25
Southwestern Hash, 29
Sticky Toffee Puddings, 187
Takeout-Style Fried Rice, 43
Tangy Key Lime Pie, 197
Tomato-Basil Eggs en Cocotte, 22—23
Turkey and Sweet Potato Egg Breakfast
    Cups, 27
Turkey Meatball Sub Sandwiches, 135
Turkey Potpie, 132—133
Turkey-Stuffed Peppers, 134
Electric pressure cookers. *See also* Multicookers
    benefits of, 2—3
    functions, 4
    types and sizes, 5
Electric pressure cooking
    best foods for, 15
    dos and don'ts, 9—10
    doubling recipes, 10
    equipment, 8—9

Electric pressure cooking (*Continued*)
  steps, 7—8
  time charts, 211—217
  time-saving tips, 14
  worst foods for, 15
Equipment, 8—9
Espresso powder
  Flourless Chocolate-Espresso
    Cake, 206—207

F

Fennel
  Cioppino, 91—92
Fish
  California Fish Tacos, 102—103
  Cioppino, 91—92
  electric pressure cooking time chart, 216
  Salsa-Poached Red Snapper, 104
  Seafood Coconut Curry, 95
  Steamed Cod and Vegetables, 100—101
  Teriyaki Salmon Salad, 105—106
  Tuna Casserole, 107
5-Ingredient, 16
  Apple Butter, 179
  Baked Apples with Coconut Muesli, 36
  Balsamic Brown Sugar Brussels Sprouts, 52
  Beef Stock, 168
  Biscuits with Sausage Gravy, 30
  Cacio e Pepe Spaghetti Squash, 41—42
  Chicken Stock, 167
  Chocolate-Covered-Strawberry Breakfast
    Quinoa, 37
  Chocolate-Hazelnut Lava Cakes, 205
  Cilantro-Lime Cauliflower Rice, 50
  Citrus Marmalade, 181—182
  Crème Brûlée, 189—190
  Easy Marinara Sauce, 171
  Fall-Off-the-Bone Buffalo Wings, 128—129
  Flea Market Kettle Corn, 57
  Flourless Chocolate-Espresso
    Cake, 206—207
  Holiday Cranberry Sauce, 180
  Homestyle Applesauce, 178
  Hot Honey Maple Carrots, 53
  Kalua Pork Rice Bowls, 151—152

Maple-Pecan Steel-Cut Oatmeal, 31
Peach Dumplings, 194
Salsa-Poached Red Snapper, 104
Savory Oatmeal with Eggs and Chorizo, 21
Stout-Poached Pears, 193
Strawberry Compote, 183

G

Ginger
  Chinese Vegetable Stir-Fry with
    Brown Rice, 68—69
  Indian Butter Chicken, 115
  Pho Ga (Vietnamese Chicken Soup), 112
  Seafood Coconut Curry, 95
  Teriyaki Salmon Salad, 105—106
  Thai Green Curry Chicken and
    Cauliflower, 116—117
  Tonkotsu Ramen, 142—143
Greek yogurt
  Lightened-Up Southern-Style
    Potato Salad, 48
Green chiles. *See also* Jalapeño peppers
  Quick Texas Chili con
    Carne, 156—157
  Seafood Coconut Curry, 95
  Vegetarian Quinoa Chili Verde, 65

H

Honey, 12

J

Jalapeño peppers
  California Fish Tacos, 102—103
  Green Chile Corn Bread, 55—56
  Red Garden Salsa, 172
  Refried Bean and Cheese
    Burritos, 70—71
  Shakshuka, 25
  Vegetarian Quinoa Chili Verde, 65

K

Kale
  Southern Beans and Greens, 51
  Turkey, Kale, and Orzo Soup, 130
  Tuscan Bean and Kale Soup, 63

Keep warm function, 4
Knives, 14

L

Lemons and lemon juice
  Apple Butter, 179
  Blueberries and Cream Clafouti, 32
  Butternut Squash and Broccoli
    Rabe Lasagna, 73—74
  Cacio e Pepe Spaghetti Squash, 41—42
  Citrus Marmalade, 181—182
  Perfect Lobster Tails with Lemon-Butter
    Sauce, 98—99
  Quick Shrimp Scampi, 87
  Shrimp and Grits, 85—86
  Steamed Cod and Vegetables, 100—101
  Strawberry Compote, 183
  Tomato-Basil Eggs en Cocotte, 22—23
  Tuna Casserole, 107
  Turkey, Kale, and Orzo Soup, 130
Lentils, 12
  electric pressure cooking time chart, 212
  Sweet Potato Lentil Soup, 64
  Vegan Sloppy Joes, 81
  Vegetable Shepherd's Pie, 76—77
  Vegetarian Quinoa Chili Verde, 65
Light and Healthy, 17
  Arugula and Feta Frittata, 24
  Barbacoa Bella Burrito Bowls, 78
  Beef and Broccoli, 163
  California Fish Tacos, 102—103
  Cheesy Broccoli and Cauliflower Soup, 62
  Chinese Vegetable Stir-Fry with
    Brown Rice, 68—69
  Chocolate-Covered-Strawberry Breakfast
    Quinoa, 37
  Greek Yogurt, 176—177
  Lightened-Up Southern-Style
    Potato Salad, 48
  Mini Crustless Pumpkin Pies, 198
  Quick Shrimp Scampi, 87
  Ratatouille, 66—67
  Refried Bean and Cheese Burritos, 70—71
  Salsa-Poached Red Snapper, 104

Shakshuka, 25
Shrimp Paella, 88
Steamed Cod and Vegetables, 100—101
Stout-Poached Pears, 193
Stuffed Acorn Squash, 79—80
Sweet Potato Lentil Soup, 64
Thai Green Curry Chicken and
  Cauliflower, 116—117
Tomato-Basil Bisque, 61
Turkey, Kale, and Orzo Soup, 130
Turkey and Sweet Potato Egg
  Breakfast Cups, 27
Tuscan Bean and Kale Soup, 63
Vegan Sloppy Joes, 81
Vegetable Stock, 170
Vegetarian Quinoa Chili Verde, 65
Limes and lime juice
  Barbacoa Bella Burrito Bowls, 78
  California Fish Tacos, 102—103
  Carnitas Tacos with Avocado Crema, 149—150
  Chipotle Chicken Fajita Lettuce Cups, 121
  Cilantro-Lime Cauliflower Rice, 50
  Citrus Marmalade, 181—182
  Cranberry Chicken Salad, 118
  Easy Chicken and Rice, 127
  Mexican Street Corn (On the Cob), 54
  Salsa-Poached Red Snapper, 104
  Seafood Coconut Curry, 95
  Tangy Key Lime Pie, 197
  Teriyaki Salmon Salad, 105—106
  Thai Green Curry Chicken and
    Cauliflower, 116—117

M

Mandolines, 14
Mangos
  California Fish Tacos, 102—103
Manual/pressure cook function, 4
Maraschino cherries
  Mini White Chocolate-Cherry Bundt
    Cakes, 203—204
  Pineapple Upside-Down Cake, 195—196
Marshmallows
  Loaded "Baked" Sweet Potatoes, 49

Mascarpone cheese
    Cannoli Cheesecake, 199—200
Meal planning, 10—11
Milk, 12. *See also* Buttermilk; Cream
    Biscuits with Sausage Gravy, 30
    Blueberries and Cream Clafouti, 32
    Butternut Squash and Broccoli Rabe
        Lasagna, 73—74
    Cheesy Broccoli and Cauliflower
        Soup, 62
    Chocolate Chip Banana Bread, 35
    Clam Chowder, 93—94
    Creamy Buttered Mashed Potatoes, 46
    Creamy Four-Cheese Macaroni and
        Cheese, 45
    Eggs and Smoked Sausage Bake, 26
    French Toast Casserole, 28
    Greek Yogurt, 176—177
    Shrimp and Grits, 85—86
    Turkey and Sweet Potato Egg
        Breakfast Cups, 27
    Turkey Potpie, 132—133
    Vegetable Shepherd's Pie, 76—77
Multicookers, 6
Mushrooms
    Barbacoa Bella Burrito Bowls, 78
    Chicken Cacciatore, 124—125
    Chicken Marsala, 126
    Chinese Vegetable Stir-Fry with
        Brown Rice, 68—69
    Mushroom Risotto, 44
    Pork Chops with Mushroom Gravy, 144
    Stuffed Acorn Squash, 79—80
    Tomato-Basil Eggs en Cocotte, 22—23
    Tuna Casserole, 107
    Vegan Sloppy Joes, 81
    Vegetable Stock, 170

N

Natural release function, 4
Noodles. *See* Egg noodles; Ramen
        noodles; Rice noodles
Nuts
    Cranberry Chicken Salad, 118

Loaded "Baked" Sweet Potatoes, 49
Maple-Pecan Steel-Cut Oatmeal, 31
Stuffed Acorn Squash, 79—80

O

Oats
    electric pressure cooking time chart, 213
    Maple-Pecan Steel-Cut Oatmeal, 31
    Savory Oatmeal with Eggs and Chorizo, 21
Oils, 12
Okra
    Seafood Gumbo, 90
Olives
    Chicken Cacciatore, 124—125
One-Pot Meal, 16
    Barbacoa Bella Burrito Bowls, 78
    Beef Pot Roast and Potatoes, 160
    Cacio e Pepe Spaghetti Squash, 41—42
    Cajun Shrimp Boil, 89
    Cheesy Broccoli and Cauliflower Soup, 62
    Chicken Cacciatore, 124—125
    Chocolate-Covered-Strawberry Breakfast
        Quinoa, 37
    Cioppino, 91—92
    Creamy Buttered Mashed Potatoes, 46
    Creamy Four-Cheese Macaroni and
        Cheese, 45
    Easy Spaghetti and Meatballs, 153
    Flea Market Kettle Corn, 57
    Hot Honey Maple Carrots, 53
    Maple-Pecan Steel-Cut Oatmeal, 31
    Mushroom Risotto, 44
    Peach Dumplings, 194
    Penne alla Vodka, 75
    Pork with Sauerkraut, 145
    Quick Texas Chili con Carne, 156—157
    Salsa-Poached Red Snapper, 104
    Shrimp Paella, 88
    Southern Beans and Greens, 51
    Sweet Potato Lentil Soup, 64
    Takeout-Style Fried Rice, 43
    Tomato-Basil Bisque, 61
    Turkey, Kale, and Orzo Soup, 130
    Turkey and Sweet Potato Chili, 131

Tuscan Bean and Kale Soup, 63
Vegan Sloppy Joes, 81
Oranges and orange juice
Carnitas Tacos with Avocado Crema, 149—150
Citrus Marmalade, 181—182
Flan, 191—192
Holiday Cranberry Sauce, 180
Oregano
Easy Marinara Sauce, 171
Vegetable Stock, 170
Vegetarian Quinoa Chili Verde, 65

P
Paleo/Paleo-Friendly, 17
Adobo Barbacoa Sauce, 175
Apple Butter, 179
Arugula and Feta Frittata, 24
Barbacoa Bella Burrito Bowls, 78
Beef and Broccoli, 163
Beef Pot Roast and Potatoes, 160
Beef Stock, 168
Bone Broth, 169
Bourbon Chicken, 114
Cajun Shrimp Boil, 89
California Fish Tacos, 102—103
Carolina Mustard Barbecue Sauce, 174
Chicken Cacciatore, 124—125
Chicken Stock, 167
Chocolate Peanut Butter
Brownies, 208—209
Cilantro-Lime Cauliflower Rice, 50
Cioppino, 91—92
Classic Barbecue Sauce, 173
Crème Brûlée, 189—190
Deviled Egg Salad Sandwiches, 72
Dublin Coddle, 141
Easy Beef Enchiladas, 154—155
Easy Marinara Sauce, 171
Holiday Cranberry Sauce, 180
Homestyle Applesauce, 178
Hot Honey Maple Carrots, 53
Maple-Pecan Steel-Cut Oatmeal, 31
Mussels Fra Diavolo with Linguine, 96—97
Pho Ga (Vietnamese Chicken Soup), 112

Quick Shrimp Scampi, 87
Quick Texas Chili con Carne, 156—157
Ratatouille, 66—67
Red Garden Salsa, 172
Red Wine-Braised Boneless Short Ribs and
Gravy, 158—159
Salsa-Poached Red Snapper, 104
Seafood Coconut Curry, 95
Seafood Gumbo, 90
Shrimp Paella, 88
Southern Barbecue Pulled Pork
Sandwiches, 147—148
Strawberry Compote, 183
Teriyaki Salmon Salad, 105—106
Tonkotsu Ramen, 142—143
Turkey, Kale, and Orzo Soup, 130
Turkey Meatball Sub Sandwiches, 135
Turkey-Stuffed Peppers, 134
Vegetable Stock, 170
Pans, 9
Pantry staples, 11—13
Parsley
Dublin Coddle, 141
Turkey, Kale, and Orzo Soup, 130
Turkey-Stuffed Peppers, 134
Vegetable Stock, 170
Pasta, 12
Beef Ragù with Pappardelle, 161—162
Butternut Squash and Broccoli Rabe
Lasagna, 73—74
Chicken Alfredo, 122—123
Creamy Four-Cheese Macaroni and
Cheese, 45
Easy Spaghetti and Meatballs, 153
Mussels Fra Diavolo with Linguine, 96—97
Penne alla Vodka, 75
Quick Shrimp Scampi, 87
Turkey, Kale, and Orzo Soup, 130
Peaches
Peach Dumplings, 194
Peanut butter
Chocolate Peanut Butter Brownies, 208—209
Pears
Stout-Poached Pears, 193

Peas
    Chinese Vegetable Stir-Fry with
        Brown Rice, 68—69
    Sweet Potato Lentil Soup, 64
    Takeout-Style Fried Rice, 43
Pineapple
    Pineapple Upside-Down Cake, 195—196
Pork. *See also* Bacon; Sausage
    Bone Broth, 169
    Carnitas Tacos with Avocado Crema, 149—150
    Easy Spaghetti and Meatballs, 153
    electric pressure cooking time chart, 214
    Kalua Pork Rice Bowls, 151—152
    Pork Chops with Mushroom Gravy, 144
    Pork with Sauerkraut, 145
    Quick Smoky Bourbon Barbecue Ribs, 146
    Southern Barbecue Pulled Pork
        Sandwiches, 147—148
    Tonkotsu Ramen, 142—143
Potatoes. *See also* Sweet potatoes
    Beef Pot Roast and Potatoes, 160
    Broccoli-Cheddar Scalloped Potatoes, 47
    Cajun Shrimp Boil, 89
    Chicken-Bacon Stew, 113
    Clam Chowder, 93—94
    Creamy Buttered Mashed Potatoes, 46
    Dublin Coddle, 141
    Eggs and Smoked Sausage Bake, 26
    electric pressure cooking time chart, 217
    Lightened-Up Southern-Style Potato Salad, 48
    pressure cooking, 15
    Southwestern Hash, 29
    Turkey Potpie, 132—133
    Vegetable Shepherd's Pie, 76—77
Pot-in-pot cooking, 4, 14
Pumpkin
    Mini Crustless Pumpkin Pies, 198

Q
Quick release function, 4
Quinoa
    Chocolate-Covered-Strawberry Breakfast
        Quinoa, 37
    electric pressure cooking time chart, 213
    Vegetarian Quinoa Chili Verde, 65

R
Raisins
    French Toast Casserole, 28
Ramekins, 8
Ramen noodles
    Tonkotsu Ramen, 142—143
Red chiles
    Thai Green Curry Chicken and
        Cauliflower, 116—117
Rice, 13
    Barbacoa Bella Burrito Bowls, 78
    Chinese Vegetable Stir-Fry with
        Brown Rice, 68—69
    Coconut-Almond Rice Pudding, 188
    Easy Chicken and Rice, 127
    electric pressure cooking time chart, 213
    Mushroom Risotto, 44
    Shrimp Paella, 88
    Stuffed Acorn Squash, 79—80
    Takeout-Style Fried Rice, 43
    Turkey-Stuffed Peppers, 134
Rice noodles
    Pho Ga (Vietnamese Chicken Soup), 112
Ricotta cheese
    Butternut Squash and Broccoli
        Rabe Lasagna, 73—74
    Cannoli Cheesecake, 199—200
Rosemary
    Beef Ragù with Pappardelle, 161—162
    Red Wine-Braised Boneless Short Ribs and
        Gravy, 158—159
    Southwestern Hash, 29
    Stuffed Acorn Squash, 79—80
    Vegetable Stock, 170
Rum
    Blueberries and Cream Clafouti, 32
    Mini Bananas Foster Cheesecakes, 201—202
    Pineapple Upside-Down Cake, 195—196

S
Sage
    Butternut Squash and Broccoli
        Rabe Lasagna, 73—74
    Stuffed Acorn Squash, 79—80

Turkey Breast, Stuffing, and Gravy
    Dinner, 136—137
Vegetable Stock, 170
Salads
    Chipotle Chicken Fajita Lettuce Cups, 121
    Cranberry Chicken Salad, 118
    Teriyaki Salmon Salad, 105—106
Salts, 12
Sandwiches and wraps
    Buffalo Chicken and Cheddar
        Quesadillas, 119—120
    California Fish Tacos, 102—103
    Carnitas Tacos with Avocado Crema, 149—150
    Deviled Egg Salad Sandwiches, 72
    Refried Bean and Cheese Burritos, 70—71
    Southern Barbecue Pulled Pork
        Sandwiches, 147—148
    Turkey Meatball Sub Sandwiches, 135
    Vegan Sloppy Joes, 81
Sauces and spreads
    Apple Butter, 179
    Carolina Mustard Barbecue Sauce, 174
    Citrus Marmalade, 181—182
    Classic Barbecue Sauce, 173
    Easy Marinara Sauce, 171
    Holiday Cranberry Sauce, 180
    Homestyle Applesauce, 178
    Red Garden Salsa, 172
    Strawberry Compote, 183
Sauerkraut
    Pork with Sauerkraut, 145
Sausage
    Biscuits with Sausage Gravy, 30
    Cajun Shrimp Boil, 89
    Dublin Coddle, 141
    Eggs and Smoked Sausage Bake, 26
    Pork with Sauerkraut, 145
    Savory Oatmeal with Eggs and Chorizo, 21
    Seafood Gumbo, 90
    Southwestern Hash, 29
    Turkey Breast, Stuffing, and
        Gravy Dinner, 136—137
Sauté function, 4
Sealing rings, 8—9
Shellfish. See also Fish; Shrimp

Cioppino, 91—92
Clam Chowder, 93—94
electric pressure cooking time chart, 216
Mussels Fra Diavolo with Linguine, 96—97
Perfect Lobster Tails with Lemon-
    Butter Sauce, 98—99
Seafood Gumbo, 90
Shrimp
    Cajun Shrimp Boil, 89
    Cioppino, 91—92
    electric pressure cooking time chart, 216
    pressure cooking, 15
    Quick Shrimp Scampi, 87
    Seafood Coconut Curry, 95
    Seafood Gumbo, 90
    Shrimp and Grits, 85—86
    Shrimp Paella, 88
Simmer function, 4
Slings, 4
Soups and stews
    Cheesy Broccoli and Cauliflower Soup, 62
    Chicken-Bacon Stew, 113
    Chicken Noodle Soup, 111
    Cioppino, 91—92
    Clam Chowder, 93—94
    Pho Ga (Vietnamese Chicken Soup), 112
    Quick Texas Chili con Carne, 156—157
    Seafood Gumbo, 90
    Sweet Potato Lentil Soup, 64
    Tomato-Basil Bisque, 61
    Tonkotsu Ramen, 142—143
    Turkey, Kale, and Orzo Soup, 130
    Turkey and Sweet Potato Chili, 131
    Tuscan Bean and Kale Soup, 63
    Vegetarian Quinoa Chili Verde, 65
Sour cream
    Broccoli-Cheddar Scalloped Potatoes, 47
    Carnitas Tacos with Avocado Crema, 149—150
    Chipotle Chicken Fajita Lettuce Cups, 121
    Green Chile Corn Bread, 55—56
    Mexican Street Corn (On the Cob), 54
    Mini Bananas Foster Cheesecakes, 201—202
    Mini White Chocolate-Cherry
        Bundt Cakes, 203—204
    Pork Chops with Mushroom Gravy, 144

Sour cream (*Continued*)

    Tangy Key Lime Pie, 197

Spinach

    Mushroom Risotto, 44

    Shakshuka, 25

    Sweet Potato Lentil Soup, 64

Squash. *See also* Zucchini

    Butternut Squash and Broccoli Rabe
        Lasagna, 73—74

    Cacio e Pepe Spaghetti Squash, 41—42

    electric pressure cooking time chart, 217

    Ratatouille, 66—67

    Steamed Cod and Vegetables, 100—101

    Stuffed Acorn Squash, 79—80

Steamer baskets, 9

Sweet potatoes

    electric pressure cooking time chart, 217

    Loaded "Baked" Sweet Potatoes, 49

    Sweet Potato Lentil Soup, 64

    Turkey and Sweet Potato Chili, 131

    Turkey and Sweet Potato Egg
        Breakfast Cups, 27

    Vegetarian Quinoa Chili Verde, 65

Swiss chard

    Southern Beans and Greens, 51

T

Thermometers, 8

30 Minutes or Less, 16

    Adobo Barbacoa Sauce, 175

    Arugula and Feta Frittata, 24

    Baked Apples with Coconut Muesli, 36

    Balsamic Brown Sugar Brussels Sprouts, 52

    Barbacoa Bella Burrito Bowls, 78

    Beef and Broccoli, 163

    Biscuits with Sausage Gravy, 30

    Blueberries and Cream Clafouti, 32

    Broccoli-Cheddar Scalloped Potatoes, 47

    Buffalo Chicken and Cheddar
        Quesadillas, 119—120

    Cacio e Pepe Spaghetti Squash, 41—42

    Cajun Shrimp Boil, 89

    California Fish Tacos, 102—103

    Carolina Mustard Barbecue Sauce, 174

Cheesy Broccoli and Cauliflower Soup, 62

Chicken Alfredo, 122—123

Chicken Noodle Soup, 111

Chinese Vegetable Stir-Fry with
    Brown Rice, 68—69

Chipotle Chicken Fajita Lettuce Cups, 121

Chocolate-Covered-Strawberry Breakfast
    Quinoa, 37

Chocolate-Hazelnut Lava Cakes, 205

Cilantro-Lime Cauliflower Rice, 50

Citrus Marmalade, 181—182

Classic Barbecue Sauce, 173

Coconut-Almond Rice Pudding, 188

Cranberry Chicken Salad, 118

Creamy Buttered Mashed Potatoes, 46

Creamy Four-Cheese Macaroni and
    Cheese, 45

Deviled Egg Salad Sandwiches, 72

Dublin Coddle, 141

Easy Marinara Sauce, 171

Eggs and Smoked Sausage Bake, 26

Fall-Off-the-Bone Buffalo Wings, 128—129

Flea Market Kettle Corn, 57

Holiday Cranberry Sauce, 180

Homestyle Applesauce, 178

Hot Honey Maple Carrots, 53

Lightened-Up Southern-Style
    Potato Salad, 48

Maple-Pecan Steel-Cut Oatmeal, 31

Mexican Street Corn (On the Cob), 54

Mini Crustless Pumpkin Pies, 198

Mushroom Risotto, 44

Mussels Fra Diavolo with Linguine, 96—97

Peach Dumplings, 194

Penne alla Vodka, 75

Perfect Lobster Tails with Lemon-Butter
    Sauce, 98—99

Quick Shrimp Scampi, 87

Red Garden Salsa, 172

Salsa-Poached Red Snapper, 104

Savory Oatmeal with Eggs and Chorizo, 21

Seafood Coconut Curry, 95

Shakshuka, 25

Shrimp Paella, 88

Southwestern Hash, 29
Steamed Cod and Vegetables, 100—101
Stout-Poached Pears, 193
Strawberry Compote, 183
Sweet Potato Lentil Soup, 64
Thai Green Curry Chicken and
    Cauliflower, 116—117
Tomato-Basil Bisque, 61
Turkey, Kale, and Orzo Soup, 130
Turkey and Sweet Potato Chili, 131
Turkey and Sweet Potato Egg
    Breakfast Cups, 27
Tuscan Bean and Kale Soup, 63
Thyme
    Beef Pot Roast and Potatoes, 160
    Beef Ragù with Pappardelle, 161—162
    Bone Broth, 169
    Chicken Noodle Soup, 111
    Clam Chowder, 93—94
    Mushroom Risotto, 44
    Southern Beans and Greens, 51
    Steamed Cod and Vegetables, 100—101
    Stuffed Acorn Squash, 79—80
    Turkey, Kale, and Orzo Soup, 130
    Tuscan Bean and Kale Soup, 63
    Vegetable Shepherd's Pie, 76—77
    Vegetable Stock, 170
Tomatillos
    Vegetarian Quinoa Chili Verde, 65
Tomatoes, 12
    Beef Ragù with Pappardelle, 161—162
    Buffalo Chicken and Cheddar
        Quesadillas, 119—120
    Chicken Cacciatore, 124—125
    Cioppino, 91—92
    Easy Marinara Sauce, 171
    Indian Butter Chicken, 115
    Mussels Fra Diavolo with Linguine, 96—97
    Penne alla Vodka, 75
    Quick Texas Chili con Carne, 156—157
    Ratatouille, 66—67
    Red Garden Salsa, 172
    Seafood Coconut Curry, 95
    Seafood Gumbo, 90

Shakshuka, 25
Shrimp and Grits, 85—86
Shrimp Paella, 88
Steamed Cod and Vegetables, 100—101
Tomato-Basil Bisque, 61
Tomato-Basil Eggs en Cocotte, 22—23
Turkey and Sweet Potato Chili, 131
Tuscan Bean and Kale Soup, 63
Vegan Sloppy Joes, 81
Trivets, 9
Turkey
    electric pressure cooking time chart, 215
    Turkey, Kale, and Orzo Soup, 130
    Turkey and Sweet Potato Chili, 131
    Turkey and Sweet Potato Egg
        Breakfast Cups, 27
    Turkey Breast, Stuffing, and Gravy
        Dinner, 136—137
    Turkey Meatball Sub Sandwiches, 135
    Turkey Potpie, 132—133
    Turkey-Stuffed Peppers, 134

V

Vegan/Vegan-Friendly, 17
    Adobo Barbacoa Sauce, 175
    Apple Butter, 179
    Barbacoa Bella Burrito Bowls, 78
    Carolina Mustard Barbecue Sauce, 174
    Chinese Vegetable Stir-Fry with
        Brown Rice, 68—69
    Cilantro-Lime Cauliflower Rice, 50
    Citrus Marmalade, 181—182
    Classic Barbecue Sauce, 173
    Easy Marinara Sauce, 171
    Homestyle Applesauce, 178
    Hot Honey Maple Carrots, 53
    Maple-Pecan Steel-Cut Oatmeal, 31
    Ratatouille, 66—67
    Red Garden Salsa, 172
    Southern Beans and Greens, 51
    Stout-Poached Pears, 193
    Stuffed Acorn Squash, 79—80
    Sweet Potato Lentil Soup, 64
    Takeout-Style Fried Rice, 43

Vegan/Vegan-Friendly (*Continued*)
  Tuscan Bean and Kale Soup, 63
  Vegan Sloppy Joes, 81
  Vegetable Shepherd's Pie, 76—77
  Vegetable Stock, 170
  Vegetarian Quinoa Chili Verde, 65
Vegetables. *See also specific*
  electric pressure cooking time chart, 217
  Turkey Potpie, 132—133
  Vegetable Shepherd's Pie, 76—77
Vegetarian/Vegetarian-Friendly, 17
  Adobo Barbacoa Sauce, 175
  Apple Butter, 179
  Arugula and Feta Frittata, 24
  Baked Apples with Coconut Muesli, 36
  Balsamic Brown Sugar Brussels Sprouts, 52
  Barbacoa Bella Burrito Bowls, 78
  Blueberries and Cream Clafouti, 32
  Butternut Squash and Broccoli
    Rabe Lasagna, 73—74
  Cacio e Pepe Spaghetti Squash, 41—42
  Cannoli Cheesecake, 199—200
  Carolina Mustard Barbecue Sauce, 174
  Cheesy Broccoli and Cauliflower Soup, 62
  Chinese Vegetable Stir-Fry with
    Brown Rice, 68—69
  Chocolate Chip Banana Bread, 35
  Chocolate-Covered-Strawberry
    Breakfast Quinoa, 37
  Chocolate-Hazelnut Lava Cakes, 205
  Cilantro-Lime Cauliflower Rice, 50
  Citrus Marmalade, 181—182
  Classic Barbecue Sauce, 173
  Coconut-Almond Rice Pudding, 188
  Creamy Buttered Mashed Potatoes, 46
  Creamy Four-Cheese Macaroni and
    Cheese, 45
  Crème Brûlée, 189—190
  Deviled Egg Salad Sandwiches, 72
  Easy Marinara Sauce, 171
  Flan, 191—192
  Flea Market Kettle Corn, 57
  French Toast Casserole, 28
  Greek Yogurt, 176—177
Green Chile Corn Bread, 55—56
Holiday Cranberry Sauce, 180
Homestyle Applesauce, 178
Hot Honey Maple Carrots, 53
Lightened-Up Southern-Style
  Potato Salad, 48
Loaded "Baked" Sweet Potatoes, 49
Maple-Pecan Steel-Cut Oatmeal, 31
Mexican Street Corn (On the Cob), 54
Mini Bananas Foster Cheesecakes, 201—202
Mini Crustless Pumpkin Pies, 198
Mini White Chocolate-Cherry
  Bundt Cakes, 203—204
Mushroom Risotto, 44
Peach Dumplings, 194
Penne alla Vodka, 75
Pineapple Upside-Down Cake, 195—196
Raspberry-Almond Breakfast Cake, 33—34
Ratatouille, 66—67
Red Garden Salsa, 172
Refried Bean and Cheese Burritos, 70—71
Shakshuka, 25
Southern Beans and Greens, 51
Sticky Toffee Puddings, 187
Stout-Poached Pears, 193
Strawberry Compote, 183
Stuffed Acorn Squash, 79—80
Sweet Potato Lentil Soup, 64
Takeout-Style Fried Rice, 43
Tangy Key Lime Pie, 197
Tomato-Basil Bisque, 61
Tomato-Basil Eggs en Cocotte, 22—23
Tuscan Bean and Kale Soup, 63
Vegan Sloppy Joes, 81
Vegetable Shepherd's Pie, 76—77
Vegetable Stock, 170
Vegetarian Quinoa Chili Verde, 65
Vinegar, 13

W

White chocolate
  Mini White Chocolate-Cherry
    Bundt Cakes, 203—204
Wine, red

Beef Ragù with Pappardelle, 161—162
Red Wine-Braised Boneless Short Ribs and
    Gravy, 158—159
Wine, white
    Adobo Barbacoa Sauce, 175
    Chicken-Bacon Stew, 113
    Chicken Cacciatore, 124—125
    Cioppino, 91—92
    Clam Chowder, 93—94
    Mushroom Risotto, 44
    Mussels Fra Diavolo with Linguine, 96—97
    Peach Dumplings, 194
    Pork Chops with Mushroom Gravy, 144
    Quick Shrimp Scampi, 87
    Ratatouille, 66—67
    Shrimp and Grits, 85—86
    Shrimp Paella, 88
Worth the Wait, 16
    Apple Butter, 179
    Beef Pot Roast and Potatoes, 160
    Beef Ragù with Pappardelle, 161—162
    Beef Stock, 168
    Bone Broth, 169
    Bourbon Chicken, 114
    Butternut Squash and Broccoli
        Rabe Lasagna, 73—74
    Cannoli Cheesecake, 199—200
    Carnitas Tacos with Avocado Crema, 149—150
    Chicken-Bacon Stew, 113
    Chicken Cacciatore, 124—125
    Chicken Stock, 167
    Chocolate Chip Banana Bread, 35
    Chocolate Peanut Butter Brownies, 208—209
    Crème Brûlée, 189—190
    Easy Beef Enchiladas, 154—155

Easy Spaghetti and Meatballs, 153
Flan, 191—192
Flourless Chocolate-Espresso
    Cake, 206—207
Greek Yogurt, 176—177
Green Chile Corn Bread, 55—56
Kalua Pork Rice Bowls, 151—152
Mini White Chocolate-Cherry
    Bundt Cakes, 203—204
Quick Texas Chili con Carne, 156—157
Raspberry-Almond Breakfast Cake, 33—34
Red Wine-Braised Boneless Short Ribs and
    Gravy, 158—159
Seafood Gumbo, 90
Southern Barbecue Pulled Pork
    Sandwiches, 147—148
Southern Beans and Greens, 51
Stuffed Acorn Squash, 79—80
Tangy Key Lime Pie, 197
Tonkotsu Ramen, 142—143
Turkey Breast, Stuffing, and Gravy
    Dinner, 136—137
Turkey Potpie, 132—133
Vegetable Shepherd's Pie, 76—77
Vegetable Stock, 170

Y

Yogurt. *See also* Greek yogurt
    Indian Butter Chicken, 115

Z

Zucchini
    Ratatouille, 66—67
    Steamed Cod and Vegetables, 100—101

ACKNOWLEDGMENTS

To my sweet husband, Abe, for trying all the recipes with me and providing that constructive criticism no matter how badly I didn't want to hear it.

To all my recipe tasters and testers, especially Amy Nash, Donna Mansour, Erin Johnson, Erin Parker-Skinner, Jen Buggica-Gutierrez, Jessy Friemann, Kelly Shea, Liz "Ix" Waddle, and Mackenzie Ryan. You have my eternal gratitude, and I owe you all cupcakes the next time I see you.

To my two dear friends: Lara Clevenger, for talking me into buying my Instant Pot on Black Friday, and Angel Petrozza, for being fabulous company and a sounding board for when my creativity well threatened to run dry, and for taking home leftovers.

Thanks especially to Marthine Satris for stumbling across my LinkedIn profile, and to Callisto Media for helping me make my publishing dreams come true.